BRICS
AND ALL
THAT

ISBN Paperback: 978-1-963271-88-1
ISBN Ebook 978-1-963271-89-8

Published by Armin Lear Press, Inc.
215 W Riverside Drive, #4362
Estes Park, CO 80517

BRICS AND ALL THAT

Are Russia and China Trying to Destroy
the Almighty Dollar?

JEFFERSON HANE WEAVER

ARMINLEAR

This book is dedicated with love and gratitude to my children: Mark, Catharine, Matthew, Caroline and Mason

CONTENTS

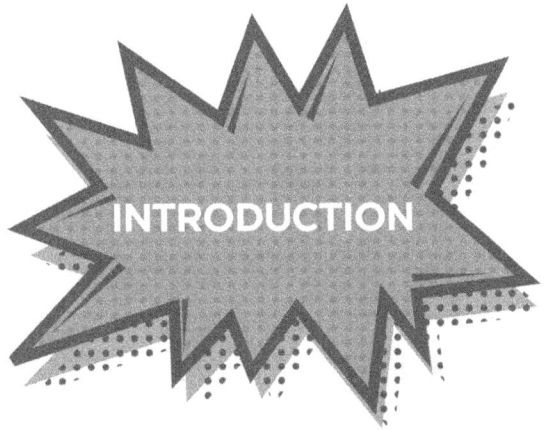

WHAT IS BRICS?

If you were asked to offer a definition of the word "brick," (pronounced *brik*), you could consult the *Merriam-Webster* dictionary and retrieve the following definitions:

1. "a handy-sized unit of building or paving material typically being rectangular and about 2 ¼ x 3 ¾ x 8 inches . . . and made of moist clay hardened by heat.

2. A good-hearted person

3. A rectangular compressed mass (as of ice cream)

4. A semisoft cheese with numerous small holes smooth texture, and often mild flavor

5. A gaffe or blunder used especially in the phrase *drop a brick*

6. A badly missed shot in basketball"

This definition would seem to be very comprehensive as it includes everything from building materials to botched basketball shots. However, you might be surprised to find that there is an entirely different definition for the plural version of the word 'brick.' This other definition requires that you delve into the world of international politics and global finance and learn about an organization known as BRICS. This definition can be found in the *Encyclopedia Britannica*, which is one of the heaviest compendiums of knowledge about pretty much anything you can imagine. Accordingly, it offers the following definition of the BRICS organization: "The acronym [BRICS]—derived from the names of the early members Brazil, Russia, India, China, and South Africa—has since been adopted as the name of a formal intergovernmental organization [founded in 2009] that aims to create greater economic and geopolitical integration and coordination among member states."

Literary giants ranging from William Shakespeare to Leo Tolstoy have long complained about the lack of a book that discusses the BRICS organization in an informative and entertaining manner. Specifically, *Hamlet* waxed poetically when he said, "To be or not to be, that is the question as to whether we will ever see a worthy book about BRICS," whereas in *War and Peace*, Tolstoy offered the mortality-driven statement "Everything ends in death, everything, but the burden would be lightened if I could read a humorous book about the BRICS organization."

For those individuals who have been living in caves and are thus deprived of news from obscure cable channels, BRICS began as a loose grouping of countries that shared little more than a desire to create an alternative financial system that was not dependent on the American dollar. Their mutual disdain for the United States coalesced into a more formal arrangement in 2009, when the founding members proclaimed the beginning of the BRICS organization and set out to restructure the global trading system. Reality has since caused the BRICS members to lower their sights and settle for assembling a group that can form the nucleus of an important mid-sized institution with a development bank that can offer infrastructure loans to developing countries.

This book has an immersive approach, eschewing the typical building block approach that is often used by lesser literary talents, to explain both the creation and the on-going operation of BRICS and its wholly-owned development bank known as the New Development Bank. Like the caring parent who tosses his toddler into a pool to force him to learn to swim in a single "tough love" lesson, this book relies on a similar technique. It begins with a Prologue that offers a fascinating account of the beginning of the BRICS organization which, like many great innovations, began almost by accident when the leaders of Russia, China, Brazil and India reportedly visited Yekaterinburg, Russia in 2009 to receive sales awards from the Famway consumer products company for their highly successful multi-level marketing programs. However, their post-award celebration in a tavern was cut short when the Russian leader's attempt to pay the bill in rubles was rejected due to the owner's dollar-only payment policy. This embarrassing incident led the four leaders to begin thinking about how they might create a new coalition that would forgo the use of the dollar.

The first part of the book begins with a two-chapter visit to the Louvre in Paris, France, where the BRICS gala affair is being held. These festivities—which amount to something akin to a debutante ball for the leaders of Russia, China, Brazil, and India—are covered by America's favorite news and entertainment show, *Comings and Goings*, which is hosted by broadcasting semi-legend Ken Roberts, distinguished foreign affairs correspondent Margaret Hill and Nobel-Prize winning Economist Stanislaw Zutnik. The three panelists provide an informative introduction to the BRICS organization and the leaders of its founding members.

The second part of the book includes two chapters which provide concise yet comprehensive histories of Russia and China—the two "ringleaders" of BRICS. The idea behind offering Pulitzer Prize-worthy stories of these two nations over the centuries was to give the reader some sense as to how their historical experiences have shaped the way they view the world as a whole and, more specifically, the Western powers—particularly the United States. This background adds some historical context (that is occasionally grounded in facts) and may help to explain better the actions of both countries in the international arena—particularly those based on their belief that they have not been given the respect they deserve by the United States and its allies.

The third part of this book offers an overview of the IMF and the World Bank—the two largest development banks. It also provides a succinct history of the post-war global trading system and the shift from a gold standard to a global economy based on American dollars—which are almost as good as gold bullion except that they are not very shiny or water-resistant and cannot be made into alluring jewelry. This chapter also provides a survey of the types of loans made by both institutions and high-lights the frustrations felt by both Russia and China with these institutions—due both to their lack of influence there as well as the control exercised over both institutions by the United States. The United States, for its part, appears to be satisfied with the outsized role that it plays in both the IMF and the World Bank.

Because any discussion about international finance involves banks and their lending practices, the fourth part of this book offers two chapters. The first follows an individual borrower as he tries to obtain a personal loan at a local bank and then tracks his efforts to secure financing for an infrastructure project at the New Development Bank. Anyone who has ever tried to get a loan from a bank to purchase a house, or a car, or even a hydroelectric dam by groveling at the feet of his or her loan officer, for example, will be able to relate to the obstacles that one must overcome to receive that coveted loan approval.

The next chapter follows Prince Freddy of the principality of Utrecht-Lorraine as he visits to the headquarters of the New Development Bank in Shanghai, China, to secure funds to build an enormous coal power plant together with the world's largest roller coaster. Prince Freddy's meeting with officials at the New Development Bank offers an insider's view as to how heads of state approach development banks and the types of questions that typically come up when these bankers are trying to decide whether making the loan will be a good idea or a catastrophic decision that could cost them their cushy C-suite jobs.

The fifth part of the book shows that the countries of BRICS are able to throw an annual party that rivals any of the charcuterie board-laden cocktail receptions put on by the stuffed-shirts at the IMF and the World Bank. It follows the annual BRICS summit in which the members meet to discuss various matters, including the admission of new members. Like the BRICS Gala Affair, the event is covered by the *Comings and Goings* crew and its award-winning broadcasters.

Some clues as to the ultimate fate of BRICS and its New Development Bank are offered in the sixth part of the book. Several factors bode in favor of the organization's long-term success, such as the sheer size of its members' economies and populations, while other factors, such as on-going rivalries between China and India, for example, may hinder its long-term cohesiveness. In any event, the founding members have invested tens of billions of dollars in the New Development Bank and, to date, have authorized dozens of development projects around the world, so they seem to be very serious about establishing the New Development Bank as a viable alternate to the IMF and the World Bank.

Finally, the book concludes with an Epilogue that showcases an episode of the pseudo-intellectual show *World Affairs*. It features an interview with President Xi of China and President Putin of Russia, the latter of whom is appearing via phone due to his outstanding arrest warrant for "crimes against humanity." The two heads of state discuss such weighty topics as their favorite movie actresses, and the prospects for BRICS and the New Development Bank.

THE TRUE (SORT OF) STORY
BEHIND THE BEGINNING OF BRICS

As with many great discoveries and inventions, the creation of the BRICS organization, unbeknownst to most historians who study such things, might not have ever occurred were it not for a fortuitous gathering of the leaders of Brazil, Russia, India, and China, in the Russian city of Yekaterinburg in June 2009. This reason for this get-together was not to hob-nob with each other and discuss weighty affairs of the world or even to redeem unused time-share vacation credits. Instead, it was a celebration honoring the leaders of the four nations for their superlative accomplishments in the rough and tumble world of multi-level marketing.

The presidents of Brazil, Russia, India and China all traveled to Russia's third largest (and most frequently misspelled) city to attend a "Diamond Circle" awards dinner. This black-tie affair was held in recognition of their outstanding sales efforts on behalf of Famway, one of the world's leading multi-level marketing firms. Famway sells a wide variety of health, beauty and household products as well as a smattering of military grade weapons for hunting enthusiasts, and prides itself on never having obtained any sort of regulatory approval for any of its products.

Indeed, it was the first year since the founding of Famway in 1960 that there was a four-way tie for the Top Sales Award trophy—which consists of a solid gold, gallon-sized cup mounted on a massive mahogany base. On the front of the cup is a solid gold label, stamped with the words, "Famway's #1 World Sales Leader." Exact replicas of this precious trophy were ultimately given to President Luiz da Silva of Brazil, President Dmitry Medvedev of Russia, President Hu Jintao of China, and Prime Minister Manmohan Singh of India. Indeed, Famway Chairman Billy Bob Famway, the grandson of Famway founders Joe Bob Famway and Bettie Bob Famway, praised all four of the leaders for their innovative efforts in constructing massive multi-level marketing enterprises in their respective countries in which every almost citizen was required to join the ranks of these companies as "sales associates" or else be sent off to labor camps.

Needless to say, each of these leaders was able to build an enormous sales force, consisting of tens of millions of individuals, all pestering each other day in and day out to purchase the latest and greatest Famway products. Because Famway was not able to verify which head of state's multilevel marketing firm sold the most products, due to widespread counterfeiting of the more popular Famway beauty and hygiene products in each of these countries, Famway's board of directors decided to declare a tie and give duplicate trophies to all four leaders.

It was only later that night, while the four presidents were celebrating their awards with their translators at a table in the Rasputin tavern in downtown Yekaterinburg and drinking vodka out of their golden cups, that they were able to relax for a few moments and enjoy the fruits of their victory.

"Gentlemen, I would like to congratulate each of you on your unprecedented sales success," President Hu's translator said, as President Hu raised the enormous cup and took a sip.

"Thank you, President Hu," Presidents Singh, Medvedev, and da Silva said together, taking a drink out of their golden cups. "I think we shocked the Famway board of directors with our innovative sales team building methods," President da Silva added.

"No doubt," President Singh of India said, though a troubled look crossed his face. "But I think it may be too much of a good thing," he said.

"Why?" President Hu's translator wanted to know.

President Singh was silent for a moment. "Our multilevel marketing company has hundreds of millions of people in it. They are constantly trying to sell their products to their families and friends so that they can win cash bonuses and valuable prizes—"

"So?" President Medvedev asked. "Isn't that a good thing?" he asked.

President Singh shook his head. "The problem is that the more time people spending selling Famway products, the less time they spend at real jobs that create actual goods and services." He shook his shoulders. "Our labor productivity has fallen dramatically," he pointed out. "Preliminary reports from the National

Bureau of Statistics indicate that our manufacturing sector may have contracted by ten percent in the last quarter."

"Uh oh," President Hu said through his translator. "I didn't think of that," he admitted.

"Neither did I," replied President da Silva. "Perhaps we focused too much of our efforts on our multilevel marketing programs—"

"Perhaps," President Medvedev agreed as the bill was placed in the middle of the table by the *ofitsiant*.

"Allow me, gentlemen," President Medvedev said graciously, picking up the receipt and fishing for his wallet. There was a murmur of 'thank yous' from the other heads of state around the table as President Medvedev retrieved five thousand rubles and handed them back to the *ofitsiant*.

"I'm so sorry, President Medvedev," the *ofitsiant* said uneasily. "But we cannot take rubles here at the Rasputin tavern," he whispered. "Only dollars."

"But we are in the middle of Russia," President Medvedev said, perplexed.

"I'm so sorry, sir," the *ofitsiant* replied. "Company policy," he added, pointing to a sign on the wall stating that rubles would not be accepted for payment.

"Young man, let me speak to your manager," President Medvedev said, irritated. "It is outrageous that a drinking establishment in the middle of Russia does not accept Russian rubles." He shook his head. "Just a minor misunderstanding," he said to his guests. "Please enjoy your vodka," he added, picking up his gold cup and taking a long swig as his fellow heads of state followed suit.

The *ofitsiant* returned with another man who appeared to be in charge. "This is Mr. Gagarin," he said, introducing his boss, who then bent over in a first-rate demonstration of obsequiousness. "President Medvedev, I understand that there is a problem with your payment," Mr. Gagarin said sympathetically.

"Quite right," President Medvedev said angrily. "My friends and I came to your establishment to celebrate having received the Famway Top Sales Award trophy and—"

"Congratulations, President Medvedev!" said Mr. Gagarin, clapping his hands together. "That is a great honor," he added. "We use the Famway deodorizer in the bathrooms here and they help keep the stalls smelling like a spring meadow even under the most trying of circumstances." He thought for a moment. "By the way, I think I am a level 28 sales associate in your Famway marketing company," he said, checking the Famway card in his pocket. "Oh, my mistake," he added, correcting himself. "I am still at level 27 but I may be able to move up to level 28 if I can get my 10-year-old daughter to sign up as a Famway distributor—"

"Oh, very good, sir," the *officiant* said, checking his card. "I just got to level 14—"

"That is quite commendable," Mr. Gagarin said. "Keep up the good work—"

"Gentlemen, I think it is wonderful that you are both involved in the Medvedev company and are doing so well, but we still have a problem here in that I cannot use our national currency to pay for my tab." President Medvedev sat back in his chair and looked at Mr. Gagarin expectantly.

"Perhaps I should get the owner on the phone," Mr. Gagarin

said, retrieving a cell phone from his pocket. He dialed the number, and a voice answered at the other end.

"Sir, this is Yuri Gagarin, the manager of your Rasputin tavern in Yekaterinburg," he said. "Yes, sir, I am fine," he added. "How is Mrs. Putin?" he continued, trying to be polite.

President Medvedev's eyes widened in horror as Mr. Gagarin continued to prattle on with his pleasantries. "I hope that your children are doing well," he added, as President Medvedev felt his shirt collar tightening around his throat like a noose. "Yes, sir," Mr. Gagarin continued. "I understand that you sometimes cannot spare the rod or else they will lose respect for you."

"This is not good," Medvedev whispered to the other three heads of state. "I didn't realize that 'you know who' owns this place!" he said nervously. "I don't want to get pushed out of a hotel window, or tied to an anchor and dropped in the ocean. or shot with a poison dart," he added, beginning to panic.

The terror he was feeling was mirrored on the petrified faces of his three fellow heads of state who were also clearly not interested in suffering such an untimely and gruesome fate.

Mr. Gagarin got to the point. "Sir, I was wondering if we can make an exception to our 'dollars only' payment policy," he asked. "We have several visiting dignitaries who would like to take care of their bill but were unaware of our dollar-only payment policy." Mr. Gagarin nodded his head and said, "I will ask them."

He turned to the table. "The owner is very sympathetic and wondered if you might be able to pay half of the bill in dollars."

President Medvedev looked at his fellow heads of states. Presidents da Silva and Singh both checked their pockets and shook their heads helplessly. President Hu examined his wallet which was stuffed with a stack of renminbi notes but then remembered his mad money stash. He retrieved a wad of slightly damp and smelly $100 bills from his sock and gave a thumb's up to President Medvedev. "How much is half of the bill in dollars?" President Hu's translator asked.

"Three hundred dollars," Mr. Gagarin replied.

The translator passed that information on to President Hu who then handed three $100 bills to President Medvedev. President Hu then stuffed the remaining bills back into his sock. "Thank you, sir," Mr. Gagarin replied, retrieving the greenbacks and the rubles from President Medvedev. He returned to the phone. "Sir, we were able to collect the bill as you requested— half in rubles and half in dollars . . . Yes, sir. Thank you for your understanding," he added, as he pocketed the phone. He gingerly handed the malodorous currency to the *officiant*, who carefully carried it over to the cash register.

"That was close," President Medvedev said, breathing a sigh of relief that was shared by his fellow heads of state. "President Hu, thank you for your kind assistance with the bill. I truly apologize for this oversight on my part."

"I am glad I was able to help," said President Hu through his translator.

"Let me pay you back," President Medvedev said, offering a handful of rubles.

President Hu's translator waved his hand and shook his head. "President Hu asked if you could send him the payment in dollars at your earliest convenience?" the translator asked. "He does not usually take rubles either," he added.

"Yes, of course," President Medvedev said, surprised and

embarrassed. He pocketed the rubles and thought for a moment. "This is truly absurd," he grumbled. "To think that I am the President of Russia, at a tavern with my fellow heads of state in the middle of Russia, and I cannot even pay a bill with rubles is absolutely appalling," he complained bitterly.

"It is ridiculous," President Singh agreed. "Last week I tried to buy a new Mercedes at a dealership in Mumbai and the owner would not accept my payment in rupees. I had to go to a bank and exchange the rupees for dollars to purchase the car."

"I know exactly what you mean," President da Silva added. "I tried to pay the caterer for my daughter's wedding in Brazilian reais but he said that he could only accept dollars. I was so angry but I had no choice but to go to the bank just like President Singh and get dollars to take care of the caterer's bill."

"Perhaps we should form our own bank," President Hu said through his translator. "A bank that is not dependent on dollars."

"A bank that does not even use dollars," President Singh said excitedly.

"A bank that uses only rubles, reais, rupees and renminbi," President da Silva added.

"Why don't we start this bank today?" President Medvedev said, no longer concerned about being shot in the back of the head or run over by his own car. The excited nods around the table convinced him that they were onto something almost as important as the bonus point schedules for their respective multilevel marketing operations. President Medvedev pulled out a pen and grabbed an unused cocktail napkin. "What shall we call this bank?" he asked.

"How about 'First Federal Savings and Loan'?" President Singh asked.

"That may be a little too colloquial," President Medvedev said gently. "We need something grander," he said. "Something that suggests a global presence."

"How about 'Citibank'?" President Hu said through his translator.

"Good try," President Medvedev said. "But I think that name is already taken," he said. "Any other suggestions?"

President da Silva was thoughtful. "Let's do something different," he suggested. "Why don't we take the first letter from the names of each of our four countries and create an acronym for the name of the bank.

"Okay, okay," President Medvedev said excitedly. "Now we are getting somewhere!" He started writing four letter combinations on the napkin. "How about 'ICRB' or 'RIBC'?" he asked the others.

"That does not really flow off the tongue," President Hu's translator said. "Yes, sir?" he asked, turning to President Hu. "Okay." His translator offered a response: "What about 'CRIB'?" he asked. "The CRIB Bank," he announced.

President Singh shook his head. "I like the fact that it is an actual word that can be easily pronounced, but to me the word 'CRIB' evokes images of cute little babies and not a gigantic international bank."

President Hu and his translator reluctantly nodded in agreement.

"How about 'BIRC'?" President Medvedev asked.

"That sounds too close to the word 'burp,'" President da Silva said.

"That's true," President Medvedev agreed. "We don't want our customers to think about vomiting every time they see our signs," he pointed out.

There was a crashing sound at the other end of the tavern as the *ofitsiant* tripped, sending a platter laden with several glasses destined for a nearby table crashing onto the floor. Drinks and shards of glass cascaded across the room as the *ofitsiant* landed face-first on the floor. He slowly pulled himself up to a sitting position as Mr. Gagarin ran over to assist him. "Are you okay?" he asked the *ofitsiant*.

"I think so, sir," the *ofitsiant* replied, dazed. He rubbed his head and looked around at the puddled drinks and scattered pieces of glass all around him. "I am very sorry, sir," he said, trying to clear his head. "I think I tripped on that brick over there," he added, pointing to a nearby broken brick that had apparently become dislodged from the wall at some point.

"Well, at least you are not hurt," Mr. Gagarin said, helping the *ofitsiant* to his feet. He clicked his fingers, and two other servers rushed over and began sweeping up the broken glass and mopping the floor. Mr. Gagarin then returned to President Medvedev's table. "I am so sorry about that disturbance, Mr. President," he said.

"Not a problem," President Medvedev replied. "I am glad that your *ofitsiant* did not get seriously hurt," he added.

"Thank you, sir," Mr. Gagarin replied. He held up the brick. "I have to get someone in here tomorrow to reattach this brick—"

"That's it!" President Singh said.

"What are you talking about?" President Medvedev asked as Mr. Gagarin floated away.

"BRICK," President Singh said. "That is the name of our new bank," he said. He looked troubled for a moment. "Of course we do not have a country that starts with a 'K'," he acknowledged.

Everyone at the table was silent for a moment. "What countries have names starting with the letter 'K'?" President da Silva asked.

"Kenya, Korea, Kazakhstan, Kuwait, Kosovo, Kiribati, and Kyrgyzstan," President Hu's translator said after consulting with his boss.

"That's very impressive," President Medvedev said. "President Hu must have been a very good student in school," he added. "So the real question is whether it makes sense to include any of these countries as founding members," he said to his colleagues. "Each of the four of us represent countries that are regional if not global powers," he pointed out. "So I don't think it makes a lot of sense to bring in a small country that will water down our own control of the bank simply to satisfy the spelling of the word 'BRICK,'" he said. "None of these seven countries are what I would consider to be major regional powers although Korea has a formidable economy and Kuwait is, of course, a major oil producer—"

"What about Kansas?" President Singh asked.

"Kansas?" President Medvedev asked, puzzled.

"Yes, you know, the place where Dorothy came from in

The Wizard of Oz," President Singh explained. "Didn't you see the movie?"

"No, I don't think so," President Medvedev said, drawing a blank.

"It is a classic fairy tale," President Hu said through his translator. "A rousing adventure featuring a memorable cast of endearing characters engaged in a quintessential battle of good versus evil." He smiled. "Judy Garland's rendition of *Somewhere Over the Rainbow* always gets to me," President Hu said through his translator, tears welling up in his eyes.

"But isn't Kansas a state in the United States?"

"Yes," President Singh admitted. "So what?"

"Why would we want to have an American state such as Kansas as a partner in our new global bank that we are setting up specifically to avoid the use of American dollars?"

"It would irritate the Americans very much," President da Silva pointed out as President Singh nodded in agreement. "That has to count for something," President da Silva added.

"I understand that," President Medvedev said. "But would we really want to have Kansas as a full-fledged partner in our bank?"

The other heads of state looked at each other and slowly shook their heads in unison. "After all," President Medvedev continued, "there is nothing that prevents us from calling our bank the 'BRIC' bank without the letter 'K,'" he pointed out.

"Oh, I see," President Singh agreed. "We don't need to spell 'BRICK' with a 'K,'" he said as the metaphorical sunlight broke through the clouds. "In fact, it looks a little more edgy to spell it as 'BRIC' instead of 'BRICK,'" he added. The other heads of state nodded in agreement. "Plus, we don't have to worry about dealing with Kansas," he added. "I would much prefer that the four of us keep control of the bank."

"Yes!" President da Silva agreed. "So much for Kansas," he added.

"Agreed," replied President Hu through his translator.

"Who needs Kansas?" President Singh said rhetorically.

"Then it's settled," President Medvedev agreed. He scrawled the word 'BRIC' on the napkin and the words "Established June 16, 2009". He then signed his name as President of Russia and then passed the napkin over to each of the other heads of state for their signatures. When the napkin came back, President Medvedev looked it over and smiled. "Gentlemen, congratulations on the creation of BRIC—an entirely new type of global organization that will be operated to benefit both the rest of the world as well as its four founding countries." He raised his gold cup. "To our success," he said, and the four heads of state lifted their gold cups and clinked them together.

PART ONE

THE BIGGEST DEBUTANTE BALL OF ALL TIME

CHAPTER 1

THE BRICS GALA AFFAIR PART ONE

"You're on in five."

"Four."

"Three."

"Two."

"One."

A crescendo of drums and bass instruments filled the air as the center camera focused on three people—two men wearing black tuxedos and one woman wearing a black formal dress— seated at a makeshift glass news desk with an enormous banner proclaiming *Comings and Goings* attached to the front. The desk was perched up on a balcony overlooking what appeared to be a cavernous, opulent ballroom in which hundreds of formally

dressed people wandered around trading pleasantries and grabbing drinks and *hors d'oeuvres* from the trays servers carried.
The music stopped as the director cued the man sitting in the
center seat.

"Good evening, ladies and gentlemen, and welcome to
Comings and Goings, America's favorite news magazine show,"
the man began, his voice's reassuring timbre honed over a 20-
year broadcasting career that began with voice-over work and
occasional employment as an extra in adult movies. "Thank you
for joining us tonight in the Louvre's Louis XIV Grand Ballroom
for the first BRICS Gala Affair." The camera zoomed in on the
speaker. "My name is Ken Roberts and I am joined tonight by the
distinguished foreign affairs correspondent, Margaret Hill, as well
as the Nobel Prize winning economist, Stanislaw Zutnik. We are
broadcasting from perhaps the most famous art museum in the
world which boasts priceless treasures including the Mona Lisa,
the Venus de Milo, the Winged Victory of Samothrace, the Raft
of Medusa, and Liberty Leading the People. What better place to
host what may be one of the most historically significant events
of this century—the formal coming out party for the leading
nations that make up the BRICS organization." He turned to
his left. "Margaret, could you tell our audience a little bit about
BRICS and why its member nations have come together to form
this entity?"

"Of course, Ken," Margaret replied, looking splendid in a
full-length, shimmering black evening gown with a giant fuzzy
yellow tarantula pinned to the left shoulder. "BRICS is an acronym that stands for Brazil, Russia, India, China and South Africa.
These nations are the founding members of the organization

known as BRICS, which was originally established to promote economic and political ties between the members—"

"By the way," Ken interrupted, "I wanted to compliment you on your dress this evening."

"Oh, thank you, Ken," Margaret replied, smiling. "It is an Eloise Wang original in silk with a complementing suede collar and cuffs. I have worn Eloise's dresses to past formal affairs because she has a unique talent for bringing together the expected and the unexpected in *haute couture*." Margaret looked a little uneasily at the dangling giant tarantula. "There are very few designers who can successfully integrate formal evening wear and arachnids in such a seamless way." She sneezed and a yellow cloud slowly wafted over the desk and dissipated. "I think I may be allergic to the fuzz," she sniffed, then gamely looked back at the camera. "Anyways, the creation of BRICS was motivated by the desire of both Russia and China to create an economic and political counterweight to the United States and the other advanced developed economies known as the G7 nations, which include Canada, France, Germany, Italy, the United Kingdom and Japan. The first formal BRIC summit was held in 2009 in Yekaterinburg, Russia, and was attended by the leaders of Brazil, Russia, India and China."

"I see." Ken looked thoughtful. "So what are some of the things that have motivated the BRICS countries to try to compete with the United States and its allies?"

"Well, Ken," Margaret began, sneezing again and sending another poof of yellow above the news desk. "BRICS represents a concerted effort by its nameplate members to set up an alternative political and economic network of member states able to operate independently of the neoliberal global economy that is currently dominated by the United States. The BRICS nations are particularly concerned about the dominant role of the U.S. dollar in the global economy. As you may know, Ken, the U.S. dollar is used in nearly 70 percent of all transactions carried out in the world. The BRICS nations ultimately hope to de-dollarize the global economy to some extent by expanding the use of their own currencies and thus weaken the financial preeminence of the United States."

"What's wrong with dollar bills?" Ken asked, puzzled, peering at several bills in his wallet. "I know they used to be a drab olive green, but they are certainly much more colorful these days what with all of the orange watermarks and the red seals and the blue magnetic strips—"

"Ken, it has nothing to do with the appearance of our dollars," Margaret said, exasperated. "It has everything to do with the prevalence of the dollar as the global currency of choice," she explained. "When everyone uses dollars to engage in international trade, it essentially gives the United States the ability to print an almost unlimited amount of dollars because there are always countries who want to acquire dollars so that they can purchase goods and services from other countries, whether it is oil from Saudi Arabia or machinery from Germany or automobiles from Japan—"

"Sort of like an unending credit card?" Ken asked, curious.

"Exactly," Margaret responded. "But it goes even further. Because the United States dollar is so ubiquitous, the American government can impose crippling financial sanctions on any individual nation by depriving the offending nation of access to the SWIFT financial system—which is a global cooperative that enables banks and other financial institutions to transfer money and information around the world. If the United States were to cut off a country's access to SWIFT (as it did to Russia after it invaded Ukraine in 2022), then that country's banks can be disconnected from the global financial system. In other words, the United States can make it very difficult for those banks to transmit or receive money and thereby essentially cripple their operations." She sneezed again. "The BRICS countries want to develop an alternate international payment system that is not controlled by the United States. They do not want to have to worry about financial sanctions being imposed upon them if they do something that would displease Washington such as, oh, I don't know, invading another country and killing hundreds of thousands of its citizens."

"Margaret, it sounds like these BRICS countries are drawn together by their mutual dislike for the American-dominated global economy," Ken observed coolly. "Thank you for that very helpful analysis." He turned to Professor Zutnik, who was sitting quietly, having apparently dozed off. "Professor?" Ken said. "Professor?" Ken tapped Professor Zutnik's shoulder. Professor Zutnik shook his head and opened his eyes. "I am sorry," he muttered. "I must have fallen asleep."

"Not a problem, sir," Ken replied. "Professor Zutnik, you are one of the foremost experts on global economics and were awarded a Nobel Prize in Economics for your work in international trade theory. Perhaps you could explain to our audience some of the problems that the BRICS countries may face in trying to set up a new global banking system?"

Zutnik stretched his arms and yawned loudly. "But of course," he replied, adjusting his thick glasses. "Before I came on the show, I prepared some simple equations to demonstrate mathematically the ways in which the BRICS nations might be able to replicate the current global trading system—albeit on a more limited basis." He motioned to a stagehand. "Can you bring over the white board, young man?" A stagehand rolled a white board onto the set behind Professor Zutnik. It was laden with a dense array of mathematical hieroglyphics that would have caused Albert Einstein to break into a cold sweat. "Ken, I thought it best to describe mathematically the basic variables and factors underpinning the international trading system," Zutnik said, turning his chair so that he could see the board. "These equations may appear somewhat daunting," he added, "but I have no doubt that members of the television audience who have a thorough understanding of Fourier analysis, differential equations and multivariable calculus, or an advanced post doctorate degree in discrete mathematics will be able to follow along without any difficulty—"

Ken looked into the camera like a deer staring at the headlights of an oncoming truck. "Professor," he stammered finally. "Although we appreciate your efforts to educate our audience about the mathematical underpinnings of the world's economic system, I am afraid that we are severely limited on time. Perhaps you could dispense with the equations and provide a more simplified explanation of the obstacles that you see facing the BRICS members."

"Ken, it took me a long time to write out all of these equations," Professor Zutnik said, visibly annoyed. "There are numerous variables and subscripts and superscripts, all of which have to be checked for accuracy. It is a very tedious job."

"Yes, sir, I appreciate the work you have done to write out these very impressive equations, but this is not exactly grade school addition and subtraction—"

"On the contrary, Ken," Professor Zutnik replied. "This is a very sophisticated and elegant description of an extremely complex and dynamic system—oh, wait, I see a boo-boo." He reached up, rubbed out a variable and then wrote in another symbol. "There!" he said. "See, this is why these equations are so intricate; if you get a single term wrong, then the whole thing can fall apart." He shook his head. "It is quite a burden to bear when you are as smart as I am," he pointed out. "What with carrying the torch of Western civilization forward and all that," he added.

"Of course, Professor," Ken said soothingly. "But for those members of our viewing audience who did not master calculus or trigonometry or even algebra, could you please provide a more accessible explanation of the barriers that the BRICS nations would encounter if they were to try to usurp the existing global economic system?"

"Well, I am nothing if not sympathetic to dumb people," Professor Zutnik said charitably. "Very well." He shoved the white board back and it rolled off camera and over the toes of the stagehand, who stifled a scream. "There are several problems with the BRICS system. First, the annual BRICS summits often appear to be little more than photo opportunities for the member heads of state to get together and talk about creating a new global economic system that will be more democratic and more equitable for all the nations of the world—"

"This of course coming from China and Russia," interrupted Margaret, "two countries that are not exactly known for their democratic traditions."

"The irony is not lost upon me, Margaret," Professor Zutnik chuckled. "Anyway, many critics have said that the BRICs summits are long on self-congratulatory speeches and short on actual deeds.

"Second, there is the sharp contrast between the lofty platitudes that each of these countries offers at the summits and the on-going disputes that are actually occurring as we speak between many of the BRICS members—"

"Such as?" Ken interjected, wanting to add to the scholarly discussion.

"Such as the on-going territorial and trade disputes between China and India," Professor Zutnik responded. "There is also a divergence of views about what each of the members want to achieve in the end—Russia and China want to take over the world and the other BRICS countries are more concerned with improving their economic fortunes and obtaining a greater degree of financial self-sufficiency."

"What can BRICS offer the poor countries of the world, Professor Zutnik?" Margaret asked, between sneezes.

Professor Zutnik shrugged his shoulders. "Not a great deal at this time," he said. "China and Russia are major powers determined to use their own currencies as much as possible in international trade. However, most poor countries have very fragile economies and often tie their own currencies to the dollar—"

"Which means?" Ken inquired, further adding to the scholarly discussion.

"Which means that if these countries stopped tying their own currencies to the dollar, then they would risk financial collapse." Professor Zutnik looked around. "It would be a very big mess."

"Doesn't BRICS have its own bank?" Margaret asked.

"They do!" Professor Zutnik replied. "It is called the New Development Bank and was founded in 2015—"

"Do they offer competitive rates on credit cards?" Ken asked. "Or double bonus miles for air travel?"

"It's not that kind of bank," Zutnik snapped. "It is supposed to be the main rival to the International Monetary Fund, or IMF, and the World Bank—which are the leading Western-dominated global banking institutions. As such, the New Development Bank or NDB was envisioned by the BRICS members as an entity that could support public or private projects and cooperate with other international organizations and financial institutions to advance the objectives of the BRICS members."

"Is it a big bank?" Ken asked.

"It was initially capitalized at $100 billion," Professor Zutnik replied. "Each of the founding BRICS member nations have pledged billions of dollars to capitalize the bank. Indeed, they have built the headquarters of the bank in Shanghai, China. The building reminds me of a bunch of oddly-stacked cardboard boxes," he added.

"Has the bank financed any development projects?" Margaret asked.

Professor Zutnik thought for a moment. "I believe that they have approved several dozen infrastructure and development projects totaling tens of billions of dollars to date. Some of these projects have been undertaken in member countries and others have been initiated in other developing countries."

"Would I be able to get a car loan from the NDB?" Ken persisted.

"As the NDB is supposed to fund infrastructure and development projects, I rather doubt that they would finance a car loan."

"Professor, I am not talking about a loan to purchase a sub-compact economy car," Ken explained. "I am considering buying an ultra-luxurious German sports car—"

"I just don't think they are interested in doing car loans of any type," Professor Zutnik said.

"Too bad," Ken said, shaking his head. "They are leaving money on the table, in my opinion."

Margaret looked thoughtful. "Professor Zutnik, what exactly are the qualifications that a prospective applicant must have to be considered for membership in BRICS?" She sneezed twice and then glared at the fuzzy yellow tarantula hanging from her shoulder. "I can't take this anymore," she said angrily, unpinning the tarantula and tossing it behind the news desk.

"Well, there are a series of guiding principles for BRICS membership which boil down to the applicant nation having a certain amount of resources. After all, the founders of BRICS are not really interested in admitting a bunch of extremely poor countries. They want new members who are able to contribute to the funding of BRICS and the NDB. They want to welcome regional powers who can help shape political events in various parts of the world." He checked his watch. "Newer BRICS members are expected to embrace the founding values and principles of BRICS, which basically means that they will parrot the views of the twin overlords of BRICS—Russia and China—on a global stage. New members agree not to impose sanctions on each other and they also promise to support measures to make the United Nations more democratic—"Professor Zutnik exploded in laughter. "I'm sorry," he said, giggling. "I found that statement about the United Nations becoming more democratic to be very funny." He cleared his throat. "Anyway, there is a lot of diplomatic gobbledygook in the standards promulgated by the BRICS organization but everything essentially boils down to new members towing the company line being pushed by Russia and China—"

"Professor Zutnik," Ken interrupted, peering at the director. "I am sorry to cut in on your very fascinating explanation, but I have just received word from our roving correspondent, Alex Marvelll, who is below us on the floor of the Louis XIV ballroom, that President Vladimir Putin of Russia is about to enter the room. Alex, take it away."

The camera cut to the ballroom floor where a bespectacled young man dressed in a brown corduroy suit was standing, surrounded by groups of formally dressed men and women engaging in conversations and enjoying drinks and delectable goodies. "Thank you, Ken," Alex replied. "We have just been told that President Vladimir Putin is ready to make his formal appearance at the BRICS gala. The fact that he is even here is surprising to some commentators because there is still an outstanding arrest warrant, issued by the International Criminal Court in 2023, against President Putin for war crimes, crimes against humanity and genocide arising from Russia's invasion of Ukraine." He looked over at a large hallway. "Of course, there are others who say that this warrant is all a misunderstanding but that is certainly a minority view—particularly among the citizens of Ukraine." He peered intently into the hall. "Wait, I think I see him now!"

The ballroom was drowned in a thundering tidal wave of sound as the Russian national anthem began. Alex pointed out that the Russian national anthem has the same melody as the national anthem of the former Soviet Union but with slightly peppier lyrics.

All eyes turned to the hallway as a shirtless Vladimir Putin rode in on a magnificent white horse while carrying an enormous golden sword. The horse walked forward toward the center of the ballroom as Putin began shifting the sword from one hand to another and twirling it. "Ken," Alex began, "I do want to give our viewing audience a little information about President Putin's wardrobe. As you can see, President Putin has chosen to go with a minimalist approach, disregarding his dress shirt entirely to display his bare chest which, like the top of his bare head, appears to be covered in shiny body oil. His belt is made of the finest black Argentinian leather which was cured, cut and sewn by craftsmen at the "Polar Wolf" Arctic penal colony. Moreover, his military-grade boots contain miniature flame throwers and machine guns. However, the real story of his wardrobe is his black silk trousers which were produced by a succession of tailors—each of whom suffered a mysterious death." Alex looked at his cards. "The first tailor fell out of a sixth-floor hotel window, the second died after being pricked by a poisonous pin, the third fell off of a yacht and was torn to pieces by the engine propeller, the fourth ran over himself with his own car, and the fifth shot himself in the back seventeen times." He shook his head. "So tragic." Then he smiled. "But the sixth tailor persevered, and managed to finish the trousers and deliver them to the Kremlin, under cover of darkness, before going into hiding. So everything worked out after all." Alex motioned for a passing server carrying a tray to come over. "Thank you," he said, grabbing a handful of crab cakes and stuffing them into his coat pocket.

"Alex, why is President Putin swinging that heavy sword around?" Ken asked, as Putin raised the sword over his head before swishing it in a succession of sideways figure-8 motions.

Alex watched Putin sling the sword over his head several times. "According to several Russian officials, Putin regards himself as the defender of Christianity and sees himself as the successor to Charlemagne, the first Emperor of the Holy Roman Empire. Charlemagne reportedly carried around a big sword called *Joyeuse* to lop off the head of the occasional heckler. This sword was later carried in the coronation processions of several French kings before finally being sent to the Louvre in the late 18th century, where it is currently on exhibit.

Putin suddenly dropped his sword. He angrily waved at an attendant who quickly ran over and handed it back to him. "I think the sword is too slippery for him to hold," Alex observed. "It must be all of that oil that he has on his body." Alex shielded his eyes with his free hand. "His head is throwing off quite a glare from the lights."

"Alex, what are all of those labels on the side of the horse?" Margaret asked. "They look like—"

"Corporate sponsors," Alex replied as the camera zoomed in on the numerous labels that were plastered like a multi-colored checkerboard to the side of President Putin's horse. "President Putin is trying to inject a greater sense of entrepreneurialism into

Russian society and so he has obtained corporate sponsors from a virtual who's-who of global corporations: Nike. Sony. IBM. Citicorp. Tesla. Broadcom. Samsung. Apple. Microsoft. Google. General Motors. It also provides him with a bit of extra spending money should his political career hit the skids."

Margaret and Ken were dumbfounded by the dozens of corporate labels blanketing the sides of Putin's horse. "Amazing," Margaret said finally. "Simply amazing."

Putin raised the sword several times and then tossed it into the air like a baton. He reached out to catch it, but it struck his arm blade-first and neatly severed his hand—which landed on the ground next to the sword. Putin began screaming in agony as he held up what was left of his arm, which was now spurting blood like the Trevi Fountain. His eyes rolled back in his head and he swayed back and forth and then slumped over on top of his horse as several attendants ran out to assist him. One man grabbed the reins of the horse and led it back down the hallway. The second attendant picked up the sword and then, after a few seconds of hesitation, the bloody hand. He looked around, rushed over to a bartender and plunged the hand in an ice bucket. He then grabbed the ice bucket and ran back down the hallway after the horse.

"Wow," was all that Alex could say. "I always thought these formal get-togethers were stuffy affairs. I would have never expected anything as exciting as seeing someone chop off their own hand—particularly while riding a horse."

"That does add to the entertainment value," Ken agreed. "Margaret, do you have anything to add?" Ken wanted to know.

"I think I am going to be sick," Margaret coughed, dashing off the set toward the restroom.

"Professor Zutnik?" Ken implored, trying to figure out how to segue-way into the commercial break.

"It was very impressive how high Putin's blood shot up in the air," Professor Zutnik observed. "Very much a parabolic curve," he added. "Putin must have extremely high blood pressure."

"Okay, thank you," Ken said, not finding Professor Zutnik's analysis to be very helpful. "Alex, who is the next guest of honor."

Alex put down an empty glass of champagne on a tray that happened to be floating by. "Ken, I have just been told that the next guest will be President Xi Jinping of China." He looked down the hallway. Suddenly, a brass fanfare rumbled through the hall and filled the ballroom. "Ken, that is the Chinese national anthem which is called *Yìyǒngjūn Jìnxíngqǔ*."

"Well, it's very catchy," Ken said, bobbing his head so that he could look "hip" to the viewing audience. "Do you see President Xi yet?"

"It's rather dark in the hallway," Alex responded. "Wait! There he is! Well, look at that!" He checked his notes. "President Xi of China is seated on a jewel-encrusted gold throne that is being held aloft by eight men—four on each side. President Xi himself is dressed in a long silk yellow robe adorned with a crimson dragon on his chest. This is a recreation of the official robe worn by the emperors of the Tang Dynasty, which flourished from 618 to 906 AD. The Tang Dynasty is widely regarded as China's most successful ruling dynasty."

Margaret returned to the set and sat down, shaking her head.

"I'm sorry about that," she said. "Alex, why would President Xi be wearing the robe of a dynastic emperor?" she asked.

Alex checked his notes. "It may be that he is trying to remind China's citizens that he wants to champion traditional Chinese values and cast himself as the modern symbol of China's 5,000-year-old civilization." Alex stopped for a second to adjust his earpiece. "By the way, I am being told that the intricate embroidery work on President Xi's outfit was performed by small children with nimble fingers at one of the Uyghurs labor camps in western China." He shook his shoulders. "But as far as Xi's choice in garments tonight is concerned, it may be that he simply likes wearing yellow silk robes." Alex looked closer. "It looks like the robe would be very comfortable. As you know, silk is highly regarded for its breathability, which makes it a top choice for emperors and presidents alike on those warm summer days when they have to attend public events like a hanging—"

"Alex," Margaret interrupted. "It looks like each of those men holding up President's Xi's throne are wearing different outfits. Are they from different parts of China?" she wondered.

Alex laughed. "No, that's what I thought at first but apparently not. I was told that each of these men is a world-class athlete from a different country that has borrowed money from China for some type of infrastructure project."

"I don't understand," Margaret said, puzzled.

"Well, the fellow carrying Xi's throne on the front left side is from Pakistan, a country that owes China nearly $80 billion. His name is Muhammed El-Farin and he is a champion powerlifter who has been handed over to the Chinese until Pakistan pays its debts off—"

"You mean he is part of the collateral for the loan?" Margaret asked, horrified.

"Apparently so," Alex said cheerfully. "And the big fellow at the end of the right side is from Angola, which owes China almost $15 billion in oil-backed loans. His name is Nongolo Odoronoku and he throws the shot put—"

"And he is also pledged as collateral?" Margaret exclaimed indignantly.

"Apparently they all are," Alex said sheepishly.

"This is absolutely despicable!" Margaret said. "For goodness sakes, we are living in the twenty-first century—"

"Well, Margaret, to be fair, we should point out that each of these countries chose to borrow money from China voluntarily," Ken pointed out, offering additional scholarly insight. "Besides, it may be a common banking practice in those countries to offer human beings as collateral. We really should not judge them if we have not walked in their shoes," he declared, putting an additional philosophical sheen on the broadcast.

The eight men carried President Xi to the middle of the ballroom where President Putin had just severed his hand and set the carriage down on the ground. President Xi climbed off the throne, gingerly stepped around the blood splatters and walked over to a lectern as the national anthem faded out.

"Ladies and gentlemen, please welcome the President of China, Xi Jinping," a voice announced. The audience erupted in thunderous applause as Xi smiled, basking in the public adulation. He retrieved a sheet of paper from his robe and laid it on top of the lectern.

"Margaret, any idea what President Xi has in mind for us?" Ken asked, wondering if President Xi knew any magic tricks.

Margaret looked at her notes. "He is going to give a speech celebrating the BRICS members and, as a special treat, will offer his own personal criticisms of the United States and its 'deviant popular culture—'"

"I suspect this will not be a balanced presentation," Ken quipped.

"Uh oh," Margaret said.

"What?" Ken asked.

"There is no English translator available. It says here that Xi will be reading his speech in Mandarin."

"Mandarin?" Ken turned up his nose. "What are we supposed to do? We don't have a translator on staff." He looked around nervously. "Alex, did you know anything about President Xi giving his speech in Mandarin?"

"That's news to me," Alex said, swiping several pigs in a blanket from a passing tray. "Back to you, Ken."

Margaret suddenly had an idea. "My phone has a translator app. Maybe it can translate President Xi's speech." She retrieved her phone from her purse. "Oh, drat!" she said. "There is no reception in here." She stood up, holding her phone with her outstretched arm and turned around in a circle. "No, nothing yet. " she said, disappointed.

"Maybe you need to climb on the desk," Ken offered, trying to be helpful. "I promise I won't try to peek up your dress," he added.

"You'll die trying," Margaret said good-naturedly, taking his outstretched hand and stepping up onto the chair and then on top of the table. She turned around in a half circle and then stopped.

"There!" she exclaimed. "I finally have a signal." She waved her free hand. "Okay, everyone, please be quiet" she said. The set was silent. They could hear President Xi beginning to speak, faintly but clearly, droning on in what they presumed was Mandarin. "Okay," she said. "I will read the translation off the phone: 'Good evening, ladies and gentlemen. Thank you for coming to the first BRICS gala affair. China extends its warmest wishes of peace and prosperity to all nations except for Taiwan and the United States and Ukraine—the last of which continues to resist the warm embrace of its Russian neighbor.

"'The BRICS organization was set up to help developing nations obtain funds to undertake infrastructure projects and expand their economies—'"

"I lost the signal," Margaret shouted. She turned around. "It's sort of spotty," she said. "The screen keeps going in and out."

"Just do your best, Margaret," Ken consoled, admiring her form.

She tilted the phone back and forth. "I am just getting scattered fragments," she complained. "I guess I should have upgraded to the premium service," she admitted. She looked again. "Okay. Xi is saying that he would like to stick his tongue in his first-grade teacher's ear."

"Is that an exact quote?" Ken asked.

"Probably not, Ken," Margaret said sarcastically. "The phone keeps fritzing out." She waited for a moment. "Here is it: 'China welcomes the opportunity to usher in a new international order that is founded on principles of equality and . . . and would like to sniff your long brown hair.'" She shook her head. "Stupid phone," she muttered. "'China and Russia have forged an eternal bond that shall enable us to establish a new global banking system . . . that will enjoy licking your inner thighs.'" Margaret tossed the phone aside. "This is absurd," she snorted, stepping back down off the desk.

"Maybe we should just guess what he is saying," Alex offered. "Let me give it a try." He cleared his throat. "'I am deeply honored to be here at the BRICS gala affair. China welcomes the opportunity to lead the developing world into a new era of peace and prosperity. All nations can rest assured that China will work tirelessly to redress the wrongs of the current global trading system which favors the war-mongering, blood-sucking crony capitalist Western powers—'" He turned to the camera. "How did you like that last phrase?" he asked, visibly pleased with himself. "Straight out of my college class in Marxist studies!" Ken nodded his approval. "Okay," Alex said, encouraged. "'China will continue to work unceasingly to bring about a new era in which the oppressed nations of the world will rise up and send their armies to occupy the lands of Europe and America and rape and pillage and burn—'"

"Thank you very much for that vivid description, Alex," Ken interrupted as the camera cut back to the set. "I'm afraid Alex was getting a little carried away there," he said. "We apologize to our viewers for the lack of an English-speaking version of President Xi's speech." He looked down at the ballroom. "It looks like President Xi has finished his speech and is stepping down away the lectern. He is now getting back on his gold throne and being lifted up into the air. And there he goes—back down the hallway being borne aloft by eight world-class athletes on loan to China."

Ken turned back to the camera. "Margaret, why do you think that no English translator was provided?" he asked.

Margaret was thoughtful. "It may be a calculated move by President Xi to underscore his belief that the events of the world will be increasingly centered around China. He may believe that Mandarin is becoming the new English language of the world. As a result, he may think it unnecessary or even insulting to China itself to provide a translator. "

"Okay," Ken said. "Professor Zutnik," any final thoughts regarding President Xi's speech?"

"I thought Alex did a good livening it up," Professor Zutnik said, chuckling. "I took a couple classes in Mandarin when I was doing my post-graduate work and from what I could hear, it sounded like President Xi was offering a bunch of platitudes but not much more. This would be typical of the Chinese leadership to wax poetically about BRICS but not really get into any specific policy details."

"Okay," Ken said. "Margaret, what value does tonight's appearance provide to President Xi?"

"Ken, I think President Xi was able to bolster his stature as a global leader even though most of us had no idea what he was saying," she answered. "The BRICS gala affair is being televised to a worldwide audience so it will provide a platform for him to try to project an image of power, particularly with him having been carried in by eight men. Certainly, the imagery underscores President Xi's belief that China is the ascendant global superpower— "

"Which is not the prevailing view among Western scholars and economists any longer," Professor Zutnik interrupted. "China faces a number of severe problems, not the least of which is the fact that its population is declining rapidly."

"Really?" Ken said, surprised.

"Indeed," Zutnik answered. "India surpassed China as the world's most populous nation several years ago. China's current population of 1.3 billion people is rapidly aging and is projected to decline precipitously over the rest of the century to less than 500 million by the year 2100. This decrease in population is being mirrored by a stagnating economic growth rate which may indeed have turned negative in the past few years after four decades of near-double digit annual growth."

"That sounds very ominous," Ken said. "I assume that this view is not popular with the Chinese Communist Party or CCP."

"No, that is a very safe bet," Professor Zutnik responded. "The CCP's official line is that China will become the dominant economic and military superpower in the next few years. Anyone who disagrees with that view will probably find themselves doing embroidery work in one of the Uyghur labor camps."

Professor Zutnik was thoughtful: "I should also point out that China's declining population will also be accompanied by both an enormous increase in retirees and an even more calamitous drop in the worker population—"

"Not a very rosy scenario," Ken interjected.

"No, it is what we call a pretty kettle of fish in the academic world," Professor Zutnik laughed. "But we shall see if these trends continue over the next few years. However, I know of no reason to think that they will be reversed anytime soon—"

"Professor, I am sorry to interrupt you but I just received an update regarding the health of President Vladimir Putin. He is currently in surgery to have his hand reattached to his arm and his doctors are cautiously optimistic that he will regain at least some function in his hand. I am also pleased to report that his horse has been bathed and is enjoying a bowl of oats.

"I'm so glad the horse is okay," Margaret said, relieved.

"Well, I see that we have reached the intermission of the BRICS gala ball," Ken announced. "We will be back after these commercial messages to see Prime Minister Modi of India and President da Silva of Brazil, the latter of whom I am told will be demonstrating his skill at juggling flaming torches. See you soon."

CHAPTER 2

THE BRICS GALA AFFAIR PART TWO

"Okay, we are coming back from the intermission.

"Five.

"Four.

"Three.

"Two.

"One."

The familiar crescendo of the overture faded as the camera zoomed in on the twelve-time nominee for best news personality, Ken Roberts, who appeared to be in deep thought. "You know," he said to no one in particular, "the tempo of our overture has always reminded me of two elephants copulating on the Serengeti Plains." He shook his head as Margaret looked at him, unsure as to whether she should shush him or cut to the chase and whack him over the head with the boom mike.

The director motioned frantically to Ken that he was on the air.

"Good evening, ladies and gentlemen," Ken began, snapping back into overpaid broadcasting form. He shuffled some blank papers that had been placed on the desk in front of him during the intermission so that he could look more serious. "Welcome back to the BRICS Gala Affair. For those of you who have just joined us, we are broadcasting from the Louis XIV ballroom of the Louvre in Paris, France. We have already seen President Vladimir Putin of Russia, who appears to need some additional sword-handling lessons and who is currently at the hospital having his hand re-attached. President Xi of China also stopped by to address the crowd, having been carried in on a golden throne while dressed in the robe of a dynastic emperor. " He turned to Margaret who had not tried to re-attach the fuzzy yellow tarantula to her black silk evening gown. "Margaret, we are still expecting to see Prime Minister Modi of India and President da Silva of Brazil this evening. Any thoughts as to what we should expect?"

Margaret nodded, relieved that Ken had not offered an opinion about the glass news desk or the weather or, indeed, anything else. "Ken, I think both of these leaders will want to make an impression on the television audience—particularly in their home countries—because they are largely overshadowed by President Putin of Russian and President Xi of China."

"Well, it is hard to compete with the Russian president cutting off his own hand," Ken pointed out.

"Indeed," Margaret said. "I don't think either of us expect

anything so dramatic from either of these two men, but the leaders of Brazil and India are acutely aware that they are not generally regarded as co-equals with their Russian and Chinese counterparts. After all, it was Russia and China that set up BRICS in the first place because they are consumed with the notion of displacing the United States as the global hegemonic power. India and Brazil have different objectives—"

"Such as?" Ken interrupted, eyeing a sheet of paper and trying to remember the steps his origami class instructor had offered for folding it into a swan.

"Ken, India and Brazil are relative newcomers to the global stage" Margaret responded. "They are both regional powers whose aspirations are less global and more continental. Brazil is the colossus of South America and India is the main challenger to China in Asia. But they have different objectives than China and Russia do. They both want to reduce their dependence on the U.S. dollar, but I think they are less enthusiastic about seeing the United States displaced by their fellow BRICS members—neither of whom is exactly known for its altruistic behavior in the international arena."

"Why?" Ken wanted to know. His pocket buzzed.

"Ken, is that your cell phone?" Margaret asked, curious.

Ken nodded. "It's my mother," he said, embarrassed. "I forgot to mute my phone."

"Well?" Margaret said expectantly. "Shouldn't you answer it? We have many mothers watching this broadcast."

Ken started to object but then thought better of that idea. "Well, since we have a few minutes before Prime Minister Modi is scheduled to appear, I guess I can speak to my mother." He retrieved the cell phone and pressed the green button. "Hello, Mother," he said, almost in a whisper.

A stagehand trying to be helpful walked over and hit the speaker button so that the television audience could enjoy the conversation between Ken and his mother. "Hello, dear," was the reply. "You look very handsome tonight."

Ken nodded. "Thank you, Mother. We all enjoyed dressing up for this event—"

"Who is that lovely girl next to you?" Ken's mother wanted to know.

Ken turned bright red and looked at Margaret who was trying not to laugh. "This is my colleague, Margaret Hill—" Ken began.

"Well, she is very pretty," Ken's mother pointed out as Margaret raised her hand over her mouth and snickered. "She has a very nice figure, don't you think?" Professor Zutnik peered over at Margaret and nodded his approval.

Sensing a potential sexual harassment lawsuit in his immediate future, Ken tried to divert his mother's attention. "Yes, Mother, but I don't think—"

"Have you asked her out on a date?" Ken's mother inquired, refusing to be diverted.

"That is a very good question, Mrs. Roberts," Margaret teased. "Ken?" she cooed expectantly.

"No, not really," Ken responded awkwardly. "She is a business colleague and an award-winning journalist," he added. "It could be very problematic with both of us working for the same employer—"

"Ken, you know I never want to interfere in your personal

life," said Ken's mother, about to interfere yet again in her son's personal life. "But I worry about you being alone. Ever since your divorce, you seem to have lost interest in dating—"

Ken looked at the camera helplessly. "Mother, I am doing fine. Everything is fine—" he declared.

"You still like girls, right?" Ken's mother asked, concerned.

"Of course I do, Mother," Ken responded tersely.

"What ever happened to that blonde woman?" Ken's mother asked. "What was her name? Angela? Abigail?"

"Her name was Angela," Ken said. "It didn't work out, Mother," he added hastily.

"Wasn't she the one who tried to blow up your car?" Ken's mother asked. Margaret looked over at Ken with wide eyes.

Ken shifted uncomfortably in his seat. "Sort of," he said. "But the police stopped her before she could detonate the explosives—"

"She did have a temper," Ken's mother added. "You must have made her mad—"

"Why do you assume that I did something to make her mad?" Ken asked his mother, apparently still oblivious to the fact that this conversation was being broadcast to millions of people around the world.

"Because you are a man and men almost always do something stupid to mess things up in their relationships," Ken's mother pointed out as Margaret and all of the female members of the studio crew nodded in agreement. "Just don't let one instance of attempted murder stop you from finding true love," she added, trying to pass on her many years of wisdom to her son.

"I won't, Mother," Ken promised, wondering if he should update his resume after the show.

"What about that girl who handcuffed you to the headboard in a hotel bedroom for a week?" Ken's mother asked, continuing to mine the endless gold mine that was his personal life.

"It was all a misunderstanding," Ken said defensively. "I forgot my safe word."

"Wasn't she a dominatrix?" Ken's mother asked.

"She was an actress," Ken said, irritated. "She said she was working her way through divinity school."

"I just want you to know that I will always love you, regardless of your personal preferences," Ken's mother declared. "There is no need to hide in the shadows—"

"I am not hiding in the shadows, Mother!" Ken said. "Everything is fine. I like girls. Preferably ones who do not know how to wire explosives to ignition switches. You have nothing to be concerned about—"

"I want grandchildren, Ken," his mother declared. "You need to get moving!"

"Mother, this is not the time or the place to discuss—"

"By the way, where is the list of the 800 numbers?" Ken's mother wanted to know, apparently losing interest in Ken's recent romantic debacles.

"800 numbers?" Ken asked, puzzled.

"Right. The 800 numbers that you call to vote for your favorite performer," Ken's mother explained, wondering if the obstetrician who delivered her son might have dropped him on his head when her attention was diverted.

A ray of light broke through Ken's sluggish brain. "Mother," he said finally. "This is not a talent show," he said. "We are broadcasting the BRICS gala affair which is sort of a debutante ball for the leaders of the founding nations of BRICS. We are not set up to have the viewing audience vote for their favorite heads of state—"

"So how do you pick a winner?" Ken's mother wanted to know.

"Ken, can I help?" Margaret asked, coming to the rescue. Ken mouthed a word of thanks. "Mrs. Roberts, this is Margaret Hill—"

"You *are* a very lovely girl," Ken's mother pointed out, returning happily to the landmine-studded field of Ken's love life.

Margaret laughed. "That is so very sweet of you to say," she said warmly.

"Have you ever thought about going out with Ken?" Ken's mother asked. "I think he makes a lot of money," she added, trying to stoke Margaret's interest.

"Oh, I am sure that Ken is doing very well," Margaret said. "But we are just friends."

"He also has a beach house in Florida," Ken's mother added, trying to lure Margaret into the family corral.

"I'm sure that it is very nice," Margaret said, agreeably.

"It *is* very nice," Ken's mother declared. "There are several bedrooms that face the water including a very spacious master bedroom," she added, almost purring.

"Mother, we need to move along," Ken jumped in, sensing that his broadcasting career might be in jeopardy. "What the—?" he blurted out as Professor Zutnik reached over, grabbed his phone and punched the "off" button. Ken looked visibly relieved as Zutnik stuffed the phone in his coat pocket. Ken made a mental note to offer to buy the professor a steak dinner. He turned back to the camera: "For those viewers who have forgotten why we are here, Margaret was about to tell us a little bit about our other two guests of honor, Prime Minister Modi of India and President da Silva of Brazil."

"Thank you, Ken," Margaret said, turning to the camera. A stagehand handed her a card. "Thank you," she said. "Oh, how thoughtful," she added. "Ken, your mother just sent me an email asking if I was available to have coffee with her—"

"Sadly you are far too busy to have coffee with my mother," Ken said hopefully.

"Fortunately, I have some time in my schedule next Thursday," Margaret responded cheerfully as Ken sank down in his seat. She turned to the camera. "Mrs. Roberts," she added, "I look forward to seeing you next Thursday. Thank you for your very kind invitation."

"Maybe we should talk about Prime Minister Modi," Professor Zutnik suggested, wondering why the servers had not brought any *hors d'oeuvres* to the set.

"Indeed, we should," Margaret said. "President Modi of India is supposed to be here in a few minutes. Here are a few facts about his background: He became the fourteenth prime minister of India in 2014 and is regarded as a conservative Hindu nationalist. He has been praised for implementing policies to encourage economic growth in India, particularly in the high tech and information technologies sectors. However, Prime Minister Modi has also been criticized for cutting back on social programs such as public health and education, and he has been vilified by many for his perceived hostility toward Muslims as he oversaw legislation that would grant Indian citizenship to members of religious groups fleeing persecution from other countries— including Christians, Buddhists and Sikhs, but not Muslims.

Nearly 80 percent of India's 1.4 billion people are Hindu and about 14 percent of Indians are Muslims—"

"Margaret, I believe Prime Minister Modi is about to enter the ballroom," Ken interrupted. "Let's go to our roving correspondent, Alex Marvelll."

The camera cut to a small room with several sinks and mirrors on one side and a row of stalls on the other side. It panned over to the single closed toilet stall, which was occupied by a man on his knees, apparently hugging the toilet bowl. The sounds of retching and vomiting reverberated against the tile walls. "Alex? Alex?" Ken asked. "Is that you in the washroom?"

The figure shifted and a hand appeared from under the door, motioning for the cameraman to hand him a microphone. "Hi Ken," Alex gasped. "Do not eat the crab cakes!" he advised, retching again. "Oh, no!" he complained. "I think I threw up on my jacket."

"Don't worry about that," Ken said, trying to be encouraging. "You need to get up and go out and do your job as a journalist. We need your firsthand expertise on the floor of the ballroom," he added as Professor Zutnik waved away a server who had finally made it to the set with a platter of crab cakes.

"I don't know," Alex said, struggling to his feet inside the stall. "It's all over my jacket." He slowly opened the door and peered out, looking as though he had been trampled by a rugby team.

"Perhaps no one will notice," Ken said, remembering that he had thought Alex's brown corduroy suit looked like someone had dunked it in a bucket of brown spew when Alex began the play-by-play of President Putin's ballroom entrance earlier that evening. "Come on, get going!" he urged. "Tell your cameraman to keep you out of frame and no one will notice—"

"That's a good idea, Ken," Alex said, wiping a vile brown substance that dripped from his mouth. "Stay off camera," he reminded himself. "That makes sense." He slowly headed out the washroom door and down the corridor, all the while licking his hand and trying to plaster down his hair—which resembled an electrocuted hedgehog. He then peered into the main hallway. "Ken, I do see a group of people waiting to come into the ballroom."

The sounds of a celebratory opening number from a Bollywood musical echoed throughout the room and a thunderous set of drums began pounding away as a phalanx of dancers dressed in brightly colored clothes surged toward the middle of the ballroom. They moved back and forth across the floor, their voices and bodies perfectly synchronized with the wailing melody, until the music suddenly stopped and the dancers parted down the middle to allow Prime Minister Modi, dressed in his traditional Indian costume, to wander out into the spotlight. The crowd applauded wildly as Modi waved to the cameras.

"Alex, could you tell us a little bit about Prime Minister's Modi's outfit?" Margaret asked as Ken now seemed to be preoccupied with folding a sheet of paper into what looked like a cat that had been run over by a lawnmower.

"Of course, Margaret," Alex said, careful to stay off camera as the applause continued and he redoubled his efforts to flatten his defiant hair. "Prime Minister Modi, as you pointed out, embraces the traditions of India. He carries this philosophy to his choice of clothing. He is one of the most colorfully dressed leaders in the world and has, to my knowledge, never appeared in public in a traditional business suit. Tonight, he is wearing a tri-color turban with a cloth tail which he customarily dons on important national events such as Independence Day. His long white shirt or *kurta* is paired with a pair of black pants called *churidar pajamas*. His red *bandi* jacket is lightweight and made of silk fabric. Indeed, Prime Minister Modi is an advocate of all things 'Made in India' and carries that philosophy everywhere he goes with his wardrobe selections—"

"Thank you very much for your warm welcome!" Prime Minister Modi said as the crowd hushed. "I am so very pleased to be here with you tonight on this most auspicious occasion." He looked around the room. "This is a celebration of BRICS—which is a collaboration of non-Western states that hope to remedy some of the economic inequities in the global trading system." The crowd applauded. "Please understand that we do not seek to engage in armed conflict with the West but instead to create a parallel economic order that will offer new opportunities for all the nations of the world." More applause. "By the way, I have heard that many of our guests tonight have asked about where they can purchase their own genuine Indian garments." He smiled as the crowd waited in hushed anticipation. "I am pleased to announce that we have many vendors in the lobby who are happy to show you a wide variety of *saris, cholis, churidars, salwars, lungis, dhotis, bandhgalas,* and turbans in all sorts of colors and fabrics and sizes. You can even get ten a percent discount as first-time buyers!" More cheers. "No longer do you have to trudge through life in drab beiges and grays. Instead, you can explore the vibrant, colorful world of Indian clothing!" He clenched his fist. "You, too, can dress like Modi every day of the week!" The crowd erupted in cheers and began chanting "Modi! Modi! Modi!" as Prime Minister Modi waved both arms in triumph and headed back toward the hallway. The Indian music restarted, and the dancers regrouped and followed Prime Minister Modi in an undulating formation that eventually disappeared into the hallway.

"Now that is what I call entertainment," Ken said, clapping his hands as the music faded out. "Professor Zutnik, what was your impression of the choreography?" Ken wanted to know.

"Ken, I really don't know anything about Indian musicals," Professor Zutnik said. "However, I would be happy to talk about India's role in the BRICS trading hierarchy—"

"Perhaps later, Professor Zutnik," Ken said, wishing to focus on more substantive topics of discussion. "Alex, it sounds as though Prime Minister Modi was given a very warm reception by the crowd."

"Indeed," Alex said, between bites, having decided to give the crab cakes a second chance. "He has a very outgoing personality and can charm almost any audience. I should also point out that you can pick up 'I heart Modi' t-shirts and tote bags in the lobby as well."

"Alex, have you seen any protesters down there tonight?" Margaret asked. "As you know, Prime Minister Modi has not exactly endeared himself to his Muslim constituents."

"No, Margaret," Alex replied. "No protesters in sight."

"Margaret, what does Prime Minister Modi hope to gain from tonight's appearance?" Ken asked, refocusing on his overpaid broadcasting role.

"Ken, I think he, like the Brazilian president, is seeking to establish himself as a global statesman. He wants to step outside of the shadow cast by China and Russia and assert his nation's independence and underscore its growing importance as the world's fifth largest economy, trailing only the United States, China, Germany and Japan."

"There lies the rub," Professor Zutnik said, finishing a candy bar that he had purchased from one of the stagehands. "India is a leading member of BRICS but it continues to be involved in an on-going rivalry with China over both territory and trade. I do not see how BRICS maintains any long-term cohesion with these on-going tensions that appear to have no mutually-beneficial solutions." He shook his head. "On the other hand, we have seen that bi-lateral trade between China and India has nearly doubled to more than $110 billion annually in the past decade. So even though they may shoot at each other in the Kashmir region every so often, China and India have a significant economic trading relationship that will probably continue to grow for the foreseeable future."

"Professor Zutnik, what are the primary products that the two countries export to each other?" Margaret asked, as Ken made mewing noises while he petted his paper cat.

"China exports machinery, pharmaceutical products and electronic components to India," Professor Zutnik said, wishing that he had bought a second candy bar from the stagehand as his stomach gurgled. "India exports refined petroleum, minerals and foodstuffs to China."

"Do you find it strange that China and India have such

a robust trade relationship even though they have occasionally come to blows along their shared border?" Margaret asked.

"It reminds me of a bad marriage in which neither partner wants to stay, but they are essentially trapped due to both their shared border and their mutual trade dependency," Professor Zutnik said, wandering fearlessly into the field of marriage counseling. "China and India depend on each other for a variety of products. However, their trading relationship is inherently fraught with tension because China exports more than $110 billion in goods to India each year—which is more than seven times the $15 billion in goods that India send back to China every year. India, like many other countries around the world, is increasingly unhappy with the ongoing trade deficits it has with China."

"And this discrepancy is due to what?" Margaret asked.

"China exports higher-valued goods, such as computers and machinery, whereas India exports lower-valued products such as raw materials," Professor Zutnik replied, suddenly noticing that he still had most of a blueberry muffin in his coat pocket left over from his breakfast earlier that day. Now he could avoid tempting fate with the half-eaten platter of crab cakes that was sitting on a table behind the director.

"But aren't there a number of countries in the world who trade with each other even though they detest each other?" Margaret asked, thinking of a few of her former romantic entanglements.

"Of course," Professor Zutnik said. "If you only traded with those countries that you like, then you would probably be limited to buying tins of butter cookies from Denmark and bottles of wine from New Zealand." He stomped his foot which tingled from having fallen asleep while he had been tethered to the desk. "Nearly every country dislikes every other country to some degree," he pointed out. "It is par for the course." He shrugged his shoulders. "But there are differing degrees of dislike evident in the international trading system. I would venture to say that China is probably the most detested trading partner in the world because it subsidizes its exports and typically runs enormous trade surpluses with most of its trading partners. China and Japan, who also have a long history of animosity toward each other, are vitally dependent on each other as trading partners. China needs Japan's technology and Japan needs China's enormous markets for its products. So they each export over $100 billion a year in machinery, electronics and computers to the other, even though they have what could best be described as a frosty relationship—"

"I can relate to that, Professor, Zutnik" Ken said, recalling the later years of his now-defunct marriage, which had been followed by a surgical carving up of his worldly wealth by a battalion of divorce attorneys.

"I have a funny story about Brazil's decision to join BRICS," Professor Zutnik interrupted, surprising everyone on the set.

"Do tell, Professor Zutnik," Ken said, surprised.

"When President da Silva was elected in 2006, Russia and China had just begun serious discussions about what would later become the BRICS organization. They contacted President da Silva and asked him if he would like to join the BRICS group. As the Brazilians tend to be more fun-loving than either the Chinese or the Russians, both the Russian and Chinese leaders referred to the BRICS organization as a club to make it sound more appealing. President da Silva, who enjoys parties as much as the next leader, thought he was purchasing a membership in an exclusive dance club in Paris called BRICS and sent over an initiation fee of $10 million to secure his place in line. He even flew to Paris and spent a week trying to find the BRICS club but to no avail. When he finally learned that he had purchased a membership in an international organization run by Russia and China, he reportedly threw a fit.

"I can understand that," Ken said sympathetically. "You pay a lot of money to join an exclusive social club where you can meet attractive women and enjoy world-class dining, dancing and drinking, only to find that you are now a member of a stodgy political organization dominated by two countries known for their dour views on pretty much anything that people enjoy doing for fun." He put the paper cat in his coat pocket. "Sort of like a bait and switch."

Professor Zutnik nodded. "Indeed. President da Silva demanded a refund but Russia and China were so anxious to have Brazil join their group that they promised they would fund the construction of a BRICS social club that would be the envy of the world."

"Did they ever build it?" Margaret wanted to know.

"They did," Professor Zutnik replied. "It is called Club Fun and is located in the sunny coastal city of Murmansk, Russia, a mere 125 miles north of the Arctic Circle—"

"And President da Silva was happy with that?" Margaret asked dubiously.

"No, not really," Professor Zutnik said. "But the Russians and Chinese promised him a free lifetime membership in Club Fun along with a special golden mug that he could fill up at the club with as much beer or vodka as he wanted whenever he happened to be passing through Murmansk—"

"That's all it took?" Margaret said, incredulous.

"No, not really. President da Silva also demanded that Brazil be the first country in the list of members of the new organization—"

"And the Russians and Chinese did not argue with him?"

"No, not really," Professor Zutnik replied. "Neither of their leaders had been able to create a catchy name playing around with those five letters—B, C, I, R, S—so they decided to let President da Silva have his way and thus the BRICS name was formed."

"Well, it rolls off the tongue better than CBRIS or SIRBC or even RIBRC," Ken said, offering mangled phonetic pronunciations of each of the acronyms—which sounded like infectious diseases—while trying to be helpful. He turned to the apparent object of his mother's affection: "Margaret, could you tell us about President da Silva?" he asked.

"Of course, Ken," Margaret said. "Luiz Inacio Lula da Silva was born in 1945 so he is the oldest of our four BRICS leaders and has been married three times. He worked as a metalworker as a young man and became active in labor strikes against Brazil's military government in the early 1980s. He was elected president of Brazil in 2003 and served as chief executive until 2011. He was then re-elected president of Brazil in 2023. President da Silva is viewed as a militant leftist by many observers but he is also very popular with his constituents. During his first two terms as president, he implemented far-reaching reforms that helped to tame inflation and reduce public debt while also helping millions of Brazilians to escape poverty. However, his administration was plagued by vote-buying scandals during his first term as president. He was also convicted of money laundering in 2017, which resulted in his serving nearly 2 years in prison. After da Silva was released from prison in 2019, he successfully petitioned Brazil's Supreme Court to have the conviction overturned. With his record expunged, he was free to make another run for president in 2022 and was ultimately successful in defeating his predecessor, Jair Bolsonaro, in a runoff, thereby completing his political resurrection—"

"Ken and Margaret, it looks like President da Silva is about to enter the ballroom," Alex said, interrupting any further discussions about either the combinatorial possibilities of the letters making up the BRICS acronym or the Brazilian president's legal entanglements. The camera switched to the ballroom floor and, careful not to veer too closely to the less-than-dapper Alex, zoomed in on the same hallway that had brought forth the three prior heads of state earlier that evening.

A blast of beats and rhythms cascaded through the hallway as a hail of confetti fell from the ceiling. Several lines of very attractive, scantily-clad dancers gyrated into the ballroom, adorned with colorful arrays of feathers and sequins and little else as they floated across the floor. They were followed by intricate formations of other dancers, who appeared to be wearing little more than body paint and strategically-placed pasties. The dancers coalesced into an elaborate circular formation, holding enormous colored plumes of feathers overhead to form a sort of ornithological dome and then fluttered apart, leaving President da Silva standing alone at the center of the ballroom. The crowd clapped for several minutes as President da Silva nodded and clasped his hands overhead, basking in the adulation of the audience.

"Good evening, my friends," President da Silva began. "Thank you for your very kind welcome. I am so pleased to be here because this gala event underscores the ascendancy of Brazil to the highest levels of global leadership. Our nation's growing population now numbers over 200 million people and our economy boasts a GDP of $2.3 trillion, which ranks it as the eighth largest economy in the world. Brazil has become the leading regional power of South America but will continue to use its newfound wealth and influence to assist its fellow nations in their efforts to industrialize and improve the lives of their people. BRICS is an important part of Brazil's on-going efforts to extend its hand of friendship and cooperation to other developing nations around the world. We hope that BRICS will continue to grow and prosper and provide an alternative source of funds for worthy public infrastructure projects throughout the world. At the same time, we still want to have fun!"

The music suddenly resumed with a thunderous bellow and the dancers, scantily-clad or not at all clad, reconverged, feathers raised, causing President da Silva to disappear in a billowy cloud of plumes. The dancers then retreated into the hallway presumably with President da Silva in tow as the music slowly dissipated.

"Bravo!" Ken and Professor Zutnik both shouted, clapping loudly. "That is truly fine entertainment," Zutnik added. "Can you imagine going to a BRICS meeting without Brazil?" he said to no one in particular. "It would be like visiting a monastery."

"Or a morgue," Margaret quipped.

"Alex, what were your impressions of President da Silva's speech?" Ken asked his floor reporter, whose hair was still proudly pointing upward.

"President da Silva gave a surprisingly short speech," Alex said, still leaning away from the viewfinder. "I was expecting at least ten minutes or so but he kept it short and sweet. No doubt the spectacle of the nearly naked Carnival dancers made a memorable impression on the viewers." Alex paused, waiting for Ken and Professor Zutnik to stop clapping. "Like Prime Minister Modi, President da Silva wanted to create a unique image to distinguish himself from his two more notorious partners—China and Russia. I think anyone who watched the Carnival dancers would certainly agree that it was a spectacular performance that will be talked about for many years."

"No doubt," Margaret said.

"Alex, how would you gauge the reaction of the audience to each of the four leaders?" Professor Zutnik asked, having given up on the idea of Ken ever asking him to present a scholarly analysis of the trade patterns among the BRICS members or anything else of substance, for that matter.

"Well, sir," Alex said. "I think that India and Brazil provided far more theatrical performances, which were not so centered upon the leaders themselves. In that way, both Prime Minister Modi and President da Silva were, in my opinion, more accessible and, ultimately, more likeable.

"I don't think anyone has ever viewed either Putin or Xi as a cuddly teddy bear," Ken opined, adding some intellectual heft to the discussion.

"No, probably not," Alex agreed. "But I think it is fair to say that both Modi and da Silva were able to take advantage of their appearances on a global broadcast and provide memorable images and impressions to the viewers. Putin and Xi probably came across as more egotistical and self-centered and, dare I say, humorless, than Modi and da Silva."

"Perhaps," Ken said, noticing that the director was waving a red card. "Well, I think that about wraps up our coverage of the first annual BRICS Gala Affair, a sparkling event in which the leaders of Russia, China, India and Brazil formally introduced themselves and the BRICS organization to the world. For Professor Stanislaw Zutnik, award-winning correspondent Margaret Hill, brown-suited Alex Marvell, and myself, eminently likeable television personality Ken Roberts, thank you for joining us. Goodnight."

"Ken, here is your phone," Professor Zutnik said, retrieving it from his coat pocket and handing it over as the theme music played. "Oh, I think you have a call," he said, noticing the lit screen.

Ken took the phone and studied the screen. "Oh, it's my mother again," he groaned.

"Shouldn't you answer it?" Margaret asked, daring him to press the green button.

"No," Ken said. "That's not necessary," he added, dropping the phone in a glass of water on the desk as the screen went dark.

PART TWO

MEET THE RINGLEADERS OF BRICS

CHAPTER 3

RUSSIA

INTRODUCTION

Serious historians, who wear tweed jackets and smoke foul-smelling pipes even in smoke-free restaurants, might suggest that we take a trip through time and look at some of the leaders and important events that have shaped the two countries that dominate BRICS—Russia and China. Indeed, these scholars might, between coughing bits of tobacco and burning embers in all directions, insist that this intellectual journey could be further improved by a cursory review of the economies of both of these countries. In this way, we might be able to understand better where both of these BRICS founders rank in the global trading system, and their objectives and concerns in dealing with other countries such as the United States. But because this book strives to be all things to all people, any serious scholarly study of the BRICS organization (minus the dense footnotes and occasional learned Latin phrases such as *bustirape* and *foetorem extremae latrinae*) and its future prospects should also include some information about the literature and music of both founding members, just to provide some insights into their respective cultures. As a result, the next two chapters will explore in succinct yet exhaustive detail the histories, the economies and the artistic legacies of these two masterminds of BRICS. Although Brazil and India were also founding member of BRICS, we have chosen to omit them, in part because they refused to respond to repeated requests for promotional fees.

RUSSIA AND ITS RULERS

Russia is the largest country in the world, spanning 11 time zones and consisting of more than 6.6 million square miles of territory— not counting those parts of Ukraine that its troops wandered into by accident in 2022. Unfortunately, these very same soldiers have been unable to withdraw from Ukraine since that time due to a lack of reverse gears on their tanks and trucks, as well as poor tow truck service. Aside from Ukraine, Russia borders 13 other countries—beginning with Norway and Finland, along the arctic tundra of its northwestern frontier, and continues south through the belly of Europe, past disadvantageously-located nations such as Poland and Belarus. The border then curves eastward through the steppes of Kazakhstan, passes the desolate tourist attractions in the Asian deserts of China and Mongolia, and finally ends at the gates of the nuclear-armed worker's paradise of North Korea on its extreme southeastern flank.

As the geographical colossus of Europe, Russia has cast a long shadow over the continent for many centuries. Indeed, eminent cartographers have described Russia in complex technical terms as a gigantic buzzard perched atop the globe casting a menacing eye over the Eurasian landmass and soiling surrounding nations with impressive regularity throughout modern history.

Notwithstanding its enormous territorial boundaries, however, Russia began as a comparatively small kingdom—the principality of Moscow—in the late 13th century. Because there was very little in the way of cultural activities in the principality of Moscow at that time, the reigning monarch, Prince Daniel (1261-1303), though technically a vassal of the Mongol invaders who had swept across Asia a century before, decided that it would be advisable to divert the attention of his increasingly unruly subjects by invading nearby territories and bringing the Word of a loving Deity to those remaining villagers who had not already been killed by his soldiers.

Over the next several centuries, the Principality of Moscow expanded northward and eastward, successfully battling the Mongol troops of the Golden Horde and ultimately winning its independence under the leadership of the 15th century Prince of Moscow, Ivan III (1440-1505) (who named himself Ivan the Great). Not having any hobbies like tennis or golf to fill his spare time, Ivan the Great engaged in a lifelong crusade of conquest and territorial expansion, fighting many battles against the Grand Duchy of Lithuania and extending the territorial boundaries of the realm to the Arctic Ocean. He was also the first ruler to adopt the title of "tsar" and use it in his diplomatic dealings with other European powers. However, visitors to the court were told that the "t" is silent because the pronunciation "ta-sar" might come across as overly dismissive (akin to spitting on the floor) and could cause the speaker to spend a few years in prison on charges of offending the dignity of the "sar")

Ivan the Great's grandson, Ivan IV (1530-1584), who was called Ivan the Terrible by everyone behind his back, did everything he could as the absolute ruler of Russia to justify his nickname. He succeeded to the throne at the ripe old age of 3, following the death of his father, and was crowned tsar in 1547 at the age of 16—an age when most other teen-agers are trying to sneak out of their houses at night to go meet with their friends. Under the guidance of a council of advisors, Ivan introduced a new legal code that provided greater self-government, loosened the control of the Russian Orthodox Church over governmental offices, and created the first professional Russian army. He also found ways to keep the army busy, sending it on military campaigns throughout central Asia and pushing the frontiers of the Russian state southward and eastward, nearly doubling the size of the country. Unfortunately, Ivan grew up to become a very unpleasant adult and did some very bad things, such as creating the world's first secret police, which he used to kill many members of the Russian nobility and carry out the massacres of thousands of civilians whom he deemed to be unfit or disloyal—including leading members of the Church.

Historians speculate that Ivan may have suffered from severe mental illnesses that manifested in symptoms of paranoia and fury, which culminated in his murdering his oldest son. No doubt his emotional instability may have accounted for (or been due to) his having eight wives, although he apparently went off the deep end only after the death of his Beloved first wife, Anastasia Romanovna.

Ivan did sometimes show his sentimental side, such as when he commemorated the death of or divorce from one of his wives with a new round of executions to rid himself of anyone in his court or, indeed, anywhere in the country, who looked like they might be planning to do something bad. But Ivan the Terrible did provide an enduring autocratic blueprint that would guide the actions of many of Russia's future leaders who saw that politics could be far more efficient and streamlined when the leader of Russia is able to imprison or, better yet, kill any potential political opponents as he or she deems necessary.

The era of the tsars came to an end in 1613, with the ascension of the Romanov dynasty whose rulers were to govern Russia for the next three centuries. Perhaps the most famous member of the Romanov line was Peter I (1672-1725) who became tsar in 1682 and chose, like Ivan III before him, to designate himself as Peter the Great when he became the first emperor of Russia in 1721, a few years before his death in 1725. Although he had a better sense of public relations than Ivan the Terrible, Peter the Great was not particularly interested in democracy and, like his predecessor, ruled Russia with an iron hand that was backed by his own ruthless secret police.

Peter the Great was consumed with the idea that Russia needed to become a global naval power and so he oversaw a grinding war against the Swedish Empire which eventually led to Russia gaining territory on the Baltic Sea. Peter the Great wanted to emulate the maritime reach of ascendant European powers, such as England and Holland, and devoted enormous resources to building an imperial fleet. He also encouraged the widespread adoption of Western ideas—particularly those pertaining to science and engineering—but he was considerably less enthusiastic about the democratic themes of the Enlightenment. Peter the Great also built a new capital city, St. Petersburg, that he named after himself as there was no better name available. This fascination with his own name carried over to his fifteen children, three of whom were also named Peter—which shortened the amount of time needed to call the children to their lessons or meals. He also brought his autocratic orientation to his own marriage, deciding that he had become tired of his first wife, Eudoxia, after she had delivered a mere three children. His solution to her lack of enthusiasm for being pregnant was to divorce her and force her to join a convent; a solution that is admittedly far simpler and less-contentious than today's lawyer-infested legal proceedings.

By the time Peter the Great dropped dead in 1725, reportedly due to urological complications caused by either gonorrhea or gangrene (historical accounts differ but neither version offers a particularly regal or heroic version of the end of his time on earth), the lands of Russia extended from what is now modern-day Poland, eastward past the Ural Mountains and across the entire length of Siberia to the Bering Sea. Russian explorers and settlers had also pushed southward to what are now the river-carved boundaries of China and the arid plains of Mongolia, thus staking out much of what constitutes the present borders of the Russian nation.

Forty years after the death of Peter the Great, Russia came

to be ruled by Catherine II (1729-1796), who, like her predecessor, adopted the moniker Catherine the Great, after overthrowing her husband, Peter III (1728-1762) (who was not known as Peter the Great or even Peter the Satisfactory). Her decision ended his whirlwind 6-month reign in 1762 during which time he managed to alienate much of the Russian military establishment by ordering that Russia—which was fighting alongside Austria against Prussia—switch sides and join Prussia in its war against Austria. This about-face by Peter, who was also the Duke of Holstein-Gottorp (a duchy located in what is now southern Denmark and famous for its happy bovines), underscored his latent Prussian sympathies and occurred after Russia's army had seized Prussian territories and occupied the capital of Berlin at a cost of nearly 140,000 military casualties.

Peter's fickle decision-making apparently prompted Catherine to adopt Ivan the Terrible's expedited marital dissolution approach. As a result, Peter was arrested and sent off to Ropsha Castle where he apparently died of natural causes following repeated attempts by well-meaning attendants to push him out a window, suffocate him with a pillow and strangle him with a rope.

Following the tragic death of her husband, Catherine, who was German by birth and born in Prussia, became Empress of Russia. Her ascension to the throne provided an outstanding example of what an enterprising young woman can accomplish when she sets her mind to it, even though no one thought to question how a Prussian princess by birth who spoke passable Russian with a heavy German accent could become the ruler of Russia. To her credit, Catherine did not let such trivial matters get in the way and promptly assembled a court of royal advisors, including Count Grigory Orlov and Grigory Potemkin, to assist her with governing the Russian empire—which was still expanding southward into territories bordering the Black Sea and eastward across the Bering Strait into the unexplored North American colony of Alaska.

Catherine's advisors took their duties very seriously and were often asked to provide late-night consultations in the royal bedchambers to discuss matters of state and offer suggestions regarding the most advantageous royal positions to adopt. Indeed, Catherine the Great developed something of a reputation as a "policy expert" as she apparently took these consultations very seriously though she never, despite rumors to the contrary, engaged in multiple consultations at the same time or with non-human species. She was also not one to "kiss and tell" and her advisors were similarly tight-lipped about the forms of assistance given to the Empress; they were appreciative of the favors afforded by the Empress and keenly aware that if they were to blab anything to anyone, their royal benefactor could have them sent off at a moment's notice into the heat of any battle that happened to be raging along the Russian frontier at the time.

Being an advisor to the court meant having to be ready at a moment's notice to go to work, but the job was rewarding as many of Catherine's court advisors received pensions, landed estates, military promotions and even hundreds of servants in exchange for their advisory services to the nation. Catherine was reportedly so generous with the payments to her advisors for their satisfactory services that the operating costs of the royal court ballooned to more than a tenth of the entire national budget by the time she hit her stride in her mid-50s—leaving the Empress with very little spare cash to run the country. Even so, she was reportedly very fond of all of her advisors, even those who were no longer physically able to engage in high-energy consultations. Although her advisors ranged widely in age, Catherine was always open to new experiences and did not let the youth or maturity of her advisors affect her views of their worthiness. Instead, she took great pains to evaluate their contributions to the royal court on a case-by-case basis, meeting with them over and over again until the best possible advice had been obtained.

Although Catherine dabbled in the occasional execution of a political rival, she was comparatively benign in the bloodletting department when compared to several of her predecessors, such as Ivan the Terrible and Peter the Great. Like Peter the Great, she encouraged the arts and sciences in Russia and oversaw the creation of new cities and universities that attracted scientists and artists alike from all over Europe. Indeed, Russia was a very popular destination for many talented individuals throughout Catherine's reign and, despite her no-nonsense view of potential rivals to the throne, was viewed as one of the more enlightened countries of Europe during that time.

However, all things must come to an end. The Romanov dynasty endured for more than a century after Catherine's death in 1792, but came to an abrupt and violent end following the Russian Revolution and the seizure of power by the Bolsheviks in 1917. The last Romanov monarch, Czar Nicholas II, along with his entire family, was executed by the Bolsheviks the following year—a barbaric act that was considered to be very uncouth by the other monarchs of Europe. The Bolsheviks were led by Vladimir Lenin (1870-1924), who, despite the similarity of his surname to former Beatle John Lennon (1940-1980), was not known for his musical talents or his upbeat lyrics. Lenin and his followers, including his right-hand man Joseph Stalin (1878-1953) (whom Lenin privately considered to be something of a crude oaf), rapidly transformed Russia into a one-party communist dictatorship that would become formally known as the Soviet Union in 1922.

Lenin was sort of the George Washington of the modern Russian state except that he did not chop down a cherry tree, was not very good at riding a horse and believed that everyone who disagreed with his political opinions should be killed. (Indeed, anyone invited over to the Lenin household to play cards was warned ahead of time that they should not offer their opinions about such things as the benefits of democratic government or else they might find themselves in front of a firing squad). What Lenin lacked in axe-wielding and horsemanship talents, and general tolerance for differing opinions, however, he made up in revolutionary zeal and his single-minded desire to transform the still predominantly agrarian Imperial Russia into a modern nation founded on the socialist principles of Karl Marx.

Lenin seized power at a time when Russia's troops were reeling from the onslaught of the Central Powers near the end of World War I. To save the nascent communist regime, he signed the Treaty of Brest-Litovsk in 1918 and withdrew Russia from World War I. The price was steep as Russia lost control of much of its western territory, including Ukraine, Poland, Lithuania, Latvia and Estonia, and was also required to recognize the independence of Finland. Russia also gave up a third of its population and nearly half of its industrial capacity with the transfer of these lands.

Not everyone in Russia was pleased with the one-sided

nature of the Treaty nor with the efforts by Lenin to consolidate his power through the implementation of the Red Terror, a name suitable for a comic book villain. Tens of thousands of real or imaginary opponents of the regime were killed or imprisoned during this purge. Lenin also sought to curry favor with the peasantry by giving them lands he did not own which, not surprisingly, irked the farmers who formerly owned those redistributed lands. For all of these reasons, Russia soon became engulfed in a bloody civil war between the Red armies of the new government and the White armies which consisted of soldiers loyal to the former aristocracy. The White armies were also assisted by troops that had been sent from several countries in Europe, whose heads of state were undoubtedly concerned that their own disgruntled citizens might try to emulate the Bolshevik method for ending their own political careers. Various countries, such as Italy, Great Britain, France, Czechoslovakia, Canada and Japan, ordered soldiers to different parts of Russia to fight the Bolshevik armies. Even the United States reluctantly agreed with France and Great Britain that the threat posed by the new communist regime warranted sending thousands of troops to occupy Vladivostok and Murmansk and enjoy the sunny, ice-covered beaches.

Unfortunately, the allied intervention was unsuccessful because it was, at best, a series of peripheral military actions with too few troops and resources to tip the balance in favor of the White armies. The very fact that French and British soldiers were wandering around various parts of Russia shooting at Russians also seemed to stoke Russian anger against these foreign invaders. Lenin was able to appeal to the widespread sense of Russian nationalism by portraying the government as defending the Russian homeland from royalist traitors and outside powers that wanted to partition the country. He also offered to give away additional lands that he did own to anyone who would take up arms in defense of the nation. By 1922, the Red armies had defeated the White armies, signaling to the allied powers that it was a good time to withdraw their own forces from Russia.

The end of the Russian civil war enabled Lenin to assume complete control of a country that had suffered enormous human losses. In the eight years from the beginning of World War I in 1914 to the effective end of the Russian civil war in 1922, Russia suffered more than ten million military and civilian deaths, a staggering toll that left the country tottering on the brink of disintegration. But there was more fun to come for the battered Soviet state as widespread crop failures led to a massive famine that killed an additional five million people and caused many desperate souls to resort to cannibalism to stay alive. All of these horrendous calamities collectively snuffed out at least a tenth of the Russian population and probably caused more than a few Russians to wonder if the whole communist takeover might have been a bad idea.

However, Lenin persevered because he was consumed with the idea of fomenting class-based revolutions throughout the world that would result in workers taking control of the factories and throwing off the yokes of their capitalist oppressors. Because he had been so good at seizing private farms, Lenin tried to hurry the whole revolution thing along in his own country by ordering the nationalization of all banks, utilities, railways and mining operations, thereby effectively ending large-scale privately-owned enterprises throughout Russia. After all, if you were unsure as to whether the working class was sufficiently familiar with Marxist doctrine or even realized that they were being oppressed, then it made sense to take the lead and point the way.

By 1922, Lenin was finding himself plagued by numerous health problems which stemmed, in part, from the herculean endeavors of hunting down and killing tens of thousands of political opponents and seizing control of thousands of factories and farms. Indeed, the stress of building enough labor camps to house all of the people whom Lenin believed to be enemies of the state would have killed a lesser man. Nevertheless, he continued with his efforts to bring joy and light to the Russian citizenry until he suffered a series of strokes which left him largely incapacitated until his death in January 1924.

Because Lenin enjoyed almost a godlike status in the Soviet Union at the time of his death, his aides decided that he could best be honored by being stuffed by the nation's leading taxidermists and put on permanent display in a mausoleum located in Moscow's Red Square. There was some debate as to how Lenin's body should be posed for viewing, with some officials proposing a standing Lenin, dressed like a svelte male model in an impeccably tailored suit, pointing at an imaginary admirer and others suggesting a heroic Lenin clad in a tunic and gazing skyward for divine inspiration. Still others favored an athletic Lenin dribbling a soccer ball. However, the fact that Lenin's rickety, desiccated remains kept falling over led everyone to agree in the end that it was best to tuck him into a fluffy bed for public viewing for all eternity, free of charge. This is where he remains, his complexion a glossy, waxy yellow, to the current day.

Even though Lenin was notorious for using terror to keep his grip on power, he was a comparative lightweight in the use of torture and assassination when compared to his successor, Joseph Stalin. Stalin has admittedly gotten a bad rap for being a psychotic mass-murdering monster because he got a little carried away with his desire to show who was "boss" in the Soviet Union. Stalin was always an enterprising individual in the area of political repression, even though he may have erred on the side of being a little too enthusiastic about disposing of his fellow Russians.

Stalin was born in Gorki, Georgia, and attended a seminary as a young man. However, he soon concluded that a career as a priest would interfere with his interests in women and political sedition. As a result, he switched careers to become a professional revolutionary and helped to bankroll Lenin's Bolshevik cabal by engaging in bank robberies and extortion schemes. Although he was arrested numerous times and exiled to Siberia, Stalin was considered to be highly capable and resourceful by his fellow revolutionaries and was invited to join the ruling Politburo after Lenin seized power in 1917.

Although not a particularly imposing figure at 5 feet 7 inches in height, Stalin was still 3 inches taller than the diminutive Lenin. He wore wedges in his shoes and blow-dried his hair to make it puffier so that he could appear even more intimidating to his fellow Politburo members. After a stint in the Russian civil war, Stalin returned to Moscow and did everything he could to ingratiate himself with Lenin—except remove the shoe wedges. Although Lenin had significant misgivings about Stalin's temperament and lack of refinement, he allowed Stalin to become his second-in-command—or at least that was how Stalin interpreted Lenin's feeble gestures as the strokes had left Lenin unable to speak. By the time Lenin died in 1924, Stalin was already over-seeing the day-to-day operations of the Soviet government.

When Stalin became the "big cheese" of the Soviet Union, he was determined to accelerate Lenin's efforts to modernize the Soviet economy. Stalin believed that rapid industrialization was the only way to transform the Soviet Union into a global power so, in 1928, he introduced the first of a series of 5-year plans to make this vision a reality. All decision-making powers regarding the economy were vested in the government, whose central planners would determine how best to allocate labor and material inputs throughout the country in order to increase industrial produc-tion. They relied on scientific and managerial principles—which involved throwing massive amounts of iron, steel, coal and other materials into the mix until they managed to manufacture the desired number of tanks or bullets or corsets. The beauty of central planning was that it left all production decisions in the hands of skilled bureaucrats who could recite long passages of Marx's *Das Kapital* from memory and whose political affiliations guaranteed that they knew what the Soviet Union's citizens wanted to buy more than the people themselves.

A centrally-planned economy is very attractive from a the-oretical standpoint because the planners do not have to wait for millions of buyers and sellers to engage in commerce with each other and determine, through their own negotiations, what items will sell in what quantities and at what prices. Unfortunately, very few central planners have unlimited knowledge about the preferences of all of the buyers and sellers in a given market. As a result, they must guess what items should be produced and in what quantities.

The other problem with a centrally planned economy is that every factory manager is judged on quantity and not quality because it is far easier for central planners to dictate how many rubber boots, for example, should be produced instead of providing detailed product specifications for each boot. Because factory managers were typically compensated based upon the sheer numbers of goods they produced, quality considerations tended to be ignored altogether so one could end up with rubber boots without soles or with multiple high heel pumps—which would still satisfy the production quotas even though they were functionally useless.

Stalin's forced industrialization of the country resulted in an enormous increase in heavy industries, including steel mills, railroads and chemical plants. However, it was an extremely inefficient and inherently wasteful process because the resources were allocated by government decree as opposed to the decisions of the on-site managers at various plants. Its success was also vitally dependent on the cheap labor provided by many landless peasants who came to the cities in search of factory work.

In conjunction with the first 5-year plan, Stalin also implemented a nationwide farm collectivization program in which the persons who had received redistributed lands from Lenin were forced (along with everyone else) to give their lands back to the government so that these properties could be combined into vast, ineptly managed collectives. This program went about as badly as one might expect and resulted in an enormous drop in agricultural production that led, not surprisingly, to another widespread famine which may have resulted in the deaths of up to 14 million people by 1933. For Stalin, however, collectivization was a win-win as it enabled him to destroy the kulaks, the wealthier farmers who controlled agricultural production in the country, and thus tighten his grip on power.

For much of the 1930s, Stalin busied himself with numerous purges of high-level military officials and political rivals. He also created the first show trials in which opponents of the regime—including many of Lenin's former colleagues—were tried on whatever trumped-up charges Stalin and his aides could dream up, thereby anticipating the slew of courtroom shows that now pollute modern daytime television. However, Stalin's own paranoia was such that many minor-level party officials, as well as other persons with academic degrees or military backgrounds, were dragged before these courts and, after the presentation of a few minutes of convincing evidence, sentenced to death or, if the judge was in a good mood, a lifetime of hard labor in the gulag. The sheer number of these sham trials coupled with the often impressively credentialed backgrounds of their victims created an enormous brainpower shortage that was to hinder greatly the Soviet Union's efforts to catch up with its capitalist rivals—who did not seem to be following Marx's blueprint of systemic economic collapse.

Stalin also became alarmed at the growing power of Nazi Germany, which had absorbed both Austria and Czechoslovakia by 1938 and seemed intent on expanding further eastward in Europe. Thus it was with some relief on Stalin's part that he and Adolf Hitler entered into a mutual non-aggression pact in 1939 in which they secretly agreed to divide Poland and otherwise leave each other alone to carry out their own mischievous deeds in their respective spheres of influence.

It was one of the great disappointments of Stalin's life

that his budding friendship with Hitler was ripped apart by the German invasion of Russia on June 22, 1941. Stalin had hoped the two dictators would spend more time together going on picnics in the country, or trading tips during giggled-filled late night telephone calls about the best ways to groom their moustaches or how best to ask female family members out on dates. After all, they both liked the same things, such as invading other countries and sending millions of people to die in labor camps. But Hitler's desire to conquer Stalin's Russia was the proverbial straw that broke the camel's back. It led to a bloody four-year war that saw Germany nearly defeat Russia and capture the capital city of Moscow before the numerically superior Russian troops were able to beat back the German onslaught and push Hitler's armies back to Berlin in 1945. The war resulted in a mind-numbing 27 million deaths in Russia, many millions of which were caused not by Hitler's armies but by Stalin ordering genocidal massacres in regions of the Soviet Union, such as Ukraine, which he believed were hostile to his own regime.

The defeat of Germany left the Soviet Union in possession of the entire swath of Eastern Europe, whose nations became little more than vassal states having nominal independence from Moscow. Stalin adopted the "finders, keepers" approach toward international politics, reabsorbing some nations, such as Lithuania, Latvia and Estonia, back into the fold, and severing territory from other countries such as Poland because the Soviet Union, at 8,650,000 square miles, was a mere 57 times the size of pre-war Poland, It needed the additional territory as a buffer in case such blood-thirsty renegade countries as Luxembourg or Liechtenstein decided to launch a surprise attack.

By the time of his death in 1953 from a cerebral hemorrhage (or blunt force trauma, if you read between the lines), Stalin's brutal legacy was indelibly stamped on the Soviet Union. His successors, despite their attempts to put a kinder, friendlier mask on the Soviet Union, did little to change its pathology as a rapacious global power seeking world domination. Stalin's successor, Nikita Khrushchev (1894-1971), was most famous for pounding his shoe on a desk at the United Nations to kill a couple of roaches and trying to sneak a few missiles into Cuba in 1962—which set off an enormous tiff with the United States. Leonid Brezhnev (1906-1982), helped to depose Khrushchev in 1964 and oversaw a massive build-up of nuclear weapons by the Soviet military, which eventually led to several international treaties with the United States capping the number of nuclear missiles that each country could keep. These treaties contained elaborate verification procedures in which both sides pinky-swore that they would not hide extra missiles inside schoolhouses or hospitals or under their own beds.

Brezhnev also decided that the Soviet military, which was already straining under the sheer weight of having to oppress hundreds of millions of people throughout Europe and Asia, should occupy Afghanistan, the crown jewel of central Asia—a primitive, impoverished mountainous country best known for its exports of opium and terrorists. Alas, the Soviet military had no better luck than the British army a century before in subjugating the Afghan tribes and was forced to withdraw a decade later, after suffering 70,000 dead and wounded soldiers. Despite having bombed hundreds of towns and villages and killing tens of thousands of Afghans, the Soviets were unable, to the surprise of scholars and politicians alike, to convince the Afghan people to embrace the values of modern civilization.

Because the Soviet Union was so firmly wrapped up in the shadow cast by Joseph Stalin, its actions in the international arena continued to resemble those of a spoiled brat who happened to be carrying a couple of thousand nuclear weapons in his pocket. Brezhnev's successors included Yuri Andropov (1914-1984) and Constantin Chernenko (1911-1985), each of whom briefly served as General Secretary of the Communist Party before succumbing to severe head colds. Both Andropov and Chernenko continued piloting the Soviet ship of state along the same rigid course originally set by Stalin. It was only after Mikhail Gorbachev (1931-2022) stepped over the prone bodies of his predecessors and assumed power in 1985 that the curtain was pulled back and the true, decrepit nature of the Soviet economy was revealed. Unfortunately, Gorbachev was tasked with trying to jumpstart the failing economy—a tougher job than Jesus had when he called the recently-deceased Lazarus from the tomb. Nothing Gorbachev did could revive the moribund nation, so he could do little more than to watch helplessly as the Soviet Union went into a death spiral before splintering into its 15 constituent republics in 1991.

The loss of the Soviet empire—including more than 2.2 million square miles of territory and nearly half of its population—haunted many Russians who believed that their country had been stabbed in the back by its leaders. Although a new constitution was adopted establishing a federalist system, efforts to democratize Russia floundered despite the best efforts of Russia's new president, Boris Yeltsin (1931-2007), to transform the Russian command economy into a market economy. Yeltsin saw economic liberalization as the only antidote for the stagnant Russian economy but he, like his predecessors, could not resist the temptation to indulge in several bloody wars, this time in the Russian Caucasus with pesky Chechen secessionists. However, Yeltsin became increasingly unpopular and resigned in 1999 in favor of the little-known Vladimir Putin, the former head of the KGB. Putin had previously channeled his anger at having been denied a tryout with the Boston Celtics basketball team into a single-minded quest for power that had brought him to the highest levels of the Russian government.

Although Russia was technically still a democracy, Putin fancied himself the true successor to Stalin and vowed under his breath to bring back the Soviet Union—even though there was a notable lack of clamoring by the other 14 former republics to rejoin Russia under the Soviet banner and relive the good times they had experienced under Lenin, Stalin and the Red Army. However, Putin did not let this palpable lack of enthusiasm trouble him and so he set about trying to rebuild the Soviet empire on his own, piece by piece.

The first thing Putin did was to give his troops some artillery and bombing practice in the newly independent country of Georgia, which was embroiled in a territorial dispute with separatists in 2008. Putin's troops occupied a fifth of the country and launched devastating attacks that killed thousands of Georgians as part of a brutal campaign to split the country. Having beaten up on a country that is less than half the size of its American state namesake, Putin then turned his attention eastward and seized Crimea from Ukraine in 2014. As the nations of the world did not do much more than send strongly worded letters expressing their disappointment with Putin's behavior, he apparently felt free to launch a full-scale invasion of Ukraine in 2022, confidently expecting that he would be rolling through the flower-strewn streets of Kyiv in a matter of weeks. However, Ukraine's furious resistance, bolstered by military assistance from both Europe and the United States, thwarted Putin's ambitions. As a result, Russia and Ukraine settled into a bloody stalemate in the easternmost provinces of Ukraine that has continued to the present day, putting a crimp in Putin's plans to reconquer the rest of the former Soviet Union in the next few years.

The invasion of Ukraine has also caused many countries in Europe and Asia to impose sanctions on Russia (including barring its leaders from enjoying the fabulous all-you-can-eat dinner buffet at the G-20 summit, which is followed by the traditional food fight between leading politicians and bankers in which they pelt each other with exquisite cream-filled pastries). These sanctions have severely impacted Russia's economy and weakened its military capabilities, and the resulting worldwide isolation forced Russia to move closer to its current best friend forever, China. This is evidenced by the two countries' deepening economic ties and their proclamations of eternal friendship—which will no doubt last for months, perhaps even a year or two.

THE ECONOMY OF RUSSIA

Due to its long-time hostility to the United States (and basically everyone else in the world), Russia was undoubtedly motivated to set up an organization like BRICS that would act as a counterweight to the economic dominance of the United States and its allies, including the United Kingdom, Germany, France, Italy, Canada and Japan. Because China was similarly predisposed to challenge the existing international trading system due to its own aspirations to become the new queen bee of the global economy (and its own dislike for everyone else in the world), it is not surprising that China decided to join Russia in the BRICS club.

Russia's economy is vitally dependent on its exports of oil, gas and coal for foreign exchange; its sales of fossil fuels constitute about a fifth of the country's GDP but make up about half of its total exports by value. Indeed, its natural gas and oil reserves are among the largest in the world and will likely serve as the main source of foreign reserves for the foreseeable future. However, many European countries imposed import sanctions on Russia following its invasion of Ukraine. As a result, Russia was forced to find new customers, such as China and India, for its energy products in order to continue funding its military activities in Ukraine and, indeed, anywhere else in the world that might need to be overrun on short notice.

The sheer size of the Russian landmass almost guarantees that it would also be a leading exporter of valuable metals such as gold, platinum, silver and copper—all of which can be crafted into fashionable rings, bracelets and leg irons. Russia also sells large quantities of exotic metals such as cobalt, molybdenum and uranium to responsible countries such as North Korea and Iran who are required to sign a form in the presence of a notary promising not to use them to build nuclear weapons. Indeed, it would be difficult to name or spell a metal that Russia does not export in substantial amounts.

Russia is also the biggest exporter of diamonds in the world and responsible for about a quarter of the world's annual diamond output. Although most of these diamonds are used for commercial purposes such as industrial machinery and cutting tools, others are polished to a bright and shiny, overpriced finish and sold to lovestruck couples beginning their journeys through life together (until they get to know each other after a few years and their marital bliss runs aground on the rocky shores of life and the muscular loins of the local tennis pro).

Russia is also a major exporter of agricultural products. Because much of Russia is what geographers describe as an "icy hellhole," its growing season is limited and its supply of arable land is less than a tenth of its entire territory. Nevertheless, it is a major producer of grains, including wheat, barley, oat, rye, and other foodstuffs that are not customarily found in hard candies. Despite the disruptions caused by its on-going battles with Ukraine in the Black Sea, Russia continues to be an important producer in the global food chain—supplying grain products to many countries in Africa and Asia.

No discussion about Russia's economy would be complete without pointing out that there has been a virtual explosion in the number of Russian billionaires in recent years. Indeed, it is heartwarming to see how numerous entrepreneurial individuals have been able to rise from the ranks of company employees to become owners of vast state-owned enterprises overnight, due to fortuitous circumstances such as their friendships with Russian leaders and their possession of incriminating photographs. This virtual gold rush of good fortune began in the 1990s when the Russian government began selling off national industries to well-connected buyers at a fraction of their true value. This fire sale of national assets made it possible for several hundred well-placed individuals to afford obscenely opulent lifestyles and buy enormous mansions surrounded by high gates strong enough to keep out the remaining 99.999999% of the population who did not share in this newest redistribution of national wealth. Unfortunately, this cascade of riches continues to benefit only a very few Russian oligarchs who have been assured that they can keep their shiny yachts and sprawling estates so long as they stay out of Putin's way and do not poke their noses into the government's business. Otherwise, they could find themselves joining other former oligarchs who died under mysterious circumstances. such as falling off a bridge or tumbling down a mountain or dying in a plane crash.

RUSSIA AND THE ARTS

LITERATURE

Russia is famous for its literature and boasts many authors who have made enduring contributions to all forms of fiction, ranging from poetry and short stories to sprawling novels that could only be published by cutting down an entire forest. Indeed, Russia's most famous author, Leo Tolstoy (1828-1910), is well-known and widely feared for his thousand-page novels such as *War and Peace* and *Anna Karenina*, both of which boast dozens and dozens of characters having multi-syllabic surnames containing nearly all of the letters of the alphabet. Not only do these books offer elaborate plots and numerous subplots, but they are so complicated and exhausting to read that most literary critics die of old age before they are able to finish either book.

More than a few of the less muscular book critics have been trapped under a copy of one of Tolstoy's works after an unfortunate fall, with several succumbing to starvation or being eaten alive by their pet cats. Indeed, one particularly ambitious critic was lugging unabridged copies of Tolstoy's collected works around when he fell down a flight of stairs and was only able to free himself a week later by gnawing off both of his legs.

Despite the sheer tonnage of his literary masterpieces, Tolstoy has been praised as Russia's greatest literary talent due, in part, to his gift for offering valuable insights about the human condition. Tolstoy suggests that material wealth will not lead to personal happiness, even though he lived most of his life on a family estate south of Moscow and was apparently able to tolerate the horror of his lavish lifestyle without too much difficulty.

For those who prefer to run half marathons in their reading ventures, Fyodor Dostoevsky (1821-1881), the other giant of Russian literature, offers the comparatively svelte *Crime and Punishment*. This book recounts the happy-go-lucky tale of an impoverished student who murders an old women and then proceeds to depress his reading audience for 500 pages by recounting, in excruciating detail, his torment and sorrow. *Crime and Punishment* focuses on the alienation of individuals from society, as well as the search by all people for redemption from the consequences of their own actions. Less clear is how many readers were alienated from the idea of reading any other works by Dostoevsky by his constant droning on about human misery and suffering in *Crime and Punishment*. However, Dostoevsky's humble beginnings made him more willing to consider whether material wealth could indeed buy happiness than his richer fellow novelist, Tolstoy.

MUSIC

Aficionados of classical music are very familiar with two of the most famous Russian composers, Pyotr Illyich Tchaikovsky (1840-1893) and Sergi Rachmaninoff (1873-1943), both of whom gained lasting fame for their stunningly beautiful musical compositions which showcased both the power and the elegance of orchestral arrangements and disdained the use of electric guitars and Moog synthesizers.

Tchaikovsky gained international recognition in the 19th century for his heartfelt ballet scores such as *The Nutcracker* and *Swan Lake*, the latter of which did not actually feature any live swans but instead loudly clucking dancers dressed up as swans with feather costumes scurrying around the stage on a pretend lake. He was also known for his *1812 Overture*, a robust anthem that celebrated Napoleon's retreat from Moscow and culminated in a fanfare of trumpets and cannon fire. Tchaikovsky was reportedly incensed that the 1882 premiere of the *Overture* "lacked authenticity" because it did not feature real cannons and cannon balls, even though the conductor, Ippolit Altani, repeatedly pointed out that shooting cannons inside the music hall would have killed numerous people in the audience and destroyed much of the building.

Despite his talents, Tchaikovsky was tormented by his own personal demons. He struggled to hide his homosexuality by marrying a former student, Antonina Miliukova, an unconsummated union, which, by all accounts, was an unmitigated disaster. Tchaikovsky did manage to live with his new wife for six whole weeks before he decided that he would rather risk condemnation by society due to his preference for young sweaty men than continue to live with the woman whom he described affectionately as a "crazed half-wit." He was also stung by the snippy criticisms of several Russian music critics—particularly in the early years of his career—that his compositions were too "European" and lacked the requisite features of Russian classical music—despite his judicious use of cannon fire in his musical works.

Rachmaninoff, for his part, was a virtuoso pianist who was not as consumed with firing cannons inside public places as Tchaikovsky. However, he composed numerous works that were emotional and dramatic, and conveyed both a sense of sadness and soulfulness. His most famous work, *Piano Concerto 2*, was a masterful composition that juxtaposed both the thundering power of the entire orchestra and the energetic notes of a single piano soliloquy. It is considered by many untenured scholars to be one of the earliest examples of heavy metal music.

Rachmaninoff was also the conductor of the Bolshoi Theatre but left Russia after the Bolsheviks seized power in 1917 and resettled in New York. He was highly sought after by the leading orchestras of the time to join them as a conductor. However, Rachmaninoff wanted to resume his career as both a composer and a performer—even though he had largely stopped writing new music after leaving Russia. Rachmaninoff spent the rest of his life performing concerts in both the United States and Europe, and was reportedly followed around the world by an aging cadre of groupies who would toss their panties and orthopedic shoes onto the stage during his concerts.

CHAPTER 4

CHINA

INTRODUCTION

Anyone who seeks to understand the history of China must first look at a map of China's modern borders and decide if China looks more like a chicken or a dragon. This is not an idle question because many people look for imaginary pictures in the clouds that float by overhead every day. The exercise may also provide some clues as to the ways in which Chinese citizens view their nation. Because the Chinese are very sensitive about their image in the world today, they might not be pleased if you suggested that the country looks like a chicken. After all, chickens—even those with very bad tempers—are not considered to be fierce animals. No doubt the fact that a chicken can be served in a variety of tasty dishes also lessens its appeal as a national symbol. A dragon, on the other hand, is arguably an apex predator because it can eat several armed warriors in a single bite and incinerate a village with a few blasts of its fiery sulfuric breath. Because it can spit fire and fly, the dragon offers a national symbol that is both intimidating and impressive. The fact that the dragon does not exist does not appear to trouble the Chinese very much because they believe that an imaginary dragon is still better than a real chicken—unless you have to serve it in a cream sauce.

CHINA AND ITS RULERS

Although Russia can claim a thousand-year legacy dating back to Prince Daniel and the Principality of Moscow, its southern neighbor, China, boasts a history that extends several millennia back in time. The earliest vestiges of Chinese civilization appeared thousands of years ago along the Yangtze River, the world's third longest waterway, which flows from the mountains of Tibet eastward all the way to the East China Sea and what is now the port of Shanghai. Although the Yangtze River has not been the inspiration for many successful popular songs in the United States (as compared to *Moon River* or *Down by the River* or even *Green River*), there have been a few foot-tapping orchestral-backed songs about it in China, such as *The Song of the Yangtze River* and *Dreaming of South of Yangtze River*. This is because the Yangtze River occupies an almost-mystical place in Chinese culture. Though Yangtze River-inspired tunes are absent from the *Billboard Top 100*, the river is the most important waterway in China and of critical importance to the Chinese economy and the welfare of the nation itself. Indeed, a third of the Chinese population resides in the Yangtze River basin, a region responsible for much of the nation's industrial production. The benefits of having a fast-moving waterway available nearby to carry all sorts of chemicals and effluents down to the ocean is difficult to overstate because it has enabled enterprising businesses to pass any waste disposal savings onto their customers for hundreds of years.

Most civilizations do not spring up overnight but instead take many centuries to develop—even when they are able to count on the assistance of aliens visiting from outer space. Indeed, it was only with the rise of the Han Dynasty (202 BC - 220 AD) that the multi-generational lineal rule that would govern China for nearly twenty centuries commenced. The influence of the Han rulers was immense as much of the modern Chinese language was created during their rule, along with what persons seeking lifetime employment consider to be one of the Han Dynasty's greatest gifts to the world—the government bureaucracy staffed by indifferent administrators. In addition, the Han Dynasty became synonymous with the predominant ethnic group in China—the Han Chinese—whose descendants have continued to dominate Chinese society to the present day while still treating the country's ethnic minorities with respect—except for those thickheaded few who dare to voice their own opinions and must be locked up for their own good.

The Han Dynasty also embraced the teachings of Confucius (551-479 BC), who offered a philosophy stressing the importance of harmony both in the family and in society as a whole. Confucianism teaches that human beings are inherently good and can improve themselves through academic study and their own good works and, failing that, the payment of large bundles of cash to government officials. That Confucius would not have been the right person to plan a bachelor party was underscored by his emphasis on morality and social virtue. He believed that people should always be kind to one another, a quaint idea from a bygone era that has little relevance in today's hyper-competitive dog-eat-dog world.

Liu Bang (256-195 BC), the founder of the Han Dynasty, was also known by his stage name, Emperor Gaozu of Han. Bang employed his own unique version of Confucianism by carrying out virtuous military campaigns to kill thousands of nomadic warriors who had attacked many settlements along the borders of the kingdom. The upside of the carnage inflicted by the imperial forces on these invaders was that China's enemies eventually ran out of nomadic warriors. China was thus able to enjoy an extended period of peace and prosperity—likened by many to the contemporaneous *Pax Romana* that had been ushered in by the brutal military campaigns of the Roman Empire.

Historians have long debated if China was the first civilization to develop its own written language and whether it was responsible for such towering achievements as the delectable treat that we now know as the fortune cookie. Unfortunately, no one has been able to provide any firm answers regarding the priority to be given to the invention of writing in China, but intrepid culinary historians have solved the more important question regarding the origin of the fortune cookie which, as it turns out, occurred in the decidedly non-Chinese city limits of San Francisco in the early 20th century. This early case of cultural expropriation provides a shocking example in which the epitome of another culture was used by devious entrepreneurs to make money— in this case by peddling folded bits of almond-flavored cooked dough stuffed with "fortunes" offering such things as lucky numbers and the launch codes for U.S. intercontinental ballistic missiles.

China has given many other inventions to the world aside from the searing invectives aimed at the United States (and pretty much everyone else) that appear regularly in the *People's Daily*, the official newspaper of the Central Committee of the Chinese Communist Party. These inventions include the abacus, gunpowder, silk, paper, porcelain, kites, the compass, movable type and alcohol, all of which have greatly shaped modern civilization and, in the case of alcohol, made the trials and tribulations of daily life much more tolerable. Indeed, it would be impossible to estimate the number of children who owe their very existence to the invention of alcohol and the impairment that it causes to the good judgment of otherwise sensible adults.

China also invented the dual column restaurant menu, which allows diners to select entrees from both column A and column B, thus bringing about a revolutionary change in the organization of restaurant menus everywhere. These menus also showcased how three ingredients could be ingeniously mixed together to create dozens and dozens of seemingly unique beef, pork, chicken and vegetable dishes.

The end of the Han Dynasty in the third century AD, was followed by centuries of political fragmentation and economic chaos. Four centuries were to pass before a new era of political unity began in the year 608 with the Tang Dynasty—which is sometimes confused with the more obscure Savory Dynasty that never got off to a good start. In any event, the Tang Dynasty ruled for three centuries and strengthened its control over China with the development of a professional civil service. It also oversaw great advances in both literature and the arts. The capital city of Chang'an became an important center of commerce throughout Asia and was for many years the world's most populous city. The lands controlled by the Tang Dynasty boasted of a population that rose from about 50 million persons at the time of its inception to more than 75 million persons by the time the Tang Dynasty collapsed in 907.

The Tang Dynasty also saw the rise of China's only female empress regnant, the Empress Wu Zetian (624-705), who proclaimed the beginning of the Wu Zhou Dynasty in 690. The Wu Zhou Dynasty turned out to be a dynasty with a small "d" as it only lasted for fifteen years, constituting a sort of brief intermission in the continuing reign of the Tang Dynasty. However, Empress Wu had been the real power behind the throne for three decades before actually deciding to sit on the throne, first as the empress consort to her husband, Emperor Gaozong (628-683), and then, after his unfortunate death in 683, as the empress dowager through her sons Emperors Zhongzong and Ruizong—who did not really have any say in matters of state as they would be sent to their rooms without their supper when they dared to disagree with their mother. Indeed, she would sometimes order that they be locked up for days until they saw the errors of their ways. But Wu had tired of playing the role of the puppet-master, so she crowned herself empress in a touching private ceremony in the year 690 and took center stage as the true ruler of China.

Wu did not start off with the proverbial silver spoon in her mouth as she initially came to the royal court as the concubine of Emperor Taizong (598-649), which was the "friends with benefits" arrangement of the day. Initially, Wu had to compete with several other women for the attention of the Emperor, including Empress Wang (628-655), the first wife of the emperor (who fell out of favor with her husband due to her inability to have children) and Consort Xiao (? – 655), who fell out of favor with the Emperor even though she bore him several children. Notwithstanding their vigorous attempts to win back the affections of Emperor Taizong (who apparently had the attention span of a gerbil), Empress Wang and Consort Xiao were unable to stop Wu from winning the heart of the Emperor. Wu then used her charms to convince Emperor Taizong to charge both of her rivals with witchcraft and exile them from the court. Showing the attention to detail that would later characterize her reign as empress, Wu ordered that both Empress Wang and Consort Xiao be tortured to death, thereby cementing her position as the "hostess with the mostest" in the royal court.

Wu had been particularly anxious to advance in status when she first arrived at Emperor Taizong's court and became his concubine due to the prevailing custom that required all palace maids and concubines be buried alive at the time of the emperor's death. This practice was intended to assure the emperor—despite being a decaying corpse at that point—would have ample servants in the afterlife and could continue to enjoy the luxurious lifestyle that he had experienced during his earthly existence. Not surprisingly, this was not a popular custom among the maids and concubines, many of whom were quite convinced that their often fleeting intimate experiences with the deceased emperor were not sufficiently noteworthy to justify being dropped into a hole and covered up with dirt. Few employment counselors nowadays would regard a career as a concubine in China's royal court to be particularly desirable in terms of either fringe benefits or promotional opportunities due to the comparatively limited upward mobility offered by such a career.

Wu eventually caught the eye of the Emperor's youngest son, Li Zhi, who became Emperor Gaozong in the year 649 following the death of his father, Emperor Taizong. Because Wu had already shared a bed with Emperor Taizong for many years, she was able to provide the compassion and gymnastic instruction that enabled Emperor Gaozong to overcome his grief over the loss of his father and assume the throne. The new ruler was young and alive but not terribly interested in running the empire, so it made sense for Wu to woo him and thereby stake her own claim to the throne. The fact that she was able to share a bed with both father and son over many years underscored her physical agility as the advanced years of Emperor Taizong meant that she had to do all of the work and the inherent laziness of Emperor Gaozong also meant that she had to do all of the work. However, she also showed great sensitivity in bridging the generations and thus paying her respects to the throne; she never let the debilitating effects of ageism derail her quest for power.

Empress Wu preceded Russia's Catherine the Great by more than a thousand years but she, like Catherine, was a strong ruler who guided China during an era in which the nation's sciences and arts flourished. Although Empress Wu was not very interested in the numerous personal consultants and court advisors so favored by Catherine, she was similarly single-minded in her use of the royal bedchamber as a weapon to advance her own *realpolitik*. Unfortunately for Empress Wu, however, she—unlike Catherine the Great—was not able to kill off all of her political rivals and was thus forced to abdicate the throne following a coup in 705. Having nothing to do but shuffle around a second-rate palace and command a handful of servants to do her bidding, Wu's health rapidly declined, and she died in December 705.

The Tang Dynasty continued on for two more centuries following the death of Empress Wu, slowly becoming economically and militarily stagnant even as its territorial boundaries expanded further east. However, the Tang Dynasty was soon followed by the Song Dynasty (960-1279), which was able to pick up the slack a little bit and rejuvenate the Chinese empire for another 300 years, particularly with the advent of movable type printing, which replaced the woodblock printing that had been in use throughout Asia for several centuries. The value of movable type printing was not loss on the leaders of the Song Dynasty, who used it to print large amounts of money far more effortlessly than had ever been possible in the past. The intellectual debt owed by today's Federal Reserve to the Song Dynasty is obvious because it would be impossible for the Federal Reserve to flood the world with dollars if the inventors of movable type printing had decided to focus their energies on some other less important invention such as plastic trash bags with drawstrings. Unfortunately, the Song Dynasty was not able to rest on its laurels and inundate the ancient world with Chinese money because it was overrun by the Mongol armies in 1271.

Because the Mongols liked the idea of dynasties so much, they went ahead and set up the Yuan Dynasty to administer their

Chinese territory—which was one of the four principal regions of the Mongol Empire. But infighting among the various family members of the Mongke Khan (who had died in 1259 without appointing a successor) had become very hostile with the Khan's family members throwing horrible temper tantrums and hurling threats of physical violence at each other.

When one considers how agitated a bereaved family can become when tussling over the decedent's knickknack collection, it would be difficult to overstate how angry the Khan's family members were at each other since they were battling for control over an empire that encompassed most of the Eurasian landmass and exceeded 9 million square miles at its greatest extent. Not surprisingly, these fights intensified and eventually led to several bloody civil wars between the claimants and their respective armies.

After decades of warfare and the loss of millions of lives (which was sort of an afterthought as the Mongol Empire would ultimately be credited with causing the deaths of up to 75 million persons), the Mongol Empire fractured into four separate regions or khanates—the largest of which was China. Although the Yuan Dynasty managed to stay afloat for almost a century, its inability to manufacture fine porcelain deprived it of the legitimacy it needed to maintain the public trust. Not surprisingly, the Yuan Dynasty (whose rulers showed little interest in the place settings of Chinese households) soon gave way to the Ming Dynasty (1368-1644), whose founders were smart enough to anticipate the pent-up demand for brightly colored vases, plates and cups.

The Ming Dynasty is perhaps best known for those priceless porcelain artifacts that are now displayed in those famous museums around the world that had the foresight to sneak these valuables out of China before such preemptive treasure grabs became a "bad thing." But the emperors of the Ming Dynasty had interests other than shiny pottery.

They realized that the northern frontier of the empire was not secure (even though their predecessors had spent several centuries building fortifications and walls here and there as they saw fit) because the Mongol raiders simply went around the military garrisons and then carried on with their plunder and looting. Many of the older sections of these walls had been constructed from little more than piles of sand and dirt, but the emperors of the Ming Dynasty took wall building to a whole new level, substituting bricks and stones for compressed earth. As a result, they were able to build much taller and wider barriers which they reasoned, quite naturally, would be more difficult for the invading Mongols to scale—particularly if the imperial soldiers were shooting arrows and throwing rocks at them. The emperors of the Ming Dynasty also became obsessed with building a single contiguous wall to protect their kingdom.

One of the heroes of the Ming Dynasty was Qi Jiguang (1528-1588), a famous general who spent much of his career fighting pirates (who were not lovable rogues like Captain Jack Sparrow) along the eastern coast of China. He was ordered by Emperor Longqing to oversee the construction and reinforcement of various sections of the border wall, including the building of numerous watchtowers in which soldiers could be permanently quartered. Indeed, the Great Wall of China could be regarded as the legacy of the Ming Dynasty because its rulers devoted enormous amounts of money and labor to connect and, in many cases, reconstruct scattered sections of existing border walls that had been built over prior centuries by the emperors of earlier dynasties. This enormous construction project ultimately extended for more than 12,000 miles and provided employment for millions of laborers—many of whom were conscripted peasants and prisoners. This exhausting and backbreaking work of cutting stones and assembling them into a vast serpentine structure that winds its way over the mountains and through the valleys across Asia was fortuitous. If it had not been available, then it is possible many of these very same people, having time on their hands, would have begun to discuss alternative employment opportunities with the enemies of the regime. Fortunately for the Ming Dynasty, the emperors were able to divert the attention of these restless people by working them so hard that an estimated 350,000 of them died during the construction of the Great Wall due to factors ranging from extreme heat and cold to disease and starvation.

The reign of the Ming Dynasty ended with the fall of Beijing to the Manchu armies in 1644 and the enthronement of the Shunzhi Emperor (1638-1661), who, despite being only 5 years old (with the birth name of Fulin) and more interested in kicking balls and throwing sticks at dogs, was appointed by a committee of Manchu princes to be emperor. Even though the Shunzhi Emperor was old enough to dress himself and put his toys away, he was not quite ready to run the empire and so he was initially supervised by the self-appointed Prince Regent Dorgon (1612-1650). To ensure that the Emperor would not have his lessons interrupted by disgruntled family members of the deposed Ming emperor staging a coup, Dorgon thoughtfully arranged to have all of them executed.

Although the Shunzhi Emperor was little more than a figurehead, he was the first emperor of the Qing Dynasty (1644-1912) to rule over China, albeit with a little help from his mentor, Dorgon. Unlike most Prince Regents, however, Dorgon was not interested in sitting around the royal palace and babysitting the Emperor Shunzhi. Instead he ordered the Manchu armies to go after the remnants of the Ming resistance. After the usual massacres of hundreds of thousands of men, women and children in the Ming-controlled cities, Dorgon's armies were able to seize control over almost all of China. Unfortunately, Dorgon was unable to enjoy his triumph for very long because he died after suffering an injury while on a hunting trip in 1650. However, there were persistent rumors that Dorgon had actually been murdered on the orders of the 13-year-old Emperor Shunzhi, who had reached the age at which a regent was no longer required. As Emperor Shunzhi was apparently something of a brat, he might have worried that he would always be in the shadow of Dorgon. As a result, he might have been very tempted to kill his mentor. After all, teenagers can be very emotional and selfish, particularly when trying to seize control of a kingdom with 140,000,000 subjects.

Although the Qing Dynasty would be the last imperial dynasty to rule China, its emperors would oversee an unprecedented territorial expansion, including Outer Mongolia, Xinjiang and Tibet, over the ensuing century—all of which reached its zenith during the reign of the Qianlong Emperor (1735-1796).

After the heady successes of the first century of rule by the Qing Dynasty, the 300-year time limit rule that seemed to bedevil nearly every prior dynasty started wreaking its karmic damage on the Qings as well. In 1839, China became embroiled in a war with Great Britain because the Daoguang Emperor refused to legalize the opium trade in China. The Emperor apparently did not understand that Great Britain was merely trying to bring the fun of smoking opium to the people of China and, coincidentally, make a little money in the process. The Daoguang Emperor's dour view of the narcotics trade did not go over well with the British who saw nothing wrong with sending a naval fleet over to do battle with the vastly inferior Chinese forces. The ensuing war ended soon thereafter with the signing of the Treaty of Nanking in which the British government was given access to several Chinese ports, repaid for the opium owned by British merchants that had been destroyed by the Chinese authorities and, as an added bonus, granted Hong Kong Island and several surrounding territories.

Other well-meaning European powers also wanted to bring the benefits of narcotics consumption to the Chinese people. They followed the example set by Great Britain and joined it in the second opium war which started with the Chinese seizure of a British vessel called the *Arrow* in 1856. The British could not allow the Chinese to seize their ship without repercussions and bombarded the city of Canton with an impressive array of artillery fire. Not surprisingly, the Chinese did not view these attacks as a gesture of friendship. Widespread rioting broke out and resulted in the destruction of several British-owned properties, which, in turn, led to the start of full-scale hostilities. The British were soon joined by the French and the Russians, each of whom sought to take advantage of an increasingly-weakened China to pursue their own political agendas.

In the end, China lost the war and, in 1858, signed the Treaty of Tientsin which opened up additional ports to the European powers, permitted European nationals to travel freely through China, freed Europeans from having to appear in Chinese courts for any crimes they may have committed in China and, most importantly, legalized the opium trade. Russia also piled on and forced China to cede Outer Manchuria, which enabled Moscow to extend its territorial reach southward all the way to the port of Vladivostok.

These treaties ushered in what the Chinese refer to as the "Century of Humiliations;" an era marked by the decline and disintegration of the Qing Dynasty. It was also, in the ensuing decades, accompanied by repeated foreign interventions in China's internal affairs in which many European powers, as well as Russia and Japan, literally carved up much of China like a giant Thanksgiving turkey. This period would end in 1945, with China's emergence from World War II as one of the major powers with a permanent seat on the United Nations Security Council. Many in China, however, have argued that the Century of Humiliations has continued to the present day, due to what they believe to be the lack of deference, indeed, the overt hostility, shown by many developed countries towards China. The depth of this anti-Western sentiment can best be understood by comparing it to the extraordinary bitterness felt by many adolescent girls who believe that their parents are doing everything they can to humiliate their daughters in front of their friends.

In any event, the Qing Dynasty, which had guided China to its greatest territorial conquests, became the unwilling participant

in a number of disastrous wars that ended with humiliating treaties, containing enormous territorial and trade concessions, that
left China's sovereignty in tatters.

But, during, the same era, China was also ripped apart by the
Taiping Civil War (1850-1864), which was one of the bloodiest
conflicts of all time and resulted in upwards of 30 million deaths.
It began when the self-proclaimed Taiping Heavenly Kingdom, a
theocratic sect, tried to overthrow the Qing Dynasty. The Taiping
Heavenly Society was founded by Hong Xiuquan (1814-1864), a
self-styled mystic and failed civil service applicant who claimed
(not unlike many upper-level bureaucrats) to be the brother of
Jesus Christ. Hong was determined to remake Chinese society
based upon his somewhat delusional interpretation of Christian
doctrines. As Hong fancied himself to be a man of action, he
founded an army consisting of farmers and peasants from the
eastern coastal region of China and went to war with the Xian-
feng emperor.

Hong's soldiers battled the Qing armies for many years,
with both sides committing numerous atrocities against soldiers
and civilians alike and laying waste to vast regions of central
China. The final phase of the war began after provincial forces
surrounded the Taiping capital city of Nanjing and tried to starve
Hong's soldiers into submission. In general, sieges are not usually
completed in a week or two but can drag on for years and years.
After all, it took the Greeks a full decade to get the residents of
Troy to roll a hollow, soldier-filled horse through the city gates
before they could storm the city.

Unfortunately for Hong and his troops, the siege continued

for months and months and the food supplies became so depleted that even Hong found himself having to eat grass and weeds to stay alive. Unfortunately, this low-calorie vegetarian regimen did not agree with Hong and he dropped dead soon afterwards. Even though his followers waited for Hong to be resurrected just like his older brother, Jesus Christ, they were disappointed to find that Hong was apparently estranged from both the Father and the Son as he never showed up. However, Hong's death did convince those few remaining soldiers who had not starved to death to surrender to the imperial armies. In recognition of their bravery, Hong's soldiers were accorded the usual military courtesies of the day and put to death.

The end of the Taiping Civil War brought some relief to the Qing court but China was still plagued by those ill-mannered foreign powers that continued to show up on China's doorstep like annoying relatives looking for yet another handout. France's victory in the Sino-French War (1884-1885) resulted in China losing its considerable political influence in both Vietnam and Indochina. This dalliance with the French was followed by the Sino-Japanese War (1894-1895) in which Japan obtained Taiwan as a colony and displaced China as the preeminent power on the Korean peninsula.

A few years later, pro-Qing, anti-foreign Chinese nationals staged an uprising in northern China that became known as the Boxer Rebellion (1899-1901). The Boxers destroyed foreign-owned properties and killed numerous Christians before laying siege to Beijing, ostensibly to support the Qing government and kill any foreigners in the capital city. This violence prompted

European, American, Russian and Japanese troops to invade China, where they were able, after a few initial setbacks, to defeat the Boxer fighters and lift the siege. The Boxer Protocol of 1901 marked the formal end of hostilities and required that all Chinese government officials who had supported the Boxers be executed, that foreign troops be stationed in Beijing and that an enormous indemnity be paid to the victorious invaders. The Russians, never ones to let an opportunity to invade another country go to waste, occupied Manchuria for several years until they were, in turn, booted out by the Japanese following Tokyo's victory in the Russo-Japanese War of 1904-1905.

Although the litany of humiliations was to continue for the first several decades of the 20th century, it remained for China to be convulsed once again by the collapse of the Qing Dynasty in 1912 and the abdication of Emperor Puyi (1906-1967), who was out of a job at the ripe old age of 6. The end of dynastic rule in China was immediately followed by the establishment of the Republic of China which was initially led by Sun Yat-Sen (1866-1925), the soft-spoken political philosopher and revolutionary. Sun is widely regarded by the people of both China and Taiwan as the father of modern China for his advocacy of Chinese nationalism and republican government' and his role in bringing the Qing Dynasty to an end.

Sun was born into a family of modest means and spent his early years in the village of Cuiheng, which is located along the southeastern coast of China. Cuiheng boasts the world's largest collection of Sun Yat-Sen tourist shops where visitors can purchase Sun Yat-Sen t-shirts, headbands, sweatshirts, banners and undergarments Fans can also buy life-sized cardboard cut-outs of Sun to prop up in their own homes and thus enjoy the sense of peacefulness and wisdom that seems to emanate from his watchful, albeit creepy, eyes. However, the Sun Yat-Sen tourist trade had not started when Sun was a young boy, so there was little reason for him to stay in Cuiheng, which, at the time, was a tiny hamlet with only a few dozen residents. His parents packed up his clothes and sent him off, at 10 years of age, to live with his elder brother, Sun Mei, in Honolulu, the capital city of the Kingdom of Hawaii. Life in Honolulu was pleasant, and Sun excelled in his studies even though there is no record as to whether he learned how to surf or juggle flaming torches. However, he did receive a Western-oriented education and became proficient in a wide variety of subjects, including history, mathematics and religion.

After spending seven years in Hawaii, Sun went back to China and continued his studies, eventually receiving a medical degree in 1892 at the Canton Hospital, a prestigious institution that had been founded by Christian missionaries. Having been exposed to Christian teachings since his time in Hawaii, it is not surprising that Sun became a Christian and began to wonder about such things as the limits of government authority and the rights of individuals. He also started hanging out with a group of friends in Hong Kong who advocated the overthrow of the Qing Dynasty but not so loudly that they might be overheard by the authorities. Sun tried to offer his views about modernizing China to various government authorities but was ignored, possibly because those same government officials had little stomach for discussing ideas that could be considered treasonous. Undeterred, Sun returned to Hawaii to work on his tan and establish the Revive China Society which was the first organization to advocate an overtly Chinese nationalist orientation.

Sun's growing interest in politics was also marked by the start of his numerous ventures into matrimony, beginning with his marriage to Lu Muzhen in 1884. It must have been a very happy marriage because Sun then married Chen Cuifen in 1891—even though he was still married to Lu Muzhen. However, there was something still missing from his life that two mature wives could not provide so he then tied the knot with Japanese teenager Kaoru Ostsuki in 1903, whom he married both for her perky explanations of Kantian philosophy as well as her flexibility. Sadly, his third marriage fell apart and was over by 1906—leaving him to tough it out with the other two wives until his fourth and final marriage in 1915 to Soong Ching-ling. He somehow managed to keep his first two wives happy until after he assumed office as the first president of the Republic of China in 1912. Unfortunately, his decision to step down from the presidency a few months later seems to have caused each of his first two wives to conclude that Sun Yat-Sen without the presidential palace and all the perks that go along with being the head of state of the Republic of China was not enough to justify sharing what had become a very crowded bed. As a result, his second wife, Chen Cuifen, called it quits in 1912, before she had even finished picking new place settings for the presidential palace. Sun's first wife, Lu Muszhen, tossed in the towel three years later, in 1915, when it became clear that Sun was not going to be returning to the glitzy life of a head of state anytime soon.

Sun's numerous marriages never caused him to lose sight of

the need for fundamental political change in China. Even before he walked down the aisle for the first or second time, he had become convinced that China could not be salvaged by tinkering with the Qing Dynasty. Sun felt that the country had become a prisoner of its own autocratic history. He believed that China could be modernized only by a sweeping revolution that would remake Chinese society from the ground up. In 1895, Sun and the other members of the Revive China Society (not to be confused with other splinter revolutionary groups such as the Revive China Group and the Revive China Association) launched a rebellion against the Qing Dynasty that was quickly crushed by the authorities. Sun was forced into exile where he continued to advocate revolution in China while attracting financial support and followers in both Great Britain and the United States.

The Qing government did not take kindly to Sun's continuing calls for its overthrow because autocrats want to keep their jobs and privileges as much as anyone else. As a result, they tried to discredit him in China while also sending agents abroad to kidnap or kill him. Indeed, Sun became trapped at the Chinese embassy in London for nearly two weeks in 1896 but was released before he could be sent back to China—where he would have been welcomed with open arms and then executed. Sun continued his travels in Canada and Japan, meeting with other "armchair revolutionaries," who wanted to overthrow the Qing Dynasty. Sun also periodically organized unsuccessful uprisings in various parts of China. He visited the United States in 1904, using a forged birth certificate to get around the law that banned Chinese nationals from entry into the country. During the following year, Sun joined a number of other individuals in Japan who also advocated revolution and a pan-Asian, anti-Western viewpoint, forming the so-called United Front or Tongmenghui.

The Tongmenghui sponsored several additional uprisings in China over the next several years—all of which failed. This lack of success by Sun as a professional revolutionary led many members of the Tongmenghui to criticize him and allege that he had somehow profited from masterminding these repeated revolts against the Qing Dynasty. Stung by this criticism, Sun focused on fund-raising activities overseas. In fact, he was in the United States when the Xinhai Revolution began with an armed rebellion against the government in Wuchang in October 1911. The unrest spread rapidly throughout the country with revolutionaries in nearly every province declaring the end of the Qing Dynasty. Within a few weeks, the government realized that it had very little popular support and so it began negotiating with the revolutionaries. On January 1, 1912, the Republic of China was established and the newly arrived Sun Yat-Sen was appointed as its president. However, Sun was not universally admired in China and so he agreed to resign his position to avoid a civil war once his prospective successor, Yuan Shikai, was able to secure the abdication of Emperor Puyi after giving him a vanilla ice cream cone.

Sun stepped down as president in March 1912, less than a month after Emperor Puyi gave up his throne and went out to play with his friends. With Yuan as the new president, Sun set about contacting political leaders throughout China, urging them to support the newly created National Assembly of China. The old Tongmenghui was reconstituted by Song Jiaoren, a longtime colleague of Sun, into a new political party called the Kuomintang or KMT—which would win almost half of the seats in the

National Assembly in the election held later that year. Unfortunately, Song was assassinated in March 1913, most likely on the orders of sitting president Yuan, who was just beginning to enjoy life as a head of state. Indeed, Yuan fancied himself as being more than just a president and would declare himself to be emperor two years later in an ill-fated attempt to revive dynastic rule in China. In any event, Song's death prompted Sun to call for a revolt by the KMT faithful against Yuan's government. Unfortunately, Sun's record of leading unsuccessful insurgencies continued and the KMT forces were brutally defeated and the party itself outlawed. Sun himself barely escaped with his life to Japan where he not only had to avoid agents of Yuan's government but also his former, now less perky but angrier, Japanese wife who had tried unsuccessfully for years to get him to pay child support for his daughter.

Over the next several years, China disintegrated into chaos as various factions struggled for power. Sun returned to China in 1916 and became head of one of several regional military factions that were jockeying for power in the south. At the same time, Xu Shichang was serving as president of the Republic of China, which controlled most of northern China. Sun worked with his political rivals in the south to create a single government that could oppose the national government in the north and unveiled a new version of the KMT known as the Nationalist Party of China. He enlisted the cooperation of the Chinese Communist Party and also solicited military assistance from the Soviet Union. Over time, Sun was able to develop a viable military force that would be headed by Chiang Kai-shek and used to attack the ruling government in 1926, a year after Sun's death from liver cancer.

Sun did not live to see the outbreak of the Chinese civil

war that saw the KMT troops led by Chiang Kai-shek wage an ongoing military campaign against the Chinese communists from 1927 to 1949. This conflict involved the usual atrocities on both sides, accompanied by several million deaths and widespread famines. However, it was interrupted by the Japanese occupation of Manchuria in 1931 and Tokyo's subsequent attempts to subjugate much of eastern China over the course of the following decade. Japan created the puppet state of Manchukuo and, in a heartwarming tip of the hat to China's imperial tradition, reinstalled, as a figurehead, the deposed Emperor Puyi who was now in his mid-twenties and ready to resume his career as an autocrat. This was something of a public relations coup for the Japanese as dynastic emperors are always in very short supply, particularly when the dynasty itself has already petered out. For Emperor Puyi, this was an opportunity to reclaim the glory of imperial China even though he was always under the thumb of his Japanese overlords throughout the entire course of his reign, which continued until Japan's surrender in 1945. As a result, he was unable to enjoy some of the pleasures of his childhood such as being able to order that members of the palace staff be flogged for his personal entertainment.

With the Japanese defeated, China was free to resume its civil war. Both the nationalist government headed by Chiang Kai-shek and the communists now headed by Mao Zedong (1893-1976) engaged in numerous bloody battles against each other and carried out massacres of millions of civilians whom they believed to be sympathetic to the other side. Despite having more troops and arms than their communist adversaries at the end of World War II, the Nationalist government troops were poorly led and inadequately supplied. The communists were able to gain the support of peasants throughout the country by taking a page from Lenin's playbook and offering to give them land that belonged to other people. This program was far more popular with the recipients than the former owners. The communists also pointed to the Nationalist government's mismanagement of the economy, which had resulted in hyperinflation and devastated the economic fortunes of millions of persons across the country. The communists also convinced many Chinese that the Nationalist government was corrupt and more interested in winning the civil war than in building an independent China free from foreign domination.

By 1949, the communists had driven Chiang Kai-shek and his army off the mainland, leaving Chiang to establish the Republic of China on the island of Taiwan. On October 1, 1949, a holiday not widely observed in Taiwan, Mao declared the establishment of the People's Republic of China. From this day forward, throughout his life, Mao would be consumed with the idea of transforming China from a backward agrarian land to an industrial power and implementing many drastic, often disastrous, policies to increase economic growth and bolster China's military capabilities.

Born into a peasant family in Shaoshan, Hunan, Mao developed a keen sense of Chinese nationalism at a young age. He read a wide variety of books on politics and philosophy by authors ranging from Charles Darwin to Adam Smith. Mao also learned first-hand about China's traditional customs when, at the age of 14, his family arranged for him to marry an 18-year old girl named Luo Yixiu, the daughter of a local landowner. Because Mao had not yet even had the opportunity to sow his oats (and may not have really known how to sow his oats at that point), he rejected his bride and left Shaoshan until both his parents and his prospective in-laws were able to calm down. His first foray into the world of marital bliss also convinced him that many Chinese customs, such as arranged marriages, were backwards and should be revised if not discarded altogether. Fortunately, Mao did not let this nuptial nightmare sour him completely on the institution of marriage as he, like Sun Yat-Sen, would take three more wives during his lifetime, two of whom overlapped by a few years due to Mao having forgotten to get a divorce.

As a young man he became acutely aware of China's exploitation by European and Asian powers and the inability of the Qing Dynasty to defend China's sovereignty. However, it was only after he went to Peking University that he discovered the writings of Marx and Lenin while working as a librarian. Their words inspired Mao to rebel against the oppressive yoke of the Dewey Decimal System. Indeed, he would take a cart of books that needed to be reshelved and, after furtive glances to make sure that he was not being followed by library spies, intentionally reshelve those books in the wrong sections of the library. However, these deeds were not enough to satiate Mao's desires to strike out at heavy-handed authority—even though he sometimes went so far as to reshelve the books upside down.

Although librarians do not typically engage in armed uprisings against government authorities, the words of Marx and

Lenin infused Mao with a revolutionary zeal that changed his life forever. Accordingly, he lost interest in pursuing a life as a librarian and instead, in the early 1920s, joined the newly formed Chinese Communist Party (CCP) which began, like most revolutionary movements, with a bunch of disgruntled, unemployed students who obviously had too much time on their hands.

Mao found the life of a professional revolutionary to be far more exhilarating than pushing carts loaded with books around the library. Indeed, he discovered that he had a talent for mobilizing people to engage in protests and strikes against the government. As time went on, the ranks of the CCP grew so much so that it became the leading opposition party in China to the KMT headed by Chiang Kai-shek. Mao used his organizational skills to help found the Chinese Red Army and draw recruits from around the country who were disillusioned with the corrupt and incompetent rule of the Nationalist government. The CCP, by contrast, struck many observers as being far better organized and more in touch with the concerns of ordinary Chinese citizens—despite its obvious top-down managerial style.

The end of World War II prompted some in China to shout "hurray" but it was only a momentary sense of relief. China soon became engulfed in a full-blown civil war between the nationalist troops of Chiang Kai-shek and the communist troops led by Mao. Although the armies of Chiang and Mao crisscrossed the country over and over again and did their best to kill millions of innocent civilians, they were only able to tally a paltry 7 million civilian and military deaths—an embarrassing performance when compared to the lethality of the Taiping Civil War. By the time the Chinese Civil War ended in 1949, Mao exercised total control over the CCP and, hence, China itself.

After completing purges of other potential rivals to the throne as payback for them being potential rivals to Mao's rule, Mao initiated China's first five-year plan, in 1953, to steer the resources of the state in ways that would facilitate the rapid development of heavy industries, including coal, electricity, iron and steel, and chemicals. At the same time, the government began to seize privately-owned farms and combine them into enormous cooperatives. Mao's plans to transform China into a modern economy were based upon the blueprint that had been used by both Lenin and Stalin in the Soviet Union. In Mao's view, there was no point in waiting for generations to transform the country if it could be done in a few years or decades through a massive reordering of Chinese society—even if it happened to cause enormous suffering throughout the country.

The forced industrialization of the Chinese economy during the first five-year plan resulted in a tripling of steel production and a doubling of coal output. This expansion in industrial output caused an enormous increase in air pollution which enabled many Chinese to experience black lung disease for the first time, without having to go near a coal mine. The government also seized control of most large-scale businesses, reasoning quite sensibly that loyal Party members should be able to motivate employees by following principles laid out in excerpts from the speeches and writings contained in *Mao's Little Red Book*—which remains an all-time bestseller in China even though it has yet to be made into a Broadway musical.

Even though Mao was often depicted as an absolute dictator in the press, he was really the first among several equals on the dais of the ruling Politburo. Mao had the final word on most decisions but he could be swayed by the opinions of other members. His colleagues included individuals such as Zhou Enlai (1898-1976)—the first premier of communist China and Mao's second-in-command (and, according to Zhou's snarkier critics, lead toady)—and Deng Xiaoping (1904-1997), who would succeed Mao as leader of China in 1978. Deng would encourage the development of a "socialist market economy" that would lay the foundation for China's explosive economic growth and insufferable smugness over the next four decades. But the Politburo was not just another social club; it exercised control over virtually every aspect of Chinese society and, unlike most social clubs, could arrange to have any persons that it found to be overly unenthusiastic about the government's policies dropped off a cliff or shot.

As the first five-year plan had proven to be very successful, Mao then decided to double down on his efforts to drag China into the modern era by announcing the second five-year plan in 1958. This plan accelerated the collectivization of farmlands and encouraged small-scale industries in the rural hinterlands of the country. Mao hoped that this "Great Leap Forward" would transform China from an agrarian economy into an industrial powerhouse by organizing China's 900,000,000 people into numerous self-sufficient communes. He ordered that all private farming be banned and that rural citizens engage in the production of steel using homemade foundries. Needless to say, the results were disastrous because the farmers had no incentive to grow food (and were, in fact, imprisoned if they tried to grow their own crops) and most peasants were not very adept at smelting iron ore in barbeque grill-sized foundries.

If Mao had wanted to surpass the deaths that had resulted from the Taiping Civil War, then he must undoubtedly have been pleased with the massive famine that resulted from the almost complete destruction of agricultural activity in China due to the government's collectivization program. In fact, Mao's Great Leap Forward resulted in upwards of 50 million deaths by 1962—the greatest human-caused disaster of all time. The sheer scale of human suffering caused by Mao's policies certainly established him as the leading cause of death in the 20th century even though he was given a good run for his money by such mass murderers as Joseph Stalin and Adolf Hitler.

The unmitigated disaster of the Great Leap Forward did not cause Mao to question his own policies; instead he blamed the "counter-revolutionaries" that were lurking behind every door for failing to implement his plans to build a true "worker's paradise." But Mao seemed to be consumed by the idea that China needed to experience an on-going state of political upheaval to prevent it from backsliding into a morass of corruption and class exploitation.

Even though Mao was no longer regarded as infallible by the year 1967, he still had sufficient power to unleash the Cultural Revolution with the avowed goal of purging China of both capitalistic and traditional characteristics. His weapon of choice was disaffected, hormonally-unbalanced young people who were happy to join the ranks of the so-called Red Guards and attack anything and anyone that Mao decided needed to be destroyed that particular day—regardless of whether it involved community governmental facilities or museums laden with historical artifacts. The Cultural Revolution was characterized by numerous outbreaks of violence across the country with many millions of men and women being persecuted or even imprisoned, including members of Mao's inner circle such as Deng Xiaoping. The country's universities were also closed repeatedly, thereby depriving tens of millions of persons of the opportunity to pursue an education. All in all, it seemed that Mao's primary interest in fomenting unrest and civil strife in China was to see how far he could push his own radical policies—no matter how much damage or suffering they caused. The only bright spot was that Mao died in 1976 and the Cultural Revolution came to an end—with only 1 or 2 million deaths to its credit.

Mao was the most important figure in modern China. Aside from dragging a backward nation of 900,000,000 people into the 20th century, he also set off a mercifully brief fashion trend by donning what is now known as the Sun Yat-Sen suit with its military-style collar and the patch pockets. Although Mao never had the opportunity to strut down a Paris walkway, his suit was all the rage in China for a while, until after his death when more traditional Western business attire began to stage a comeback in the closets of China's political leaders.

After the turbulence and destruction and the tens of millions of deaths that accompanied Mao's regime, Deng Xaioping offered a more pragmatic vision for China's future in which ceaseless revolution was deemphasized in favor of economic development "with Chinese characteristics." Deng argued that China's economy should be guided by market principles—but still subject to the benevolent guidance of the CCP. To that end, he initiated numerous reforms designed to jumpstart the nation's economy while reordering the nation's political system and rehabilitating millions of persons who had been victims of Mao's political witch hunts during the Cultural Revolution. Indeed, economic development became the mantra of Deng's China. Accordingly, the Maoist ideology of unending social upheaval (which had become stale after two decades) took a backseat to concerns about labor productivity and industrial expansion. Over time, the Chinese economy was opened up to foreign investment and tens of millions of persons streamed into China's cities to work in factories (where they could learn first-hand about Marx's theory of labor exploitation) whose products helped China to become the world's second largest economy by the year 2012.

Deng engaged in negotiations with Great Britain to secure the return of the colony of Hong Kong—which evoked feelings of elation throughout China similar to those you might feel if your neighbor unexpectedly returned a shovel he had borrowed eight years before. Deng also ordered an invasion of Vietnam in 1979, ostensibly to punish Vietnam for toppling the murderous Pol Pot regime in Cambodia. Although China advanced nearly 387 feet into Vietnamese territory and occupied several villages and an apparel factory filled with boxes of t-shirts declaring "My Grandparents went to New York and all I got was this Lousy T-Shirt," the battle-hardened Vietnamese fought the Chinese army to a standstill. As a result, China decided to declare victory and withdrew its forces, having achieved nothing except for a few thousand military casualties and a truckload of those highly sought after t-shirts.

In the years after Deng Xiaoping's death in 1997, China had a series of leaders such as Li Xiannian, Yang Shangkun, Jiang Zemin and Hu Jintao (all of whom should not to be confused with the law firm of the same name), who carried on Deng's policies of economic liberalization but who, unlike Deng, were not featured as *Time's* Man of the Year or even offered lucrative greeter positions at any of the leading Las Vegas casinos. However, this succession of short-term leaders ended with the ascension of Xi Jinping, who became the General Secretary (i.e., Dr. Evil) of the CCP in 2012.

Xi's rise to the top of the Chinese government marked the end of the Deng Xiaoping era because Xi, who became President of China in 2014, believed that the CCP needed to reassert its primacy over the Chinese economy. As Xi viewed himself as the ultimate hall monitor of China, he advocated numerous policies to clamp down on dissent and to reinforce the CCP's grip on power. He also launched widespread anti-corruption campaigns that conveniently resulted in the disappearance of many of his political opponents. As a result, Xi became the undisputed heavyweight champion of Chinese politics, having secured unprecedented third terms as the General Secretary of the CCP in 2022 and the President of China in 2023. However, it is unclear whether Xi received commemorative belts with brass plates to wear if he wanted to strut around the Great Hall of the People like a prized peacock. In the interest of avoiding the messiness of future presidential elections, Xi has reportedly suggested that the Party simply elect him for another ten 5-year terms ahead of time so that he can continue serving in office until the age of 129 without having to bother with the inconvenience of gathering all the delegates together to rubber-stamp each new term every five years.

As part of his on-going efforts to reassert the CCP's control over Chinese society, Xi also started a campaign against China's leading technology companies in 2021, imposing huge fines and severe restrictions on their operations, ostensibly to rein in their monopolistic pricing policies and chaotic marketing practices. Unfortunately, this effort nearly destroyed China's internet companies, wiping out nearly half of their $2.5 trillion market capitalization in less than two years. This clampdown on China's most dynamic companies did have one bright spot, however, as it apparently caused many tech moguls to reconsider any criticisms they might have otherwise voiced about the government, thus contributing to the social peace so ardently desired by Xi and his colleagues.

Xi's campaign against China's internet companies also coincided with the outbreak of the COVID-19 global pandemic in 2019. Xi spent much of the following three years denying that the actual virus had been engineered at a laboratory in Wuhan, China, pointing out (quite logically) that there were no signs on any doors at the building that contained the words "COVID-19 Virus." Instead, he argued convincingly that the virus had originated in a hot dog cart at 57th Street and Park Avenue in New York City because that would be the most likely place that you would find an infected bat.

Emboldened by the explosive growth of the Chinese economy over the past four decades, Xi also set his sights on the United States, predicting that it was only a matter of time before

China would become the preeminent global superpower. Unfortunately for Xi, the wheels started to come off of the Chinese juggernaut as other countries cut back their purchases of Chinese exports and China's own population began to shrink in 2023. The economy was further battered by the collapse of the real estate market and the virtual disappearance of foreign investment due to increasingly punitive government policies. However, Xi did not let the disintegrating economy get in the way of his desire to bully his neighbors, picking fights with almost everyone he could find—including India, Vietnam, Japan, the Philippines and South Korea.

Xi was also famous for his unique interpretation of international law in which he ordered the Chinese military to create a number of artificial islands in the South China Sea so that China could claim enormous areas of the surrounding waters as its own. Other nations, such as the United States—which advocate the more traditional freedom of the sea's doctrine—contested Xi's claims and delighted in sending naval vessels through the Taiwan Strait in order to give Xi the proverbial poke in the eye. Xi also reportedly considered a plan to dig up and dump the entire Himalayan Mountain chain into the South China Sea so that China could expand its coastline eastward and landlock some of its adversaries, such as Taiwan and the Philippines. However, Xi later abandoned the idea when he realized that shoving the world's tallest mountain range into the ocean would cause sea levels to rise so much that it would flood China's existing coastal regions and defeat the whole purpose of expanding China's territorial reach.

Xi also unveiled the Belt and Road Initiative in 2013 in which

China made many development loans to countries throughout Europe, Africa and Asia, to assist in the construction of dams, bridges, roads and harbors. However, this program—loosely modeled on the very popular loan shark lending programs popularized by both gangsters and credit card companies in the United States—has been denounced by many borrowers as unconscionable "debt traps" in which the terms were often so one-sided that it was almost impossible to repay these loans. The fact that many of these projects were geared toward encouraging a more China-centered global economy has also been widely criticized.

THE ECONOMY OF CHINA

The rise of China from an almost primitive, devastated country torn apart by centuries of warfare and famine to the world's second largest economy is one of the most impressive stories in history. Although Mao was the father of modern China, his twice-purged, second- or third- or fourth-in command (depending on the day of the week), Deng Xiaoping, was the key figure in China's economic development. Deng's 12-year stewardship of the Chinese nation—following the death of Mao and the enormous disasters of the Great Leap Forward and the Cultural Revolution—brought important economic reforms and sparked the beginning of more than four decades of economic growth averaging nearly 9 percent a year. Indeed, it was only in the past few years that China's superheated economy—the so-called "factory of the world"—has begun to slow down, beset by a rapidly aging and declining population, an imploding real estate market, dwindling exports and falling foreign investment.

China's rise in the global economic hierarchy was greatly aided by its being granted admission to the World Trade Organization (WTO) in 2001. This event enabled China to gain greater access to the markets of most developed countries in exchange for solemn, cross-your-heart promises to refrain from stealing sensitive technology and exporting goods made with forced labor. WTO membership also gave China greater access to foreign direct investment which made possible the construction of thousands of factories that would employ tens of millions of workers who would eventually produce more manufactured goods than any other country in the world. The United States had supported China's application for membership in the WTO in the hopes that an expanding market economy would lead to the democratization of the CCP—even though China's leaders never expressed any interest in cultivating a kinder, gentler, cuddlier CCP.

China remains a very important economic and military powerhouse with ambitions to control the global economy and reshape the international system. To that end, it has sought to take the lead in high technology fields ranging from semiconductor manufacturing to artificial intelligence. Its manufacturing capabilities have been greatly aided by numerous joint venture agreements with Western companies that have typically required both the sharing of proprietary technologies and the construction of manufacturing facilities in China so that these companies could market their products to China's billion-person consumer market. Not leaving anything to chance, the CCP has also restricted foreign access to its domestic markets and subsidized exports to gain market share in other countries—while denying that it is doing these very same things in order to portray itself as a victim of hostile propaganda from those very same countries. This is an ingenuous version of the old complaint that the other person started the fight by hitting back.

China was arguably the biggest beneficiary of the globalization of the world economy as its plentiful low-cost labor and stable (i.e., autocratic) government attracted numerous investors who were anxious to make their fortunes in China. Unfortunately, the flip-side of China's ability to produce a wide variety of manufactured goods with an almost endless supply of cheap labor was that it drove thousands of domestic manufacturers in the United States and Europe out of business. This tectonic shift in global manufacturing capabilities has resulted in the United States and Europe having a much greater dependence on Chinese supply chains for products ranging from pharmaceuticals to solar panels. Fortunately, the United States labor market has remained resilient with plentiful job opportunities for short order cooks, bell hops, maids, waitresses and bank clerks—thus demonstrating that the United States can continue to be a major power in low-wage industries for the foreseeable future.

China's breakneck growth over the past forty years has fueled an arrogance on the part of its government which has confidently predicted that its economy will be two or three times the size of that of the United States by the year 2050. However, China's severe population control programs—most notably its notorious one-child program—has caused its fertility rate to drop to 1.0— which is less than half of the 2.1 children per couple necessary to maintain a stable population. As a result, many scholars who were ready to crown China as the new hegemon of the global economy are now predicting that China's population could fall from 1.3 billion people to less than 400 million people by the end of the century. They are also asking who is going to buy all of the additional appliances, cars, apartments and clothing that would have to be produced and sold by this future super-economy with the collapsing population.

If China's population were to decline by 70% to 400 million by the year 2100, for example, its consumer class would shrink accordingly as there would be proportionately fewer workers and younger families around in this new, slimmed-down China. For China's GDP to triple from its present size during that same time period, each of these consumers would have to purchase 8, 9 or even 10 times the current amount of goods as today's consumers in order to prop up the Chinese economy. Unfortunately for China, it cannot ignore the most fundamental feature of the marketplace: A country cannot continue to produce goods and services without limit if there are not enough consumers around to buy them.

CHINA AND THE ARTS

PAINTING

Anyone wishing to get on the good side of their Chinese friends might toss out the name of China's most beloved painter, Fan Kuan (960-1030), who is known for his extraordinarily detailed landscapes. His most famous surviving work, *Travelers Among Mountains and Streams*, anticipated the concept of the vanishing point by several centuries. This idea was a breakthrough discovered by the Italian master Brunelleschi (1377-1446) (not to be confused with bruschetta—the tasty toasted bread topped with flavorful vegetables, fruits and meats) in which all lines on a canvas converge at a single point. Fan came up with a unique approach which hinted at the vanishing point concept by utilizing three overlapping perspectives—near, middle and far—to create a three-dimensional painting that did not look stilted or distorted like most of the stuff today that passes for modern art.

Fan's work focused on the beauty of the natural world. Like all great artists, he made a number of false starts, as evidenced by certain unfinished works such as *Parking Garage by the Yangtze River*, *Man in a Barrel Over the Waterfall* and *Chow Chows Playing Poker*. But his interest in Daoism caused him to seek a greater oneness with the cosmos and to look to the natural world for artistic inspiration. Accordingly, his most famous works such as *Travelers* showcased the beauty of the living world itself and underscored the insignificance of human beings in the universe.

Those who prefer their trees to be bulldozed and their meadows to be paved over with asphalt might prefer Zhang Zeduan's (1085-1145) jubilant masterpiece *Along the River During the Qingming Festival*, which has been called the "*Mona Lisa* of China." Zhang captured numerous depictions of everyday life along the Bian River on a 17-foot-long silk scroll which unrolls to reveal a succession of scenes ranging from the quiet of the countryside to the hustle and bustle of the villages and features hundreds of people from all walks of life—a living panorama of Chinese society. Indeed, some art critics have pointed out that *Along the River During the Qingming Festival* depicts more than 800 people—which, by their calculations, makes it at least 800 times better than Leonardo Da Vinci's portrait of a single young woman with poor dental work.

The intricate details of Zhang's painting have mesmerized China's citizens to the present day. Not surprisingly, art collectors and emperors alike have taken turns stealing the painting from each other over the past thousand years. In fact, Emperor Puyi, whom the Japanese had placed in charge of the puppet Chinese state of Manchukuo during World War II (as discussed above), was caught with the painting in his suitcase while trying to flee the advancing Russian army in 1945. Although the Soviet government kept the painting for a few years, Stalin eventually decided that it would be too difficult to pass it off as a rendering of life in a 20th century Russian steel mill, so he ordered that it be handed back over to the Chinese government. Zhang's painting has been exhibited a few times since its return and has always drawn thousands of spectators during its public displays. Otherwise, it remains under lock and key at the Palace Museum in the Forbidden City to the present day.

LITERATURE

The golden age of the Tang Dynasty also gave the world China's most famous poet, Li Bai (701-762), who composed over a thousand poems during his lifetime while wandering across the countryside. His poems evoked a heartfelt reality and imagery that embraced the simplicity of everyday life— which was enhanced, in many cases, by his prodigious consumption of wine. Indeed, one of his most famous poems, *Drinking Alone Under the Moon*, continues to be widely celebrated in China to the present day, recalling an evening in which he toasted himself, the moon and his shadow. However, this poem was barely more than a dozen lines, reflecting Li Bai's ability to express his thoughts about loneliness, homesickness and having a blood alcohol level several times the legal limit in a very spiritual and moving way.

Many of Li Bai's poems focused on the sadness of being separated from family and friends even though he was the one who typically took off and spent long periods of time away from home—perhaps seeking peace and quiet from the complaints of one or more of his four wives who may have been unhappy with the size of his poetry royalty checks. But his wanderings gave him a perspective about 8th-century China that infused his writings with an authenticity that could only come from stumbling around the land with a fine rice wine in hand.

Because many of Li Bai's poems were very short, he enjoyed a true advantage over later writers such as Russia's Leo Tolstoy because his entire life's work of poetry would have fit inside the pages of a single copy of Tolstoy's *War and Peace*. Hence, Li Bai's poetry was eminently portable and could be carried around and enjoyed by anyone who happened to be on the run or had ample leisure time due to their own adverse attitude toward full-time employment.

China's other literary titan was Cao Xuequin (1710-1765), a novelist who rose to prominence during the Qing dynasty and who, like Li Bai, enjoyed full-time social drinking. Although he was born into a prosperous family that had entertained the Kangxi Emperor on several occasions, the family fortune was lost and Cao spent most of his formative years living in extreme poverty. This cruel turn of fate colored Cao's view of the world and caused him to consider the capricious nature of life itself. This sense of lacking any meaningful control over his own life manifested in his novel *Dream of the Red Chamber*, a.k.a. *The Story of the Stone*, which is widely regarded as the greatest novel of Chinese literature. It has been compared to Shakespeare's most famous play, *Romeo and Juliet*. However, Coa realized that it would not make much sense to use European names in a tale about two doomed Chinese lovers, so he gave his Romeo the name of Pao-yu and his Juliet the name Tai-yu and made no reference to the Italian city of Verona.

Coa's novel offered its readers all the features of a first-class trash novel burnished with the veneer of literary respectability. There are numerous conflicts percolating throughout the book between masters and their servants, and wives and the concubines of their husbands. Some of the characters are noble and others are despicable, but none are Presbyterian. Cao manages to cover the spectrum of human emotions and behavior in a single sprawling tale. However, the book itself can be very frustrating to follow for almost any reader trying to make his or her way through the narrative because there are dozens of characters who share similar family names—making a quick read virtually impossible. Indeed, many readers report that they must create wall-sized ancestral diagrams in order to keep straight which family member is trying to kill or kidnap or rob or seduce which other family member.

PART THREE

THE WONDERFUL WORLD OF GLOBAL BANKING

CHAPTER 5

MEET THE IMF AND
THE WORLD BANK

INTRODUCTION

The motivation for Russia and China to set up the BRICS organization in the first place stemmed from their shared antipathy toward the United States and its dominance of the international banking system. Both President Putin of Russia and President Xi of China see the United States as the primary obstacle standing in the way of their plans to reorganize the global economy around Moscow and Beijing. This is not to say that both Putin and Xi do not enjoy certain uniquely American guilty pleasures. Putin likes singing country music tunes and wearing a cowboy hat when taking bubble baths, while Xi secretly watches Russ Meyer's family-oriented movie classics such as *Supervixens* and *Beneath the Valley of the Ultra-Vixens*. However, both Putin and Xi are openly hostile to the United States as a political entity and the influence that it has exercised over the global economy since the end of World War II. Xi's dislike for the United States was also fueled by the fact that Shari Eubanks, the voluptuous star of *Supervixens*, was snubbed for the Best Actress award by the Motion Picture Academy.

BRETTON WOODS AND THE POST-WAR ECONOMIC ORDER

In 1944, delegates from 44 countries met for a 22-day sleepover at the Mount Washington Hotel in Bretton Woods, New Hampshire to discuss the establishment of a new worldwide economic regime. Unfortunately, some of these delegates were disappointed to find that New Hampshire is not next-door to Los Angeles, California, thus greatly limiting their opportunities to see their favorite celebrities. Although the hotel concierge nearly provoked an international crisis by refusing to drive these delegates 3,019 miles so that they could take the movie stars' home tour in Beverly Hills, California, he did smooth things over by ferrying the delegates around some of the local landmarks such as the Mount Washington Cog Railway and the Bretton Woods Lumber Yard.

What prompted all of these important people to travel to the quasi-tropical paradise of Bretton Woods in the first place? Although a few may have been trying to burn up some leftover travel points on their credit cards, most of these representatives were genuinely concerned about creating a new global financial system. In particular, they wanted to avoid a recurrence of the problems that many believed had led to the collapse of the international trading system in the early 1930s and the rise of fascism in both Germany and Japan.

THE GOLD STANDARD VS. THE SALTED FISH STANDARD

Before the outbreak of World War II, most countries followed the gold standard which meant, in theory, that a citizen of any one of these nations could go to a bank with a handful of paper notes and redeem these bills for their equivalent value in gold bullion. As you might expect, most countries did not like being tied to the gold standard because it meant that they had to retain significant amounts of gold bullion to back their respective currencies with something of tangible value. Because gold is very expensive and difficult to mine and refine in large quantities, one might wonder why these nations did not back their currencies with something else of value that might have been more easily acquired, such as salted fish.

Although there is nothing that would have precluded any or all countries from dumping the gold standard in favor of the salted fish standard, gold has long been regarded as a valuable asset and used as a medium of exchange both domestically and internationally. Gold has been sought by kings and thieves alike for thousands of years, due to its luster, its brilliance, its portability, its resilience and its scarcity. It has been used in jewelry since antiquity and continues to be viewed as both a symbol of wealth and an enduring store of value.

What if the nations of the world had adopted the salted fish standard instead of the gold standard? In the beginning, their leaders might have been very excited about the fact that you can catch a fish far more easily than you can mine an ounce of gold. It is easier to drop a baited hook into a river than to dig up tons of dirt and rock in search of a few gold nuggets. Fish are readily available around the world so that a country following the salted fish standard would be able to expand its fish-backed currency much more rapidly than those fuddy-duddy nations still clinging to the gold standard. After all, fish provide a far more plentiful and widely-available form of collateral to back a nation's currency. If a country using a fish-backed currency wanted to double the amount of money in circulation, it would merely need to double its supply of salted fish. Nations using the gold standard, by contrast, can only expand their money supply as they are able to increase their gold reserves—which is a slower and more expensive process.

Even though the widespread availability of salted fish could enable a country to expand its money supply, there are several problems with using a salted fish standard. First, the value of the currency would be dependent on it being redeemed for salted fish—which is a perishable commodity that will start to smell after a while. Second, this convertibility presumes that everyone wants to hold salted fish which, quite frankly, may not be the case, particularly as the fish rot. Some people do not like fish at all (the so-called "anti-pescatarians") whereas other people do not want to carry around reeking fish carcasses in their wallets and purses.

So salted fish may lack the universal appeal of gold—which would reduce its value as a convertible asset. Third, decaying salted fish will cease to exist after a certain amount of time, just like some of the bank employees forced to scrub the salted fish vaults at the banks. Gold, by contrast, does not corrode and will last longer than almost any object except for preservative-laden fast food hamburgers. Fourth, salted fish are not very portable due to their perishability and their stench; gold, by contrast, can be transported in all sorts of conditions without any adverse effects. Fifth, salted fish are arguably not a valuable enough commodity to anchor the value of a nation's currency because salted fish can be easily obtained by everyone from children with fishing poles to the crews on commercial fishing trawlers. Gold, by contrast, is difficult to extract and process (unless you are an entrepreneurial dentist) which ensures that it is a scarce element. Even so, it is still common enough to be used in the coinage of a country.

Anyways, most of the leading industrial nations tied their currencies to gold for much of the 19th and early 20th centuries. The problem that arose for any country linking its currency to its gold reserves was that it might not be able to expand its money supply quickly in case of a national emergency. So if a country was falling into a depression, for example, its government might want to increase domestic spending in order to pump up the economy. However, its leaders would have to acquire sufficient additional gold reserves to back the increased amounts of money that they wanted to pump into their economy—which might be made even more difficult due to the country's lack of reserves. In other words, these leaders, who would certainly be concerned about their prospects for re-election, would have no meaningful way to stimulate the economy and offer increased employment opportunities to those restive individuals who are always looking for an excuse to riot and burn down cities in the name of democracy. Needless to say, the inherent rigidity imposed by the gold standard on the ability of leaders to act in times of national emergency weighed heavily on the minds of the visiting delegates.

The delegates who came to Bretton Woods in the summer of 1944 were led by representatives from the United States and Great Britain, who were keen to set up a new international economic order. Many of the delegates had already concluded that the gold standard was not the best way to ensure worldwide economic stability. Indeed, some of the delegates blamed the inflexibility of the gold standard for having plunged the world into the Great Depression. They believed that the gold standard prevented individual nations from taking aggressive measures to inflate their economies following the onset of the Great Depression in 1929 and the ensuing decade-long contraction in global economic activity.

Although World War II had not yet ended, the delegates were optimistic about the future and worked together to establish a new international monetary system that was dubbed the "Bretton Woods" system—a more elegant title than other site-related proposals, such as the "Gulag in New Hampshire" banking system, offered by the more disgruntled delegates chaffing under the monotony of their daily routines.

The delegates wanted this new banking system to avoid the flaws of the prior gold standard regime and discourage nations from erecting barriers to trade such as tariffs. Indeed, the delegates wished to set up a new global trading system that would discourage countries from devaluing their currencies excessively and, through a lowering of barriers to trade, encourage worldwide economic growth.

This is not to say that the delegates showed up at the Mount Washington Hotel with open minds, blank pads of paper and brightly colored, dinosaur-shaped pool toys because discussions regarding the possible structure of the postwar economic system had been going on for more than a year. However, the delegates were aware of the need to establish some sort of system that would stabilize international trade and finance.

Because the prewar gold standard was now blamed for everything from global poverty to gonorrhea, it fell to John Maynard Keynes, British tea connoisseur and very tall economist, to propose the creation of a central global bank that would issue a new international currency called the *bancor*. These *bancor* notes would be issued to member nations who could then utilize these funds to settle balance of payments deficits between themselves.

Keynes realized that the devastation of World War II had left the United States as the only economic power that had not been ravaged by warfare—which meant that it had no meaningful competitors for its products in the international arena. As a result, the United States could increase its exports dramatically and pile up huge surpluses of *bancor* notes. To avoid this potential problem, Keynes suggested that any country that ran persistent balance of payment surpluses would have to remit its excess holdings of *bancors* back to the central bank to bring the system back into equilibrium.

Keynes' idea that a world central bank could act as a stabilizing force in the international arena was thematically popular with many delegates, even though they were finding it difficult to tan in the lukewarm New Hampshire sun while lounging by the hotel pool. However, the concept did not appeal to the representatives of the United States, who were concerned about the threat that such an international banking institution could pose to the nation's sovereignty. They were also unhappy with the idea that the United States would have to power the global economy for the foreseeable future with nothing more than a pile of *bancors* to show for its exports—which it would then have to remit back to the bank so that the whole system did not fall apart.

Fortunately, the delegates resisted the temptation to call each other vivid multi-syllabic names and pledged to work toward some sort of compromise solution that would satisfy those who favored a global bank and those who preferred to rely on more state-centered solutions. After three weeks of "constructive" talks (which were marred by only a single physical altercation that occurred when a French delegate slapped the *sous* chef with a glove after claiming that the truffles were soggy), the delegates finalized an agreement to set up two new global organizations that would one day be staffed with self-important, multi-lingual bureaucrats with impressive titles. The first was the International Monetary Fund (IMF), which would monitor exchange rates and provide funds to settle balance of payment deficits between member countries. The second was the International Bank for Reconstruction and Development (IBRD) (now the World Bank), which would lend funds to assist with the postwar reconstruction of Europe.

The Bretton Woods Agreement tried to incorporate some of the discipline that had been a feature of the gold standard while bringing greater flexibility to global currency markets. Due to the overwhelming economic and military power of the United States at the end of World War II (which resulted from the fortuitous destruction of much of Europe and Asia), the dollar became the new standard by which other currencies were valued. As a result, gold was pushed aside and a set of fixed rates of exchange was established in which brightly-colored currencies such as the British pound, the French franc and the Italian lira were pegged to the U.S. dollar—even though they were permitted to float freely in value relative to each other. However, gold was not totally forgotten as the dollar was in turn pegged to gold, which was valued at $35.00 per ounce.

This system would continue for nearly two decades until it became unsustainable due to the decline of America's economic power relative to the recovering economies of Europe and Asia. The Bretton Woods system's reliance on a single currency also made it difficult for nations to adjust their balance of payments accounts in an efficient manner. This system effectively ended in 1971 when President Richard Nixon "temporarily suspended" the convertibility of dollars to gold due to Washington's persistent balance of payment deficits throughout the 1960s. In short, more and more dollars were being sent abroad to pay for imports ranging from British toothpaste and French mayonnaise to Italian frozen pizza and Japanese gizmos, thus creating a growing balance of payments deficit. Many of the holders of these dollars converted them to gold. As time went on, the United States became increasingly alarmed that its rapidly-shrinking gold reserves would dwindle to nothing if it did not take some sort of corrective action. Government leaders were also concerned about what they would do with the spacious, granite-lined Fort Knox depository in Kentucky if the United States did not stop this outward flow of bullion. Because it would have been politically impossible to rein in the government spending that was funding both an explosion of social programs and the Vietnam War in the 1960s, Nixon decided to sever the dollar's link to gold. Needless to say, the convertibility of the dollar to gold was never reinstated and the dollar—though still the reserve currency for much of the world—was permitted to float freely along with all other currencies.

Because other countries could no longer convert their dollars to gold, there was no longer a tangible asset to back the dollar and, hence, the world's other currencies. As a result, every currency became a *fiat* currency in which its value was rooted solely in the willingness of individuals to hold that particular currency. The value of these currencies would thus be determined by the actions of governments and central bankers, as well as the conditions of their respective economies. Henceforth, no one with a pocketful of dollars would be able to go to a bank cashier and demand that he or she be given a bunch of gold coins in return.

A MODEL FOR THE NEW DEVELOPMENT BANK

To understand BRICS and its scope of operations, we need to understand how both the IMF and the World Bank operate because they are the anchors of the international financial system. Their activities over the past eighty-odd years have established norms and practices that have shaped the ways in which nearly all of the world's nations engage in trade and finance. Indeed, some economists refer to the IMF and the World Bank in more technical terms as the "athletic supporters" of the global economy.

When China and Russia first began to discuss the possibility of setting up some sort of alternative international bank that they would fund and control, they were very ambitious about the scope of this new institution. The founders of BRICS initially believed that they could set up a parallel global financial system that was not under the thumb of the United States and its allies. It is not a coincidence that the primary actors behind the creation of BRICS were Russia and China—who have never been well-known for their enthusiasm for truth, justice or the American Way. Moreover, both countries seemed to view their positions relative to the United States in the international hierarchy as a zero-sum game. If they could increase their financial heft at the expense of the United States, then it would be a very good day in the neighborhood. However, both countries believed that the structure of the IMF (and the World Bank, for that matter) reflected a somewhat outdated balance of financial power among the member states. This balance of power could not be radically changed because the United States and its allies (including the United Kingdom, Germany, and Japan) exercise *de facto* control over the decision-making processes of both the IMF and the World Bank.

Although China has been a member of the IMF from 1945, for example, it has only about 6% of the votes whereas the Russian Federation, which joined the IMF in 1992, has a meager 3% share of the votes. The United States, by contrast, has the largest single voting share of about 17%, which irks China and Russia to no end—particularly since Washington can veto any proposal in the

IMF due to the requirement that any motion or proposal must get 85% of the votes in order to pass. Russia's attitude towards the IMF has also been soured by the IMF continuing to release portions of Ukraine's multi-billion dollar loan to Kyiv which, of course, makes it possible for the Ukrainian military to purchase guns and bullets and fire back at the invading Russian troops who have not been warmly welcomed in Ukraine by its citizens.

As time wore on, however, more pragmatic voices shifted the debate to the role a new BRICS bank could play. As a result, the focus shifted from the idea of creating an entirely new global banking system to a more modest, incremental approach of building a new international bank that could provide an alternative source of funds to countries that might not be able to satisfy the rules and requirements often imposed on borrowers by the IMF and the World Bank.

Even though Russia and China are developed countries, they both eventually concluded that they did not want to try to set up a new banking system to compete with the IMF and the World Bank because they would have to build up a new operation from scratch. Instead, they decided to copy those features of the IMF and the World Bank that would help them to operate their own bank. In essence, they would reverse engineer the IMF and the World Bank, which would be right up the alley for Putin and Xi. However, Russia and China wanted to make sure that they set the bank up so that they could exercise meaningful control over its operation and oversee the admission of new members. After all, what is the point of going through all the time and effort to set up an entirely new global banking operation that can cater to the whims of the world's dictators and tyrants if the founders cannot exclude the United States and its traditional allies from joining the party? All the liberal democracies would do is to mess it up for everyone else with their insistence that the bank promote democracy and freedom in its lending practices and encourage such annoying things as human rights around the world. All bankers know that these types of frivolous concerns interfere with the profitability of lending institutions and invariably gunk up the creation of such innovative banking products as triple digit interest rate credit cards and foreclosures that not only recover the property securing the loan but also secure the indentured lifetime services of the family that borrowed the money in the first place.

INTRODUCING THE IMF

The IMF was one of the singular achievements of those delegates who were fortunate enough to visit Bretton Woods in July 1944, after the town was engulfed by the annual pilgrimage of dozens of visitors who congregate there every June 1st to celebrate the first and last day of spring. Once the Bretton Woods summer begins on June 2nd, the crowds disperse and the town returns to a less frenzied, almost comatose, pace, the perfect place to keep visiting delegates from around the globe from getting into too much trouble.

Because the Bretton Woods night life has been unfavorably compared to spending a night in a mortuary or taking your great aunt (or uncle) to your high school prom as your date, its lack of distractions compelled the delegates to focus on the matter at hand. The IMF was inspired by Keynes' vision of an international banking institution that would promote the economic growth of its member nations by supporting policies that would stabilize the global financial system and encourage sound banking practices. As such, the IMF was established to increase monetary cooperation and expand trade among its members.

The IMF, like all other global organizations, is fortunate today to be stuffed with many employees who view themselves as the "guidance counselors" of the global financial system. If you are able to climb over the backs of your colleagues to the top of the heap at the IMF, then you can be a member of the IMF's Board of Governors—which oversees all major policy decisions ranging from the underwriting of loans to member nations to the allocation of covered parking spaces at the IMF headquarters in Washington, D.C. Each of the 190 member nations of the IMF is represented by a single governor and—if the governor is unable to fulfill his or her duties on the cocktail circuit—an alternate governor. Most governors have backgrounds in finance and occupy prominent government positions in their respective countries—which means that they enjoy a certain degree of diplomatic immunity. As a result, they can ignore those annoying parking tickets that get pasted on their double-parked limousines on almost a daily basis.

Because members of the Board of Governors must often attend to such weighty matters as black-tie receptions at national embassies or the bracket rankings of the monthly beer pong tournaments, they are far too busy to oversee the day-to-day operations of the IMF—which is carried out by the 24-member Executive Board and its staff. The IMF itself is divided into 18 departments which employ impressive numbers of persons who analyze the economic policies of debtor nations and offer advice that is always greatly appreciated by the recipients. Some of the most impressive titles in the world can be found in the catacombs of the IMF bureaucracy including, for example, "Institute for Capacity Development Director," "Financial Counsellor and Monetary and Capital Markets Department Director," and "Economic Counsellor and Research Department Director." But most of the day-to-day work is delegated to various underlings who must do something to get paid. As a result, a request by a country in South America for a loan to help stabilize its currency, for example, may be reviewed by a recent college graduate who majored in European literature but who is not exactly sure where the country in question is located or how to pronounce the name of its capital city.

The IMF has developed something of a reputation for being "bossy" because it does not simply welcome a loan applicant to the bank, issue a check and send the applicant on its way. Instead, it will evaluate all aspects of the applicant's economy. If the loan is approved, the IMF can provide advice to the applicant as to how it can improve its fiscal and monetary policies and, hopefully, repay its loans in a timely manner. For some reason, the IMF calls its advice "surveillance," which simply adds to the warmth and fuzziness that borrowers typically feel towards lending institutions in general. The term "surveillance" is merely another way of saying that the IMF is going to be in the "business" of its borrowers at both the global and regional levels—which is not as sensuous as it sounds.

Like other banks, the IMF must underwrite each loan request. This process usually involves sending various personnel to make on-site visits to the borrowing country. These employees will generate wordy reports that only a handful of people will peruse, let alone read and digest. These reports will describe the economic conditions in the applicant country and offer suggestions for actions that the country should take as a condition for receiving funding from the IMF. Of course some countries are far more desirable to visit than others. The more senior officials get to go to the countries with scenic alpine mountain ranges and pristine white sand beaches while other, lower ranking, employees of the IMF may find themselves having to tiptoe through a minefield-laden desert, swim across a snake-infested swamp or belly-crawl over a field while being shot at by warring factions in order to conduct their on-the-ground research about a particular applicant.

Although there have been very few hit television shows, or even a single memorable commercial jingle, dealing with the IMF, it is difficult to overstate its importance in the global economic system. The IMF boasts reserves in excess of $1 trillion and has loaned more than $320 billion to nearly 100 countries, many of which are beset by economic and political crises, to provide financial support. It also offers special drawing rights (SDRs) which are a sort of supplemental asset that holders can redeem as needed for additional financial assistance. SDRs are priced using a basket of the world's leading currencies such as the dollar and the euro, but not the conspicuously absent Albanian lek.

Unlike the New Development Bank of BRICS and some of the other multilateral development banks, the IMF does not fund specific infrastructure projects. A sub-Saharan country, such as Chad, that wishes to boost its nascent tourism trade by building the world's tallest roller coaster ride (the proposed name borrowed from NASA: *The Vomit Comet*) would not be warmly received by the IMF. Chad would instead have to convince the New Development Bank or, perhaps, the African Development Bank, to bankroll its ground-breaking roller coaster project. However, Chad could approach the IMF for a loan to help stabilize its economy. This is not to say, however, that an imaginative loan administrator in Chad could not utilize some of the funds to encourage tourism there and, perhaps, throw in a few dollars for roller coaster infrastructure improvements.

The IMF does not typically release the borrowed funds in one fell swoop because it is always concerned that the leaders of certain borrowers will blow the money on such things as shiny yachts, European mansions or even enormous statues of themselves towering over their capital cities. Instead, the IMF employs a sort of "learning curve" disbursement schedule, doling out funds over time as it determines that a particular borrower is doing the right thing such as cutting back excessive government spending or improving revenue collection. In this way, the IMF can restrain the profligate tendencies of some of its less disciplined members by conditioning their next loan disbursement on their good behavior. If the borrower is insistent on pursuing destructive economic policies (perhaps by employing millions of idle peasants for highway beautification projects to paint the country's roads a variety of pastel colors to prevent them from thinking about storming the presidential palace), then the IMF can decide to withhold additional funds until the offending country gets its affairs in order and reins in unsustainable government spending.

You will not find a local IMF office in your town because the IMF has never embraced the idea of retail banking for the masses.

The IMF lends money only to national governments. It does not make loans to private individuals or corporations, so you should never give your private information to anyone who calls you on the phone and offers to give you your own IMF gold credit card. At first blush, lending to national governments would seem to offer greater assurances of repayment because individuals and, indeed, companies, can go bankrupt. However, making loans to national governments is not always without risk. After all, the IMF does not have the ability to repossess an entire country should it fail to repay its loans. Moreover, its desk-bound analysts and bankers are ill-suited for donning military equipment and seizing control of a defaulting country. But the IMF's ability to withhold additional funds from a defaulting borrower and essentially tag that country as a "deadbeat" is a very powerful motivation for borrowing nations to try to work with the IMF. Undoubtedly, it is more compelling than any threat by the IMF to parachute its loan underwriting division into the capital city of a defaulting member. After all, if a country defaults on its loan obligations, other lenders—even the ones whose officers worry more about their corporate perks than the occasional non-performing loan—may sit up and take notice. By spacing out the release of the loan installments, the IMF is able to condition continued access to credit on that particular nation following the guidelines and conditions laid out by the IMF when the loan was authorized.

Or at least that is the theory behind the "deadbeat borrower" thesis. However, there are a number of countries that have defaulted repeatedly on their loan obligations but then returned to the negotiating table with the IMF to try to restructure their loans. One of the most successful practitioners of this "wash, rinse, repeat" approach toward debt financing is the country of Argentina. It has defaulted on its sovereign debt loan nine times in the post-war period, including three times during the past two decades. This record of financial recklessness has set the gold standard for economic mismanagement; a lofty position in the pantheon of fiscal ineptitude about which most other floundering countries can only dream. Indeed, Argentina and the IMF have become very familiar with each other (e.g., "If this is Tuesday, Argentina must be in default.") as each default has been rectified, typically by a restructuring of the debt payment schedule. But hope springs eternal that Argentina will eventually figure out how to get its financial house in order and learn how to live within its means—even though it would be more fun to go dance the tango at the leading Buenos Aires nightclubs than to try to fix the Argentinian economy.

The question arises as to why Argentina has been able to default on its loans so many times and still come back to the IMF for additional relief. One possibility is that the IMF party planners were worried that the collapse of the Argentinian economy would deprive them of tasty beef products to serve at official functions. Another possibility is that the decision-makers at the IMF have short-term memory issues and approach each new loan request as though it was the first time that Argentina had sidled up to the trough. However, the most likely explanation is that the IMF knows, from its thousands of prior loans, that things do not always work out as originally planned and that it is preferable to rework the terms of a loan instead of simply consigning an entire country to banking oblivion. Besides, when you are talking about billions of dollars of loans being flushed down the toilet, it makes sense to try to fix the problem. Otherwise, the collapse of a middle-sized power such as Argentina could have a disastrous effect on many of its trading partners—thus undermining the IMF's work in those other countries.

INTRODUCING THE WORLD BANK

The World Bank is the behemoth of development banks in the world today. When it was set up in 1944, along with the IMF, the delegates at Bretton Woods envisioned it as a lender that would help to finance the reconstruction of war-torn Europe, particularly its charming sidewalk cafes and gourmet restaurants. Unlike the IMF, however, the World Bank was designed to be a source of funds for specific development projects as opposed to a source of funds for helping national governments smooth out the hiccoughs in their economies. Although the World Bank's focus was originally limited to Europe, its mandate soon expanded to include loans throughout the world to assist developing nations in the construction of infrastructure projects ranging from highways and dams to power grids and water systems. To date, the World Bank has made over 11,000 loans to various recipients—many of whom are non-state actors such as multilateral organizations and even private companies. Since 1945, the World Bank has provided more than $1.3 trillion in loans, grants and credits to member countries around the world.

The World Bank's lending operations are divided between two different organizations—(1) the International Bank for Reconstruction and Development (IBRD), which was created at Bretton Woods and which focuses on middle-income and credit-worthy poorer countries and (2) the International Development Bank (IBD), which was created in 1960 to focus exclusively on the world's poorest countries. The IBRD provides loans, guarantees and advisory services—offering an enormous staff of heavily-credentialed specialists who are pleased to share their expertise with borrowing members whether they want it or not. The IDA, by contrast, provides loans with little or no interest and generous repayment periods of up to 40 years to the most impoverished countries of the world that are not typically featured in the *Fodor's* travel guide series. Unlike the IRBD, the IDA's capital comes from the voluntary contributions of World Bank members, which can change from year to year. In recent years, the IBRD and IDA have collectively committed about $70 billion per year to member countries in the form of loans, grants and credits. Because the IBRD and the IDA are somewhat traditional in their loan product offerings, however, they do not, as of yet, offer their borrowers holiday gift debit cards or World Bank "debtor dollars" featuring the likenesses of various countries (who have defaulted on their loans) which can be redeemed at fine stores everywhere. The World Bank has also been slow to try to augment its revenue sources by offering, for example, sleek "World Bank" branded sports apparel or athletic shoes with the snazzy "WB" logo. Its ill-fated network sitcom *World Bank Officials Discuss Loan Underwriting Rules* was not a success and was cancelled after the airing of only the first two of its 54 one hour-long episodes. Indeed, one of the program's more charitable television critics likened the show to "a frontal lobotomy without the benefit of anesthesia."

Although some executives at the World Bank would probably prefer to loan funds to wealthier countries in North America and Europe, due to the greater likelihood of repayment and fatter executive bonuses, the World Bank's mission is to eliminate extreme poverty in the world by funding sustainable development projects. This noble-sounding charter precludes it from acting like a traditional, profit-oriented bank because it must exclude those very borrowers that would be coveted by private bankers. However, it can fund a wide variety of projects ranging from roads and dams to schools and power plants. As with the IMF, the need for on-site reconnaissance also provides numerous opportunities for World Bank staff members to visit countries all over the world that they would never voluntarily set foot in otherwise.

In recent years, the IBRD and IDA have loaned nearly half of their funds to Africa, followed by about one-eighth each to South Asia, Latin America and the Caribbean, Europe and Central Asia. These regional groupings are deceptive because some of the countries, such as Australia and New Zealand in Asia, and Germany, France and England in Europe, for example, do not borrow money from the World Bank. As a result, the bulk of the funds supplied by the World Bank each year tends to be concentrated on a fairly small number of countries even though the loan proceeds are spread out among dozens of borrowing members.

In recent years, India has become the leading debtor at the World Bank, and, as of the end of 2022, owed $38.3 billion, followed by Indonesia at $20.6 billion, Bangladesh at $18.2 billion, Pakistan at $18.1 billion, and Colombia at $15.1 billion. Other notables include Vietnam at $15.1 billion and Nigeria at $14 billion. Somewhat surprisingly, China, which portrays itself as either a global superpower or a poor country barely able to rub two chopsticks together (depending on its intended audience), owes the World Bank $16 billion. Much of China's debt stems from its emergence as a global manufacturing power over the past few decades but it has steadily repaid back its loans as its economy has expanded.

Like borrowers at private banks, the rankings of the World Bank debtors change over time because some countries repay their loans and other countries increase their borrowings. The more destitute the country, the fewer borrowing options it has in the international banking system. As a result, the poorest countries have little choice other than to go to the IDA because they simply lack the collateral to entice more traditional lenders. Unfortunately, bankers at blue-chip lenders such as Citibank and JP Morgan Chase do not consider artesian pottery and tribal costumes to be sufficient collateral to mitigate the risks of default on a multi-billion dollar loan.

As countries move up the development ladder from the not-so-highly coveted "dirt poor" and "comfortably impoverished" rankings, however, they become more stable and more attractive to a wider variety of banks. Over time, these developing countries tend to shift their borrowings to other lenders and reduce their dependence on the World Bank. Among the gallery of IDA borrowers, nearly all of the top borrowers as of 2022 are from Africa except for Bangladesh. Fortunately, all of these countries are able to offer a seemingly endless supply of development projects for consideration by the World Bank.

Like the IMF, the World Bank boasts its own impressive list of 25 Executive Directors, each of whom has an alternate who must patiently wait until the existing Executive Director dies from a poisoned quiche Lorraine or gets run over in a parking lot before they can step up and assume Executive Director status. Moreover, each alternate must perform a number of vital tasks for their respective Executive Director, such as fetching the Executive Director's laundry, washing the Executive Director's car, de-worming the Executive Director's dog, unclogging the Executive Director's executive toilet or baby-sitting the Executive Director's hyperactive children on very short notice—all the while insisting with gritted teeth that he or she is happy to miss his or her mother's funeral so that the Executive Director can attend the premiere of a new musical or run out for a few drinks with the other Executive Directors.

Like the IMF, the World Bank is governed by its member nations. The United States, thanks to the foresight of its Bretton Woods representatives— who believed that Washington should always be number #1 in all things—has about 17% of the vote. As a result, the United States (as with the IMF) can veto any proposals submitted by other members of the World Bank that it finds to be objectionable. The other major stakeholders, in descending order, at the World Bank include Japan, China, Germany, France, the United Kingdom, India, Saudi Arabia, Canada, Italy and Russia. Not surprisingly, both China and Russia consider their comparatively small stakes in the World Bank—4.8 percent and 2.5 percent respectively— to be an insult and certainly not reflective of their status as leading global troublemakers. This inability to influence the World Bank in any meaningful way has undoubtedly fueled their determination to build up the New Development Bank and at least challenge the hegemony of the IMF and the World Bank.

Because the members of BRICS have lowered their sights on upending the entire global economic system in favor of creating their own development bank, the World Bank provides a structural blueprint the BRICS countries can use as they expand the scope of the New Development Bank. This is not to say that Russia and China are merely content to create another multilateral development bank that will quietly take its place in the international system. On the contrary, the BRICS countries hope to reduce the influence of the United States and its allies by using their own currencies instead of American dollars to fund development projects through the New Development Bank and to carry out trade among themselves. In this way, both Putin and Xi hope to reduce the prevalence of American dollars in funding global transactions. By weaning itself off of dollars, Russia, for example, could reduce the ability of the United States to impose crippling economic sanctions on it should Russia decide to launch any more unprovoked attacks against smaller border countries that start with the letter "U" or "P" or "B" or "L" or "E" or "F" or "G" or "A" or "K" or "M" or "C" or even "N." After all, Russia has a habit of invading other countries which it has not been able to shake since the time of the Tsars.

Unfortunately, President Putin refuses to go to therapy and feels that he is not being given enough credit for seeking to impose the superior Russian culture by force on other countries that are clearly in need of a civilizing invasion. Putin also appears to exhibit the classic signs of denial in that any military actions by Russia against its neighbors should not, in his opinion, be subject to punitive measures that would freeze Russia's offshore assets or cut it off from the international banking system as occurred following its invasion of Ukraine.

In any event, the New Development Bank represents the culmination of the efforts by Russia and China to build their own hybrid version of the World Bank and the IMF that can be used to enhance their own economic and political power. Moreover, it could serve as a piggy bank that can be tapped by its founding members for funds should the need arise. The New Development Bank also offers an alternative source of funds for countries whose projects might not be fully funded by existing development banks as well as a platform for expanding the influence of Russia and China around the world.

PART FOUR

GETTING MONEY
FROM BANKS

CHAPTER 6

HOW INDIVIDUALS APPLY FOR LOANS

INTRODUCTION

The following two chapters outline some of the ways in which prospective borrowers can approach lenders to borrow money. In this chapter, we follow prospective borrower, John Kimble, as he attempts to apply for a personal loan at his local bank and then for a development loan at a so-called multilateral development bank or MDB. The next chapter will highlight the ways in which actual governments apply for funding from global lending institutions such as the New Development Bank (which is operated by BRICS) in order to fund all sorts of development projects.

APPLYING FOR A PERSONAL LOAN AT YOUR LOCAL BANK

If you need a loan to purchase a home, buy a car or even send your child to an overpriced Ivy League college where they can learn all about grievance and the plight of the upper middle class, then you may want to wander over to your local bank to secure the necessary funds. The process of obtaining a loan is straight-forward. You must first drive over to the bank where you will be greeted at the door by a person who will ask how you are doing without appearing to be very concerned about your actual physical or emotional condition. This individual—whom you suspect may not be on the fast track to the C-suite—may also offer you a shiny brochure describing the bank's newest credit card offering, known as the Freedom card, which is an innovative financial product that is exempt from the state's usury laws. You will then be directed to go over to the lobby to sit in one of several chairs or couches that feel as though they were made by the same old-world craftsmen who hammered together steerage class seats for airline passengers. You might glance around the lobby and watch the one teller on duty wait on a line of several hundred individuals that extends out the front door and snakes around the building out to the street. You would marvel at the patience of the bank's customers who slowly shuffle forward, taking care to step over the occasional patron who has fainted from exhaustion while waiting in line. You would also see several offices in which well-dressed executives make phone calls and hit buttons on their computer keyboards, updating their knowledge about the latest banking regulations or perhaps watching pay-per-view championship mud wrestling matches.

After ten or twenty minutes or so, one of these very import-ant bankers might decide that they have spent enough time searching through their drawers for their favorite black pen or perhaps a toothpick to remove a stubborn piece of yesterday's steak dinner gristle from their upper left molar. As this banker slowly but surely looks in your direction, he will raise his hand ever so slightly and motion for you to enter the inner sanctum of his glass-walled office so that you can discuss the business at hand. A little nervous at first, you rise to your feet and, slowly but steadily, walk thirty feet over to the office which, according to the brass plate on the glass wall, is occupied by one J. Robert Evans, Assistant to the Second Vice President of Lender Operations for Megabank. "Good morning, Mr. Evans," you say, grateful to have made it inside the office of such a high-ranking bank executive. "My name is John Kimble, and I appreciate you taking the time to meet with me today." You take a deep breath of exalted air. Mr. Evans nods ever so slightly and rises from his seat, studying you for any signs of concealed weaponry, and extends his hand in temporary friendship. "What can Megabank do for you today?" Evans asks.

"Well, I need to borrow some money to send my daughter to college—" you begin before Evans raises his hand. "Let me stop you right there," he warns. "Do you know how many people come into my office each day asking to borrow money?" he asks. "Dozens and dozens." He shakes his head. "It's like an on-going parade of sadness and tragedy that can be very depressing—"

"Well, you do work for a bank," you point out, trying to be helpful.

Evans takes a deep breath. "It is unending," he complains,

exhaling heavily. "Everybody is so needy," he continues. "But what can we do?" he says. "We have to push the money out to keep the lights on." He suddenly straightens up and retrieves a brochure from his desk. "By the way, do you have a Megabank Freedom credit card?" he asks. "It can help you consolidate all of those annoying high-interest rate credit cards into one *single* high-interest rate credit card," he points out. "It can help you organize your affairs much more efficiently so that you do not have to deal with dozens of creditors month after month—particularly if you need to get your financial records together in a hurry to flee the country or declare bankruptcy—" He points to the picture on the brochure. "Did I mention that you can have a picture of your favorite pet put on your Freedom card?" he asks. "I have a picture of my pot-bellied pig on my card," he adds proudly, retrieving a card from his wallet. He looks at the card fondly. "Pigs are really quite intelligent," he points out. "By the way, did I mention that the Freedom card is made of metal—not that chintzy plastic that you see in most credit cards." He taps the corner of the card on his desk. "Solid steel," he points out. "Let me show you a little secret," he adds, lowering his voice and leaning forward. "Each corner of the Freedom card has a razor-sharp edge so that you can use it to defend yourself from an attacker." Evans stands up, holding a corner of the card between his right thumb and fore-finger. "Watch this!" he says, flicking his wrist. The card whistles through the air and plunges deep into the doorframe. Evans quickly retrieves it and returns to his seat. "The managers don't like to see us throwing these cards around like death stars," he says, lowering his voice.

"Pretty impressive," you remark, wondering if you should consider switching your accounts to another bank.

"There's no other credit card like it," Evans says, stretching his arms upward. "However, you do have to practice throwing it a few times," he points out. "The first time I tried to throw it, I sliced off the tail of an elderly lady's Labrador comfort dog in the lobby." He shakes his head. "That accident almost cost me my job. But I apologized profusely, paid the dog's medical bills, dated the customer for a few weeks and everything worked out fine." He looks thoughtful. "By the way, did I point out that you can get Freedom credit cards for every member of your family—even the little ones attending elementary school?" Noticing your apparent lack of interest in such an intelligent credit management approach, Evans adds: "You should know that the Freedom moniker is not an empty promise; we also give these cards to people who have been declared legally incompetent because we do not think that having a guardianship imposed upon one of our customers should prevent him from exercising his constitutional right to go spend his money as he sees fit." Evans raises an eyebrow. "Any interest?"

"No, not really," you answer, shifting uncomfortably in your chair, almost forgetting why you had come to the bank in the first place. "Look, Mr. Evans," you say, trying to be polite. "I need to borrow some money for my daughter's education. My wife and I have scrimped and saved to send our Abigail to college, but we simply cannot afford to pay for everything on our own."

"Higher education is such a noble endeavor," Evans says. "What does your daughter want to study?"

"She is very interested in becoming an art historian," you answer.

"I see," Evans responds. "Does that sort of career path not strike you as being an enormous waste of money?" he asks earnestly.

"Not at all," you respond defensively. "She will receive a classic liberal arts education and—"

"And move back in with you and your wife after graduation," Evans says calmly. "Not judging," he adds hastily. "I would not be in too much of a hurry to convert her bedroom into a crafts room when she leaves for college," he cautions, trying to be helpful.

"Art history is her passion," you respond, growing more irritated. "It is her career. I am merely here to help her pay for college."

"Ah, yes," Evans says, clasping his hands and appearing to be in deep thought. "Let's be very clear so that there is no misunderstanding," he declares. "You need a loan," he says, the mist beginning to clear. You nod your head. "For your daughter," he adds. You nod your head again. "To go to college," he concludes. You nod your head a third time, cautiously optimistic that the synapses have finally begun to fire in Evans' brain—albeit at the rate of a pop gun.

"Well, let's see if we can fund the education of another art historian!" Evans declares, suddenly energized. He turns to his computer. "Why don't we try to get you preapproved," he announces. "Can I see your driver's license?" he asks. You retrieve your driver's license and hand it over. Evans inserts it into a scanner. "This will save us so much time," he says, looking at your photograph for a second. "Not a very good picture," he adds, shaking his head sadly. "You should have opened your eyes wider when they took your picture," he volunteers. "It makes you look so old and tired—"

"I *am* tired," you say, wondering how many more hours you will have to spend with your newest banking buddy.

"Okay," Evans announces. "We have preloaded your personal data, which will save us a great deal of time in the application process." He looks at the screen. "It says that you have a checking account and a savings account with Megabank," he observes. "Very good," he adds. "We are always happy to go that extra step for our loyal customers." He looks closer. "You spent a lot of money on liquor last December," he observes. "Should we be concerned?" he asks warily.

"No," you reply, indignantly. "I had to pick up the drinks for our company holiday party," you explain. "I rarely drink alcohol," you add.

"It would be very sad if you were to go on a drinking binge and squander your daughter's tuition," Evan says, eyeing you suspiciously. "How embarrassing it would be for you to wake up in your front yard wearing your underwear on your head with an empty whiskey bottle in each hand." He shakes his head disapprovingly. "I hope you will exercise greater self-control in the future—if only for your daughter's sake."

You are about to respond when Evans asks, "Did you bring copies of your last three years of tax returns?"

"I did," you reply, handing over your files. "I also filled out the bank forms and emailed them to you."

"Yes, you did," Evans says, eyeing the screen. "Now I need to get your permission to pull credit," he adds. "Do you agree to allow me to pull your credit report?" he asks.

"Of course," you answer.

"Very well," he says, pushing a button. A couple of minutes pass and then a chime rings. "Here we are," Evans said. "We have your credit score."

"Good," you say.

"Not so good," Evans responds glumly. "You are in the bottom third of all borrowers in the United States." He peers at the screen. "There are several unpaid medical bills that have been placed in collection—"

"I was in a very bad car crash last year," you reply. "I broke both of my legs and my left shoulder blade. I spent three weeks in the hospital. As you can imagine, the costs of the hospital, the doctors, the drugs, and the physical therapy have been horrendous—"

"I am so sorry for what you have been through, Mr. Kimble," Evans says soothingly. "But you must persevere and overcome the obstacles that life throws out at you." He pointed at a white bandage on his left index finger. "I cut myself while chopping vegetables last week and had to get several stitches, so I know what you are going through." Evans takes a deep breath and looks back at the screen. "You have a good income and a stable work history despite your accident so Megabank should be able to help you with your daughter's college tuition—"

"That is a relief," you say, breathing easier.

"Do you own your own home?" Evans asks.

"No," you reply sadly. "We had to sell the house to pay for my medical bills."

"That is too bad," Evans says, sympathetically. "We could have offered you the Megabank home equity line of credit which allows you to borrow against the equity in your home until you lose it in foreclosure—"

"That's not really an option for us," you respond despondently.

"How much money do you want to borrow?" Evans asks, suddenly laser focused on you.

"Fifty thousand dollars," you reply.

"Beg pardon?" Evans says, leaning forward and making choking sounds.

"Fifty thousand dollars."

"That's what I thought you said," Evans says, sinking back in his chair. "I am afraid that we cannot loan you that much money."

"Why not?" you ask. "I am an existing customer. You know, the type of customer that you said the bank would go out of its way to help."

Evans sighs. "Unfortunately, the bank bases all lending decisions on your personal data such as your income and expenses and your employment history—which are all evaluated by extremely sophisticated computer algorithms and by our branch manager, Carl Rhodes." He points through the glass at a man seated at a desk across the hall who seems to be engrossed in a picture book about Scandinavian nude volleyball. "Carl!" Evans shouts. Carl looks up, startled. "This is Mr. Kimble," Evans continues, shouting through the glass. "He is applying for a loan."

Carl gives an enthusiastic thumbs-up and returns to his study of Norwegian techniques for massaging cramps in sensitive private areas. "Anyways," Evans continues. "Carl's approval is a mere formality once the loan underwriting is complete."

"Okay," you say cautiously. "I suppose we can tighten our

belts a little bit. I can work a second job and maybe limit my sleep to three or four hours a night. Could we get forty thousand dollars?"

Evans shakes his head. "Thirty thousand dollars?" you ask. Evans looks down at the floor without saying a word. "Twenty thousand dollars?" you plead. "I'm afraid not," Evans whispers. "Ten thousand dollars?" you beg. Evans appears to shed a tear but it is actually a drip from a leaking AC conduit line in the ceiling striking his cheek. "I am sorry, but we cannot loan you any money at all."

"Nothing?" you ask, slumping into your chair.

"Nothing," Evans replies, wondering why you are having such a difficult time understanding his succinct responses. He notices that your hand is very close to a pointy letter opener on his desk so he gently slides it toward himself and into an open desk drawer. "Mind you, if it were up to me, I would give you the entire fifty thousand dollars but, alas, the decision is out of my hands."

"But you said that your bank would be able to help me!" you cry out.

"Of course we can help you," Evans says comfortingly. "We just can't give you any money," he adds, trying to clarify his position.

"Then how can you help me?" you shout, about to burst a blood vessel.

"With the Megabank Freedom card," Evans smiles, passing the brochure back to you. "Financial freedom can be yours as you load up all of your dear daughter's college costs onto a single account that will provide you with an up-to-date record of every cost, every fee, every charge and every other expense that you will incur over the next four years so that your daughter can join the ranks of thousands of other unemployed art historians following graduation." He smiles. "You can even have your daughter's picture put on your Freedom card," he adds. "You don't have to have a pot-bellied pig on your card," he says, trying to explain that the choice of photographs for a Freedom credit card is not limited to animals with porcine features.

You shake your head, trying to make sense of Evans' explanation of the situation. "Your bank does not want to loan me any money but is willing to give me a Freedom credit card and allow me to strangle myself financially to finance my daughter's college education." You look at Evans who seems to be distracted by a fly that is buzzing around his head. "Is that correct?"

"Absolutely," Evans says, slapping the fly out of the air in mid-flight. "The Freedom credit card offers an alternative form of financial assistance to our valued customers such as yourself who do not qualify for one reason or another for more traditional loan products."

You take a deep breath. "My concern about using a credit card to pay for four years of college—"

"Four years, if you're lucky," Evans points out. "More and more students seem to take five or six or even seven years to make it through to graduation. If they do, in fact, graduate at all."

"Okay," you say, gritting your teeth and suppressing a desire to wrap your hands around Evans' neck. "My concern about relying on a credit card is that it will have a much higher rate of interest than a more conventional personal loan."

"Oh, that is not necessarily true," Evans replies. "Our conventional loans typically have interest rates ranging from six to eight percent. Our Freedom card, by contrast, has an introductory 30-day 0 percent interest rate which converts to a variable rate that is tied to the Carl Index—"

"The Carl Index?" you ask. "Is that like the Prime Rate?"

"No, not really," Evans replies. "It is better than the Prime Rate because it is not set in Washington, D.C., by out-of-touch policy makers but instead by our very own branch manager, Carl Rhodes." He points across the hall to Carl who has apparently finished his study of Scandinavian sunbathing practices and is now wearing a virtual reality helmet and moving his hands around in front of him as though he were either trying to find his way through a dark cave or imitate a mime having a seizure.

"Carl?" you ask, incredulous.

"Carl," Evans responds as Carl's flailing arms knock his desk lamp over.

"Carl sets the interest rates on the Freedom card?" you ask, still incredulous.

"Every single day," Evans replies. "You see, the Freedom card has a daily variable rate that is set by Carl every morning at 9:00 a.m., unless, of course, Carl is nursing a hangover and does not get into the office until after lunch—"

"So the rate changes every single day?" you ask, unsure if you are missing something important.

"Every single day," Evans answers.

"Well, most credit cards have double digit interest rates," you point out cautiously. "What sort of rate does the Freedom card have?"

"Oh, it can vary all over the place," Evans explains. "If Carl has been thrown out of his girlfriend's house, then he might pick a rate of 45%. But if he has purchased a new shirt and tie, he might be in a good mood and set a rate of 16%—"

"So there is no rhyme or reason as to how Carl sets the interest rates for the Freedom card," you observe.

"Well, if Carl is in a good mood when he comes to work, he usually sets the rate lower. But if he is in a bad mood, then he could set the rate up in the stratosphere."

"Does Carl like coffee and pastries?" you ask, suddenly having a thought.

"Oh, yes," Evans replies. "Pastries are one of his favorite foods."

"Not a fruit and vegetable guy, I assume," you say.

"I don't think Carl's body could digest an actual vegetable," Evans replies. "Why?"

"Well, if I were to get a Freedom card and brought a coffee and pastry to Carl every day, then perhaps he would be so happy that he would keep the interest rates lower."

"That is a very clever thought," Evans agrees. "So would you like to apply for a Freedom card after all?" he asks expectantly.

You sigh. "I don't see what choice I have at this point," you respond. "I just need to make sure that I don't forget to drop off the pastry and coffee to Carl every morning."

"That would be a very good idea," Evans replies. He begins filling out the application. "Would you like to apply for a hundred-thousand-dollar credit limit?"

"Oh, no," you answer. "Fifty thousand is more than enough—"

"Before you close the door on the idea of obtaining a one hundred-thousand-dollar credit limit, I might remind you that you do not have to use that other fifty thousand dollars in credit for your daughter's expenses—even if it takes her a decade or more to get through school. I mean, you and your wife could take a trip or buy a new car or refurnish your house—" Evans shakes his head. "I'm sorry, I forgot that you had to sell your house." He clears his throat.

"I think we will stick with the fifty-thousand-dollar credit limit," you declare. "I will also have to set aside some cash for Carl's coffee and pastry fund—"

"I am sure that he will be very grateful for your generosity," Evans replies. "Shall we finish filling out the application?"

"Yes, indeed," you reply as Carl, still wearing his virtual reality headset, accidentally puts his fist through his computer screen.

APPLYING FOR A PERSONAL LOAN AT A MULTILATERAL DEVELOPMENT BANK (MDB)

Nearly every one of us has had to apply for a bank loan to purchase a home, or an automobile, or even business equipment or inventory. However, some of us want to do more than simply buy a shiny new car or a luxurious home, or even start a business selling do-it-yourself taxidermy equipment. Indeed, there are a few of us who have much greater ambitions that cannot be funded by the typical neighborhood bank.

Suppose you wake up one day and look around your neighborhood of single-family homes and suddenly realize that it would be a good idea to build a 500-foot-tall hydroelectric dam at the end of the street to block off a twenty-foot-wide drainage canal. This dam would make it possible to create a new reservoir that would provide a variety of water-oriented recreational activities. Unfortunately, it would drown everyone who lives on the other side of the proposed dam. recreational activities. Because such out-of-the-box thinking is not typically appreciated (let alone encouraged) by most bankers, you would probably have to focus on a different type of bank to obtain the funds for such as massive project in a residential area. As a result, you might want to contact a multilateral development bank (MDB) to discuss your idea.

Before going to the banks, however, you realize that you are proposing to erect a 500-foot-tall wall of concrete that will probably have an enormous aesthetic impact on the neighborhood and, as such, may need to be approved by your neighborhood's homeowner's association. You are certainly familiar with the homeowner's association as they have repeatedly cited you in the past for violations of the association's covenants and restrictions, such as your failure to keep your sidewalk mildew free, and your use of "offensive" inflatable holiday toys (a naked Santa Claus) to aggravate the more prudish members of the association.

As you think about the reaction that the homeowner's association will likely have when you admit that your project will drown all the families on the other side of the hydroelectric dam, you realize that you need to see if there is a loophole to get around the need for homeowner association approval. As a result, you hire an attorney (who specializes in the law of homeowner associations) to review the covenants and restrictions line-by-line to see if there is any language that expressly bans the construction of hydroelectric dams in the neighborhood. A few days later, your lawyer calls you and informs you that the covenants and restrictions do not say anything about prohibiting hydroelectric dams or, indeed, any other types of power-generating facilities such as oil refineries or nuclear power plants. As the drafters of the covenants and restrictions apparently had no concerns about hydroelectric dams being constructed in the neighborhood, you decide that you will not bother informing the homeowner association about your plans since they evidently have no authority to prevent you from moving forward. Armed with this new knowledge, you then proceed to search for the financial backing to fund the construction of your project.

Because you like to view yourself as being hip and on the cutting edge of all things, you peruse the internet and discover that there are several multilateral development banks that might have an interest in your neighborhood hydroelectric dam. Some of the biggest actors in this field include the World Bank, the Inter-American Development Bank and the European Investment Bank. Your research also reveals a few other promising banks such as the Asian Infrastructure Investment Bank, the African Development Bank, the Islamic Development Bank and the New Development Bank (NDB), the last of which is the bank that was set up by the BRICS countries in 2015. Being somewhat new at trying to obtain a loan from a multilateral development bank, you start making calls to try to contact bankers who can assist you with your new project.

Unfortunately, you find out very quickly that you are at an enormous disadvantage because you are a private individual who is seeking to build a hydroelectric dam in his neighborhood. Indeed, you are told over and over again by call center employees that development banks do not work with private citizens but essentially limit themselves to national governments and non-governmental organizations (NGOs). This is, of course, very disappointing as you have already bragged to all of your neighbors that it will only be a matter of time before everyone will start getting free electricity with the completion of your as-of-yet undisclosed neighborhood improvement project. However, you are not quite ready to throw in the towel, even though the representatives of the Asian Infrastructure Investment Bank, the African Development Bank and the Islamic Development Bank have rejected your application out-of-hand due to the flimsy reason that your proposed hydroelectric dam is located in the United States—which, to your dismay, is apparently not considered at least spiritually (even by so-called "globalists") to be part of Asia, Africa or the Middle East. You are also ignored entirely by the World Bank, the Inter-American Development Bank and the European Investment Bank—all of whom refuse to return your repeated phone calls to their general operator. Because the operator at the European Investment Bank has an extremely sultry Czech accent, however, you call her seventy-five more times so that you can listen to her tell you repeatedly that the European Investment Bank has no interest in your hydroelectric dam— until you are served with a restraining order prohibiting you from ever contacting anyone at the European Investment Bank for any reason ever again.

A little miffed at the haughty attitude of these MDBs, you then pick up the phone and call the last name on your list of potential lenders: the New Development Bank. You had been reluctant to call them before due to your belief that the NDB is dominated by Russia and China, but you conclude that you really have nothing left to lose so you give it a try:

"Good evening," says a pleasant voice answering the phone. "This is the New Development Bank."

"Good evening," you respond, surprised at having gotten so far in the loan approval process so quickly.

"To whom may I direct your call?" the voice asks.

"I need to speak to someone who is in charge of funding for hydroelectric dams," you respond, hoping to zero in on the one person who can get your hydroelectric dam project underway.

"Sir, we do not have a specific person who deals with hydro-electric dams," the voice replies. "Let me forward you to our Infrastructure Department so that they can better serve you. May I say who is calling?"

"Kimble," you say, "John Kimble."

"Mr. Kimble, which country do you represent?"

"The United States of America," you say proudly.

"Oh, dear," the voice says. "Sir, the New Development Bank only makes loans to member countries and other developing countries. I am afraid that the United States of America is not a member of the BRICS organization—which operates the New Development Bank—and would therefore not qualify for a loan."

"I see," you reply, downcast. "Thank you for your help," you add, hanging up the phone.

"Have a good day," the voice says.

You think about the operator's comments for a moment and decide to do a little research on the New Development Bank. You soon discover that the NDB is owned by BRICS which consists of five original founding members—Brazil, Russia, India, China, and South Africa—and four new members—Ethiopia, the United Arab Emirates, Iran and Egypt—who joined its ranks in 2021. The NDB was ostensibly created to provide a lending source for developing countries seeking to undertake large-scale "sustainable" infrastructure projects such as roads, ports, hospitals, bridges, water purification plants, railroad lines, and, yes, hydroelectric dams. To date, the NDB reports that it has approved funding for nearly 100 projects with a cumulative value of $33 billion—most of which are located in its member nations. You do some quick math and conclude that your hydroelectric dam would fit in very nicely with the NDB's project criteria if only you can get around the fact that your neighborhood is not located in a BRICS-approved country. As the United States is not a member of BRICS and, hence, not able to take advantage of the NDB's lending programs, you realize that your only hope may be to call the NDB operator back and try a different approach—outright lies. So you dial the number and take another shot.

"Good evening," says the same pleasant voice. "This is the New Development Bank."

"Good evening," you respond. "May I speak to the president of your infrastructure department?"

"Sir, your voice sounds very familiar," the voice replies suspiciously. "Were you the American who called a little while ago?" the voice asks.

"No, not at all," you respond, crossing your fingers behind your back to maintain some sense of integrity. "I am actually a representative of—" you look at the BRICS membership list—"of the Russian government and I need to speak with the head of the infrastructure department to discuss our new development project."

"I see," the voice answers, still not satisfied. "Hold, please."

You wait for a moment and then a new voice picks up. "This is John Horton," a voice says.

"Mr. Horton," you reply. "Thank you for taking my call. I understand that you are the head of the infrastructure department at the bank."

"I am," Horton answers.

You are at a loss for words but only for a moment. "Good afternoon, sir. My name is, uh, Victor Putin—"

"Putin?" Horton asks, suddenly interested. "Any relation to President Putin?"

"Distant cousin, twice removed," you respond, thinking quickly on your feet.

"Well, this is indeed an honor!" Horton responds warmly. "Any member of the Putin family is always welcome to contact us at the New Development Bank."

"Well, that is wonderful to hear," you respond, encouraged by his enthusiastic response. "May I get to the point of my call?"

"Yes, sir, of course," Horton replies anxiously.

"My cousin, President Putin, is interested in building a hydroelectric dam on the Yenisei River and asked me to give your bank a call and see about getting this project started."

"Of course," Horton said. There was a pause. "It looks like there already is a dam on the Yenisei River in Khakassia, Russia." He pauses. "Indeed, it is the largest power plant in Russia and one of the largest hydroelectric power plants in the world—"

"As you can see, the Yenisei River has been a very good place for us to build dams," you point out.

"Yes, I suppose," Horton replies. "Where about would the proposed dam be built in relation to the existing dam?"

"Oh, at least two or three miles upstream," you respond, thinking quickly on your feet.

There is a pause. "Mr. Putin, I am a little surprised that you would want to build a new dam so close to the existing dam. Would that not render the existing dam superfluous?"

"No, not at all," you respond, quickly retrieving and flipping through a couple of articles on hydroelectric dam engineering principles accompanied by stick figure illustrations. "The idea that placing a new dam a couple of miles upstream from an existing dam will cut off the water supply to the existing dam is an outdated concept in hydroelectric dam engineering," you add, surprised at your own ability to make up such innovative and nonsensical technical jargon under pressure. "Nowadays many of us in the dam building business subscribe to the automobile dealership model of hydroelectric dam placement—"

"I am afraid I am not familiar with that concept," Mr. Putin," Horton says, perplexed. "I am an engineer myself and I am embarrassed to say that I have not read anything in the professional literature about this automobile dealership paradigm that you are talking about—"

Your gift for gab goes into overdrive. "Simply put, the more automobile dealers you have in a given area, the greater the number of patrons," you respond confidently. "In short, I can expect a certain number of persons shopping for cars will visit an individual agency. But if I build a string of automobile dealerships next to each other in a single geographic area, then I can expect that they will cumulatively draw more visitors than they would otherwise if they were all located in separate areas. The same principle applies to dam construction," you add. "The more dams you build in close proximity to each other, the more water flow you will get and the more power you will generate." You pause. "What makes this concept so revolutionary is that it is so counterintuitive. I mean, you would think that sticking a bunch of dams next to each other would cause the water flow to slow to a trickle, but the opposite is the case." You pause. "The more dams you have, the more water you get."

"I see," Horton responds, wondering how he could have missed such an obvious point in his professional education. After all, he had attended several of the leading engineering schools in the world. "Do you have any technical articles that you could forward to me so that I might better understand this concept?"

"Of course," you answer, crossing all of your fingers and your toes for good measure. "I would be happy to send the seminal article by, uh, Baskin and Robbins, which was one of the earliest to suggest that there is a direct relationship between the geographical proximity of dams to each other and the resulting volume of water flow." You quickly scan your computer screen. "This idea was anticipated in several other articles such as Lorentz's famous essay which concluded that a greater concentration of fast food restaurants in a given area would lead to increased sales. I might also suggest you review the encyclopedic work by Schultz and Haberstein, which drew the same conclusions regarding the increased concentration of clothes shops in shopping centers that cater exclusively to teenagers invariably leading to increased revenues."

"This is truly fascinating," Horton says, sounding impressed and perplexed at the same time.

"There is just one hitch," you point out.

"And what might that be?" Horton asks.

"My cousin would like to build this hydroelectric dam in the United States in a small town which, unknown to almost everyone, boasts the single greatest concentration of hydroengineering talent in the world. Once the dam is completed, it would be disassembled and them shipped over to Russia to its final destination several miles upstream from the existing dam."

You hear a deflating sigh at the other end of the phone. "Unfortunately, Mr. Putin, the New Development Bank is specifically limited to building infrastructure projects in member countries and select developing countries," Horton points out.

"But we would be moving the dam to Russia once it is completed," you declare, trying to maintain the ruse. "The United States would merely be the site of construction—"

"Mr. Putin, it is really not very cost effective to build a dam in one country and then dissemble it and move it halfway around the world to a completely different location—"

"I don't think my cousin would be very happy to hear that sort of negativity," you declare. "Bad things happen to people who disagree with my cousin," you add.

"I have no desire to displease your cousin," Horton responds. "But the New Development Bank was set up to fund sustainable infrastructure projects in the developing world. Obviously, the United States is not a developing country—"

"No, not really," you admit. "But there are a few rough areas in the cities that you would not want to venture into after dark—"

"Even so, that would not solve the problem." Horton sounds as though he is beginning to lose his enthusiasm for the conversation. "Mr. Putin, even if you had your cousin's full backing, the other members of BRICS would have to agree to allow this project to be built, at least initially, in the United States. Given the geopolitical tensions between the United States, on the one hand, and Russia and China, on the other hand, it is very unlikely that this request would be considered."

"Mr. Horton, I hate to pull rank, but I must demand that you permit me to speak with your supervisor—"

"Oh, very well," Horton says wearily. "Hold on a minute." A buzzing sound fills the air.

"Good evening," a voice says.

"Good evening," you reply. "My name is Victor Putin. Who am I speaking with?"

"Forgive me, Mr. Putin," the voice says. There is the sound of a chair falling over and a shattering of glass followed by grunting noises. "My name is Carl Rhodes." You hear more crashing sounds and then silence. "How may I be of assistance to you?"

"Never mind," you respond, hanging up the phone and admitting defeat.

CHAPTER 7

HOW COUNTRIES
APPLY FOR LOANS

Like other multilateral development banks (MDBs), the New Development Bank (NDB), started by the BRICS nations in 2015, was set up to provide funds to both member nations and emerging countries so that they could build infrastructure projects. Its founding members portrayed it as an alternative financial source for countries concerned about the stringent policies that the IMF often imposes on debtor nations as a condition for obtaining loan approval. Russia and China, the two leading BRICS nations, also viewed the NDB as an institution that could be used to extend their political influence throughout the developing world. Indeed, they have wasted little time in presenting the NDB as a new type of lender that will be more sympathetic to the aspirations of less developed countries. These emerging nations are suspicious, if not outright hostile, toward the United States and its allies, who dominate the international economic order.

However, Russia and China will have had to use some verbal sleight of hand in order to present themselves as benevolent protectors of the world's downtrodden countries due to their own histories of engaging in armed border skirmishes against or even outright invasions of neighboring countries. China has an ongoing border dispute with India, which has occasionally spilled over into armed conflict. Russia has taken aggressiveness to an entirely different level with its periodic invasions of countries ranging from Georgia to Ukraine.

Those nations located on the opposite side of the world, or at least a few countries away, from either China or Russia may be a little more sanguine about the incongruity between their sympathetic public statements and their often blatantly self-serving actions. Also, many emerging countries—rightly or wrongly—see the current so-called neoliberal economic order as being fundamentally skewed against their own interests. In essence, they believe that the United States and the other leading developed countries, such as the United Kingdom, Germany, France and Japan, have rigged the global trading system to prevent poorer countries from producing higher-valued goods and services for export. Even if many of these countries are not so easily persuaded that they are being held down by the nefarious industrial democracies, they see the NDB as a way to hedge their financial dependence on the IMF. The NDB could provide another source of money and, perhaps, offer a potentially less severe underwriting standard than the IMF—which is viewed as the megalodon of the international banking system by its more vocal detractors.

One of the countries that is not so enamored with the IMF or the World Bank is the kingdom of Utrecht-Lorraine, a European principality that is sandwiched between Switzerland and Austria. It was founded in 1639 by geographically challenged Dutch and French explorers. The principality was always viewed as something of a poor stepchild to its more famous neighbors—a land which boasts ten times as many sheep as citizens. While Switzerland is world-renowned for its watchmaking and chocolates, and Austria is famed for its ceramics, crystal and jewelry, Utrecht-Lorraine is known for more prosaic products, such as finely crafted "ugly Christmas sweaters," mutton steaks and a distilled potato vodka having one of the highest concentrations of alcohol of any fermented beverage in the world.

Although Utrecht-Lorraine has a proud artisan heritage, its citizens are sensitive to the fact that very few tourists bother to visit their country. This paucity of visitors may be partially due to the fact that marauding bands of drunken shepherds, wearing hideous holiday sweaters, prey upon the few tourists that do visit so often that Utrecht-Lorraine is routinely blacklisted by the state departments of most of the world's nations. Indeed, Utrecht-Lorraine only has one hotel, in the capital city of Scrotal, and any travelers who wander into the country by accident can usually find a spare room—even during the annual sheep-tossing championship games.

However, Utrecht-Lorraine's current monarch, Prince Freddy, is determined to change the public perception of his country from a backwater pariah to a wealthy enclave that will rival its Swiss and Austrian neighbors. Prince Freddy wants to attract the rich and famous elites of the world to his mountainous realm and has come up with various ideas over the years to rebrand Utrecht-Lorraine as a luxury destination. Indeed, he has tried to build world-class ski resorts with near-suicidal runs atop the towering alpine mountains, but the one resort that was completed had so many fatalities that it was eventually closed down. He has also attempted to encourage the world's leading hoteliers to build new luxury hotels in Utrecht-Lorraine, but was repeatedly rebuffed by their concern that Utrecht-Lorraine would not attract the "right type of tourist." Finally, Prince Freddy has endeavored to establish an offshore banking industry to cater to the tyrants and dictators of the world whom he believes have long been underserved by the world's traditional banks. Sadly, he has found few takers in the banking world as there is apparently a widespread belief among those very same tyrants and dictators that Utrecht-Lorraine would not be a desirable banking destination.

Prince Freddy's thoughts about the future of Utrecht-Lorraine are not new; he has tried for years to secure loans from both the IMF and the World Bank. Unfortunately, the IMF has never been very interested in providing a loan to Utrecht-Lorraine because its currency–known as the *fleg*–is not very stable. It is printed primarily to cover Prince Freddy's gambling debts. Indeed, the IMF only found out that Prince Freddy has a gambling problem after two of his castles were seized by casino officials in Monaco for the non-payment of gambling debts. As a result, the IMF declined to entertain any further loan requests from Prince Freddy, perhaps fearing that the fun-loving royal would continue to pile up gambling losses and thumb his nose at any IMF demands for repayment.

Hoping to find a more sympathetic ear at the World Bank, Prince Freddy and his recently hired finance minister, Carl Rhodes, decided that they would take a contrarian approach and seek funding for an enormous coal power plant, even though the plant's construction would scar many acres of the country's tree-covered topography. However, Carl Rhodes had been very convincing in his argument that a massive coal-burning power plant would lure hundreds of eco-tourists and, failing that, numerous environmental activists who would pay a lot of money to come to Utrecht-Lorraine to participate in protests at the front gates of the plant.

Prince Freddy had filed a loan application with the World Bank, hoping that his project would inspire its loan officers. To further entice the bank's loan officers, he had even borrowed the idea of building the world's tallest roller coaster in front of his coal power plant from the government of Chad. His finance minister had supported this two-project approach, arguing that the World Bank might not be overly enthusiastic about funding the construction of a massive coal plant. But if you add a gigantic roller coaster to the mix, then you can appeal to people of all ages and backgrounds. After all, almost everyone who is not an expectant mother, or who does not suffer from motion sickness, vertigo, high blood pressure, headaches, sinus congestion, nausea, a heart condition, back or neck pain, or similar physical infirmities, can enjoy a thrill-packed ride on a roller coaster. And then, if all goes to plan, they can then visit the coal power plant gift shop and pick up such things as drawstring vomit bags, coal-dusted candy and pre-gift-wrapped lumps of coal to give to naughty children.

Unfortunately, the World Bank was no more sympathetic to Prince Freddy's vision for Utrecht-Lorraine. The underwriters at the World Bank had been particularly critical of the idea of building a coal power plant in the middle of the Alps, fearing that it would create an environmental catastrophe. Even though Prince Freddy and his finance minister, Carl Rhodes, had gone to great lengths to reassure the World Bank that the coal power plant would be a green coal power plant and that the buildings themselves would even be painted in a soothing emerald green color to underscore Utrecht-Lorraine's commitment to an environmentally -friendly coal power plant, the World Bank officials had not been impressed. Instead, they had summarily rejected Prince Freddy's application, concluding that the project did not promote sustainability objectives.

After having tried a few other development banks and finding that they had little interest in lending to a downtrodden European country located in one of the most expensive and scenic areas of the continent, Carl Rhodes, had suggested that they reach out to the New Development Bank to try to get funding for the coal power plant. Prince Freddy, seeing no other options, asked his finance minister to set up a meeting at the NDB headquarters in Shanghai, China.

Three weeks later, they pulled up in a limousine to the New Development Bank at 1600 Guozhan Road, in Shanghai. "Are we all set, Carl?" Prince Freddy asked, as the car idled in front of the iconic tower that seemed to resemble a bunch of misshapen boxes piled on top of one another.

"Absolutely, your excellency," Carl Rhodes said hurriedly, shutting off his laptop and watching the *Nordic Naughties* website go to black. He retrieved a large leather case and stepped out of the vehicle followed by his employer. "I forwarded all of the documents to the bank ahead of time so they should have everything for our meeting."

"Thank you, Carl," Prince Freddy said, emerging from the limousine in a splendid black military uniform that was lined with several rows of shiny medals. He grabbed the jewel-encrusted golden crown that had fallen on the floor of the car and placed it on top of his head. "Carl, how do I look?" he asked his finance minister.

Carl studied Prince Freddy. "You look absolutely regal, Your Highness," Carl said soothingly. "I think that the bank officials will be very impressed to have an actual monarch visiting them," he added.

"Quite so," Prince Freddy said, studying his reflection in the back window of the limousine. He bent inside. "Driver, please stay here until we return." He did not wait for an answer but shut the door and motioned for Rhodes to follow him into the building. They stepped into a modern glass lobby and were greeted almost immediately by an attractive young woman dressed in a bright red business ensemble with matching designer high heels. "Good afternoon, Your Highness," the lady said, smiling and extending her hand. "My name is Miss Chang. I am the senior loan under-writer who will be working on your loan request—"

"It is a pleasure to meet you, Ms. Chang," Prince Freddy said putting on a white glove and shaking her hand gently.

"My name is *Miss* Chang," Miss Chang responded firmly.

"I am not a 'Ms.' Although I have many suitors, I have not yet allowed a man to climb on top of me and defile me," she declared.

"Who needs that?" Prince Freddy answered sympathetically. He nodded his head to underscore his empathy with the anti-defilement point of view.

"And you must be the finance minister," Miss Chang said to Carl Rhodes, extending her hand.

"I am," Carl Rhodes replied, wondering if Miss Chang was familiar with Norwegian massage techniques as he gently caressed her soft hand. "My name is Carl Rhodes," he added.

Miss Chang looked puzzled. "Your name sounds so familiar. Have we met before?" she asked.

Carl Rhodes shook his head. "I don't think so," he replied.

"Well, we are pleased that you have come to visit us in Shanghai," Miss Chang responded. "Your Highness and Mr. Rhodes, please come with me." Prince Freddy and Carl Rhodes followed Miss Chang over to the elevator.

Five minutes later, they walked into an enormous glass-walled conference room anchored by a massive rectangular table flanked by a dozen leather office chairs on each side. "Gentlemen, please have a seat," Miss Chang said, pointing to two chairs at the far end of the table. She then took a seat on the opposite side. "First of all, I would like to thank you both for applying for a loan with the New Development Bank."

"We are pleased to be here," Prince Freddy said. "Where do we begin?"

Miss Chang leafed through a thick file that was laying on top of the table when they entered the room. "Your Highness, our project team has completed an initial review of your proposed coal power plant. They wanted me to ask you if it is necessary for you to build the roller coaster next to the coal plant?"

Carl leaned forward as Prince Freddy was about to wax poetically about the symbiotic relationship between carnival rides and power plants in general. "Miss Chang," Carl said, "we were trying to diversify the risk of this project from an underwriting point of view. We realize there is risk involved with any type of large-scale engineering project such as a power plant. As a result, we thought we could offset some of the risk by throwing in the world's tallest roller coaster. Just imagine the tourist trade."

"That is another concern that came up," Miss Chang said, flipping through the file. "Your country doesn't have any tourists," she said after scanning a few pages.

"You have obviously never attended our sheep-tossing championships," Prince Freddy interjected.

"No, Your Highness, I have not," Miss Chang replied. "But the loan officers are concerned about committing additional funds to this project to build the roller coaster—"

"The world's tallest roller coaster," Carl interrupted.

"The world's tallest roller coaster," Miss Chang said, correcting herself. "Utrecht-Lorraine is not exactly inundated with tourists—"

"That is why we want to build a gigantic roller coaster," Prince Freddy pointed out. "Build it and they will come," he added, quoting someone famous whose identity had slipped his mind. He straightened up his crown which had slipped down over his forehead.

"Sir, we think that it may make more sense to focus on the

coal power plant and leave the roller coaster out of this project," Miss Chang added.

A door opened and a man dressed in a black pinstripe suit walked into the room. "Your Highness and Mr. Rhodes, I would like to introduce you to my boss, Neelam Sharma, who is the bank's senior risk management officer—"

"Gentlemen, welcome to the New Development Bank," Sharma said, crossing the room and shaking the newly white-gloved hand of Prince Freddy. Sharma was a short, balding man who was wearing blindingly shiny black shoes. "Your Highness, it is a true honor to welcome you to our corporate headquarters!" he added.

"And this is Mr. Carl Rhodes, the finance minister of Utrecht-Lorraine—" Miss Chang began.

"Good to see you again, Carl!" Mr. Sharma said, pumping Carl's arm furiously.

"You two know each other?" Miss Chang asked, puzzled.

"Of course," Mr. Sharma replied. "Carl used to work remotely with the New Development Bank on a project-by-project basis. I was very sorry to see him move on but it seems as though he landed on his feet as the finance minister of Utrecht-Lorraine—"

"It's a great gig," Carl agreed.

"You are a man of many talents, Carl," Prince Freddy said.

"Well, why don't we sit down?" Mr. Sharma said, pointing toward the table. He and Miss Chang took their seats across the table from Prince Freddy and Carl Rhodes. "Miss Chang," Mr. Sharma began, flipping through some of the papers. "Why don't you review the status of the project with His Highness and Mr. Rhodes?"

"Yes, sir," Miss Chang said. "Gentlemen, the first part of the underwriting process here at NDB involves a formal assessment of the project. As there was little enthusiasm for the roller coaster, the underwriters focused on the coal power plant. As you know, the NDB loans monies to countries on a project-by-project basis and focuses on infrastructure projects that will help to assist the development of countries such as Utrecht-Lorraine."

"Very good," Prince Freddy said, lending his regal wisdom to the conversation.

"There was some concern about the fact that you want to build a coal power plant," Miss Chang added. "As you may know, the NDB has a mandate to fund infrastructure and sustainable development projects that have minimal environmental impacts. To date, the NDB has approved 96 projects totaling nearly $33 billion ranging from roads, bridges, tunnels, canals, railroads, schools, sewage treatment plants and, yes, even several coal power plants—"

"Have you ever approved a casino?" Prince Freddy asked, remembering the spectacular night in Monte Carlo two years before when he had amassed a fortune of several hundred thousand *euros* at the craps table over the course of the evening. Unfortunately, a bad run of luck at the end wiped him out so badly that he had to hock his royal signet seal ring to avoid washing dishes in the casino's kitchen. For three weeks, Prince Freddy had been forced to ship every royal decree to the *maître d'* to be embossed with the royal signet seal, until he was able to send over a trunkful of *flegs* and a half dozen Medals of Merit, Utrecht-Lorraine's greatest civilian honor. Prince Freddy then awarded these medals *in absentia* to the *maître d'*, the head chef, the *sous* chef, the head waiter, the chief cashier and the most senior busboy, and then secured the return of the ring.

"No, Your Highness," Mr. Sharma replied. "Casinos are not really viewed as development projects by the bank. They do not typically contribute a great deal to the infrastructure of a country—"

"I would beg to differ," Prince Freddy responded. "There are countries such as Monaco whose economies are based on luring wealthy people to their casinos so that they can lose vast amounts of money and contribute to the public welfare."

"I understand, sir," Mr. Sharma said. "But a casino is a project that is beyond the scope of the mandate given to the NBD by its founding members—"

"Speaking of casinos," Prince Freddy continued. "Do you have any casinos in Shanghai?"

"No, sir," Miss Chang responded. "Not really." She thought for a moment. "Casinos are forbidden in China."

"That's too bad," Prince Freddy said sadly, wondering why he had bothered to travel to Shanghai in the first place.

"But there are some casinos in Macau on the coast," Mr. Sharma added. "Macau is about 1,300 kilometers to the southwest." He sat back. "It is referred to as the 'Las Vegas of Asia' due to its many gambling establishments."

"I see," Prince Freddy said, still disappointed. "Perhaps we will visit Macau another time."

"Sir, if I may continue," Miss Chang added. "Although the coal power plant is not the most common type of project funded by the NDB, we have financed a few such projects in the past.

Indeed, one of our most ambitious projects is an enormous coal power plant in Brazil—"

"But we still have to be mindful of the ecological impacts that these projects may have on the environment," Mr. Sharma added. "We have also approved funding to cover the costs of the paving the Trans-Amazonian Highway which has, unfortunately, caused a great deal of damage to the Brazilian rain forest."

"Which brings us to one of the concerns expressed by the underwriters regarding your project," Miss Chang said. "The proposed location of your coal power plant is in the middle of an alpine forest. The underwriters were concerned that huge areas of the surrounding forests would have to be destroyed to build the plant itself as well as any ancillary facilities and roads."

"Well, we do have a lot of trees in Utrecht-Lorraine," Prince Freddy pointed out, drawing upon his vast knowledge of forestry. "If we have to chop down a few thousand trees, so be it." He thought for a moment. "My country is almost completely covered with trees. Indeed, you would find it difficult to locate an area, aside from the meadows—which are filled with sheep poop—and our towns and villages, where you can see your own shadow in the middle of the day."

Carl Rhodes shifted forward. "Miss Chang, nearly eighty percent of Utrecht-Lorraine is covered by forests. Indeed, it is the most heavily forested country in the world. There are trees everywhere. Trees to the left of us. Trees to the right of us. So many trees!"

"Your point, Mr. Rhodes?" Miss Chang snapped.

"My point is that the footprint of the coal plant would

necessitate the removal of perhaps twenty acres of trees. In addition, we would have to clear additional lands so that we could build several access roads up to the power plant. However, this will be little more than a blip in the scheme of things because we have so many trees!"

"Okay, okay," Miss Chang said. "Perhaps the loss of tree cover would not pose too much of a danger to the surrounding ecosystem," she concluded. "I will retrieve the forestry surveys of Utrecht-Lorraine and run them by the underwriters and see what they say." She scribbled some notes on a page and moved on.

Mr. Sharma pulled the file over in front of him. "The underwriting team also expressed some concerns about the creditworthiness of Utrecht-Lorraine and its ability to pay its bills in a timely manner." Mr. Sharma dug into the file. "They were concerned about the foreclosure by Monaco on two castles owned by yourself—"

Prince Freddy waved his hand dismissively. "It was all an unfortunate misunderstanding," he said. "I had opened a credit account with the casino and secured it with the deeds to two castles—which were just run-down country cottages in the middle of nowhere that I had been trying to sell for years without success. So when I had a string of bad hands at the baccarat table, I put my checkbook away and told the casino to go ahead and keep the two properties. 'Good riddance!' I said, as I left the casino."

"I see," Miss Chang said. "We were under the impression that the properties had been claimed by the casino due to the government's lack of money—"

"Oh, no!" Prince Freddy said comfortingly, raising his hand. "Utrecht-Lorraine has enormous amounts of money. Vaults and vaults full of money! We print it all the time!" He gave a thumbs-up sign to underscore his point.

"That is true," Carl Rhodes agreed, lending his expert opinion to the discussion. "You could paper the streets of Utrecht-Lorraine a foot deep with all of the paper money that we have available." He retrieved a 100 *fleg* bill from his pocket and opened it up to reveal a brightly colored watermarked note with a portrait on the front of a disheveled 16-year-old Prince Freddy that had been taken after he was arrested for public drunkenness. He flipped it over to reveal a picture of an angry-looking sheep on the back. "I thought you might find it interesting to see what a 100 *fleg* bill looks like as our engravers are renowned for their artistic skills."

"That is a very nice-looking note," Mr. Sharma said, admiring the bill.

"It also has a number of features designed to frustrate the two counterfeiters who have tried to create fake 100 *fleg* notes in the past decade." Carl pointed toward the edge of the note. "If you look closely, you will see in very tiny print, the very first poem ever written by His Highness Prince Freddy." He traced his finger around the four sides of the bill. He cleared his throat and read the literary masterpiece: "'I like my dog. I like my frog. Jump on the log. Walk through the fog.'" He nodded at the beaming Prince Freddy. "It still gets to me every time." Carl appeared to wipe a tear from his eye. "Your Highness, I still can't believe that you were able to express such profound sentiments at the tender age of seven—"

"Actually, I was six," Prince Freddy said, gently correcting his finance minister. "But I felt that I had something important to say, even at such a young age."

"So why do you need this loan in the first place?" Mr. Sharma asked.

Carl Rhodes cleared his throat. "Even though we have billions of *flegs* in circulation, the exchange rate of the *fleg* to the American dollar is about 100,000 *flegs* to one dollar. We have a very impressive supply of paper money, but it is not worth a great deal. As the coal power plant itself may cost upwards of $1 billion, we have no choice but to seek funding from the New Development Bank."

"But the needs of our own citizens are not great," Prince Freddy pointed out. "Aside from the occasional disgruntled would-be assassin who tosses a rock through one of the ground floor windows of the palace, the people of Utrecht-Lorraine are content and live simple lives. My hope is that much of the energy generated by this power plant can be sold to other countries which would enable us to earn much needed foreign exchange—"

"Which would facilitate the development of your economy," Miss Chang interrupted.

"And help to repay the loan," Carl Rhodes added. "Our thought is that most of the power will be exported to those snobs—"

"Now, now, Carl," Prince Freddy said, comforting his finance minister. "We mustn't call names."

"Okay, okay," Carl said, calming down. "Our plan was to export most of the power to residents in Germany, Switzerland and Austria. Any remaining power could be used by our own citizens to meet our own domestic energy needs." He thought for a moment. "Our expectation is that the monies received from the sale of power to other countries would more than cover the debt service costs."

"Well, that's good to hear," Mr. Sharma responded. He rifled through the file. "Another question raised by the underwriters was the general condition of your country's economy. From what we understand, your primary exports are holiday sweaters, livestock products and very corrosive alcoholic beverages." Mr. Sharma rubbed his eyes. "However, your imports are only about one tenth of your exports by value and seem to be limited to such things as trampolines, traffic cones, kayaks, suntan lotion and sheep-shaped latex companions—"

"Our shepherds live a very solitary lifestyle," Prince Freddy said defensively. "In general, however, you will find that Utrecht-Lorraine is self-sufficient and prides itself on not having to rely on other nations for much of anything." He added: "Our citizens may not be very wealthy, but they are able to make almost everything they need for their daily needs."

"That is not necessarily a bad thing," Mr. Sharma pointed out. "Many loan applicants import far more goods and services in terms of value than they export—which of course makes lenders such as ourselves very concerned about their ability to repay their loans." He smiled. "You do not appear to have that problem—"

"Well, not too many people use the *fleg* currency so it does hinder our ability to engage in trade with other countries," Carl Rhodes admitted. "Perhaps that is a good thing as it makes it virtually impossible for us to overextend ourselves."

Miss Chang turned to the Utrecht-Lorraine finance minister. "Mr. Rhodes, could you tell us a little more about the sources of energy currently supplying the needs of the citizens of Utrecht-Lorraine?"

Carl Rhodes stared at the ceiling for a moment. "At the present time, most of our energy comes from burning wood, geothermal energy provided by a few geysers, several hydroelectric dams, a couple of small coal power plants and a rickety 80-year-old nuclear power plant that was purchased from the United States and installed by His Highness's grandfather, King Harold. He bought it at a scratch and dent sale when the American government was trying to free up some warehouse space."

"Why coal? Mr. Rhodes?" Miss Chang asked. "Why not solar or wind or maybe even another nuclear power plant?"

Carl took a deep breath. "Well, we tried to install a few wind turbines on the side of one of the mountains but two of the propellers flew off into the sky. One of them landed on a railroad car, severing part of its roof and injuring nearly 50 passengers— who are now suing the Utrecht-Lorraine government for millions of dollars of damages in a class action lawsuit. The other propeller sliced through a passing flock of migratory birds that happen to be on the European Endangered Species List so we are now having to pay a fine for the harm caused to these birds." Carl took a deep breath. "In any event, His Highness has decided not to pursue wind power any further at this time as it is simply too dangerous."

"I see," Miss Chang said, surprised at the perils posed by what she assumed were harmless windmills.

Prince Freddy shook his head in agreement. "It is simply not worth the risk." He looked up. "Plus, we have all these lawyers showing up at the royal palace every day to ask questions." Prince

Freddy's eyes narrowed. "Unfortunately, we can't toss lawyers in the dungeon like my grandfather, King Harold, used to do during his reign." Prince Freddy smiled at the recollection. "He would pack them in like canned sardines." He dropped his hands in his lap. "If I tossed a single lawyer in a dungeon, I would find myself being called a monster by broadcasting companies around the world."

"Your Highness, you just have to be subtle about how you deal with these lawyers," Carl said, trying to be helpful. "Just douse them with chloroform when they show up at the front door and put them on a non-stop bus to Belarus. If anyone comes looking for them, you can deny everything and eventually the media will lose interest and go onto the next scandal."

"Okay," Mr. Sharma said, anxious to move on with the meeting. "I believe that the bank might be on board with the idea of funding the coal power plant. Just to be clear, there is no interest in funding the roller coaster—"

"The world's tallest roller coaster," Carl pointed out, just in case anyone had forgotten about this crucial point.

"Yes, Mr. Rhodes," Mr. Sharma acknowledged. "The world's tallest roller coaster."

Prince Freddy raised his hand excitedly. "What if we built a water park instead?" he wanted to know. "People love water parks," he pointed out. "Plus, they are fun for the whole family—" He shook his head. "I can see why you would be reluctant to approve a roller coaster because not everyone can ride a roller coaster." He continued with his brainstorm: "You can't put young children on roller coasters because they can fall out of the seats," he explained. "You can't put older people on roller coasters because they could suffer a heart attack or motion sickness." He clasped his hands together. "But water parks can be enjoyed by people of all ages—"

"Except for those people who don't know how to swim," Carl added, trying to be helpful.

"Well, there is *that*," Prince Freddy admitted. "But the point is that a water park would appeal to a much wider audience except, of course, those people who sink to the bottom of the pool and drown."

"I don't think we can consider a water park, Your Highness," Mr. Sharma said. "Besides, it would be at the top of a mountain," he added. "You would probably only be able to use it for a few months out of the year."

"It could be an ice skating rink in the winter," Prince Freddy said hopefully.

"I'm afraid not, Your Highness," Mr. Sharma said, showing a discernable lack of interest in anything fun.

"Very well," Prince Freddy said, suddenly dejected.

Mr. Sharma returned to the file. "I am encouraged by the fact that even though the national currency of Utrecht-Lorraine—"

"The *fleg*," Carl added.

"Yes, Carl," Mr. Sharma continued, irritated. "The *fleg*. Even though the *fleg* is a devalued currency, Utrecht-Lorraine has a significant balance of payments surplus which will only be further enhanced by the construction of this coal power plant and the sale of power to foreign customers. As a result, I think that the Board of Directors of the New Development Bank should be sympathetic toward this project."

That sounds promising," Prince Freddy said, straightening his crown.

"Gentlemen, we also have to discuss the method by which the proposed coal power plant is to be financed and constructed," Miss Chang announced.

"I assume it is a very straightforward process," Prince Freddy said breezily. "You approve the project and release the money and we hire the finest engineers in Utrecht-Lorraine to build the coal power plant—"

"Do you have any engineers in Utrecht-Lorraine who can build a $1 billion coal power plant?" Mr. Sharma asked skeptically.

Prince Freddy looked puzzled. "I assume we must have somebody who can tackle this job," he said, looking at his financial minister for reassurance. "Carl, don't we have some pretty talented bladesmiths who could build a coal power plant?"

"Your Highness, I think it would be a bit of a stretch for a dozen elderly craftsmen who make ceremonial swords out of steel to build a coal power plant," Carl responded, throwing cold water on the regal initiative.

"Perhaps," Prince Freddy agreed reluctantly. "All the same, they do make very sharp swords," he pointed out. "You can toss an apple in the air and slice it in half with one swing," he added.

"It doesn't really work that way," Mr. Sharma interrupted. "Because the New Development Bank is run by Russia, China, Brazil, India and South Africa, they will usually require that the plant be financed using one of their own currencies—most likely the Chinese renminbi. They may also require as a condition of the loan that the work be performed by firms based in one or more of these countries—most likely China or Russia."

"Well, how would our bladesmiths learn how to build a coal power plant if all the work is being done by a company from

Shanghai or Moscow?" Prince Freddy wanted to know, having an unexpected moment of clarity. "This would be the biggest infrastructure project ever built in Utrecht-Lorraine, and we would certainly want much of the work to be performed by our own citizens so that it benefits the local economy."

"Well, I am not sure this suggestion would be acceptable to the bank," Mr. Sharma said gently. "Although the bank can take your request that the local labor force be employed wherever possible in the project under consideration, you must understand that a coal power plant is an enormously complicated structure. It does not necessarily lend itself to employing unskilled labor."

"Surely somebody has to carry the coal to the plant," Prince Freddy pointed out. "You don't need to be a mechanical engineer to lug a bag of coal."

"I think your workers could transport the coal to the plant," Mr. Sharma said. "As far as the actual construction of the facility is concerned, however, I believe that the bank would insist that one of its own pre-approved engineering firms be used to build the plant."

Prince Freddy looked surprised. "If I am borrowing the money, I would want to bid the project out around the world to try and get the best possible price—"

Miss Chang nodded her head. "Your Highness, you will be able to pick from a wide variety of companies," she said soothingly.

"Such as?"

"Such as China Huaneng Group or China Energy Investment Corp. or China Datang Corp.," she answered. "They are among the largest coal power plant construction firms in the world." She pointed at the yellow hazy Shanghai skyline. "These companies have been instrumental in helping China to achieve its status as the world's biggest polluter," she bragged. "So they know what they are doing."

"But they are all from China," Prince Freddy pointed out. "There are other companies in the world that build coal power plants, several of which are based in Europe."

"Your Highness, I don't make the rules, I just follow them," Mr. Sharma pointed out.

"Utrecht-Lorraine is not a rich country," Carl Rhodes said. "It needs to build the coal power plant for the lowest possible price. His Highness is clearly concerned about the costs of the project and wants to make sure that he gets the best possible deal for his country."

"I would also point out that your Chinese workers would have to bring bagged lunches," Prince Freddy said. "We do not have any Chinese restaurants in Utrecht-Lorraine."

"Not to worry, Your Highness," Miss Chang interjected. "These firms are very self-sufficient. They will set up camp on the job site, build the project and then leave as soon as the construction is completed."

"Not to beat a dead horse," Prince Freddy responded, "but I must insist again that the local labor force to be used as much as possible in the actual construction of the project." He looked out the window at the yellowish-brown sky. "We have many unemployed and underemployed citizens in Utrecht-Lorraine. They will not be very happy to hear that they will not be given any opportunity to work on this project." He stood up and walked over to the window. "We do not need any social unrest," he pointed out. "I would have to fill the moat around the royal palace with water again."

"Perhaps I can discuss the bidding process with the board of directors," Mr. Sharma said. "We do not want you to feel like you have a gun to your head."

"Thank you, Mr. Sharma," Prince Freddy said graciously.

Miss Chang coughed. "Another item to be considered is the extent to which this project will comply with Utrecht-Lorraine's environmental laws."

"Why?" asked Prince Freddy.

"Well, our mandate requires that all projects funded by the bank be in compliance with local environmental laws and regulations."

"That won't be any problem," Carl Rhodes said.

"Why not?" Miss Chang asked.

"We don't have any environmental laws," Prince Freddy replied. "My father, King Dennis, abolished our country's environmental laws several decades ago—"

"Why did he do that?" Miss Chang asked.

Prince Freddy took a deep breath. "King Dennis was a social Darwinist," he said. "He believed that there should be no limits on the ways in which humanity and nature interact with each other. For him, it was a matter of the survival of the fittest. My father believed that environmental laws protect the weak and unfairly restrict the actions of the strong. For him, it was more a matter of live and let live and see who comes out on top. Hence, he saw no reason to restrict the ways in which humanity develops the resources of the earth."

"Is your father still alive?" Mr. Sharma asked, wondering if King Dennis might have spent a lot of time in a padded room.

"Very much so," Prince Freddy said. "That is why I am still a prince. But my father turned over the day-to-day management of Utrecht-Lorraine to me many years ago. He lives in Paris, France, and spends most of his time on the Champs-Elysees posing for pictures with tourists and enjoying the theaters, cafes and luxury shops with his many girlfriends."

"I see," Mr. Sharma said. "Does your father have to approve the loan application?"

"Not at all," Prince Freddy said, waving his hand. "He is retired for all practical purposes."

Carl Rhodes offered an explanation: "When King Dennis decided to step down as the ruling monarch, he did not want to abdicate so he and his son signed an agreement whereby King Dennis would retain his title, his crown and his scepter for the remainder of his life but his son would take over the royal duties and do whatever royal things needed to be done."

"We would need to see a copy of that agreement," Mr. Sharma said.

"Here you go," Carl Rhodes answered, retrieving a single sheet of paper from his coat pocket and sliding it across the table to Mr. Sharma. "It is very simple agreement," he added as Mr. Sharma read the document. "His Royal Highness Prince Freddy agreed to assume all duties of the sovereign including all public functions such as showing up at the grand openings of any new stores or restaurants, performing ribbon cutting ceremonies at any new factories or sewage treatment plants, judging the winner of the local grammar school's tug-of-war contest or overseeing the military maneuvers of the vaunted Utrecht-Lorraine royal guardsmen." Carl stopped. "The list is all-inclusive. The point is that King Dennis wanted to remain king in name only because he wished to do something different during his remaining years, i.e., enjoying life in Paris and meeting ladies who are enthusiastic about sovereign prerogatives. Fortunately, he had a dutiful son to whom he could delegate his sovereign authority." Carl gestured at Prince Freddy, who had returned to his seat and was now trying to remove something from one of his teeth with his fingernail.

"This document certainly appears to vest Your Royal Highness with all the powers needed to approve the loan from the bank," Mr. Sharma said. "If we have any questions for King Dennis, is there a way to contact him?"

Prince Freddy was silent for a moment. "My father does not have a telephone," he said. "We usually have to send a letter to his house in Paris if we need to reach him," Prince Freddy added. "If we have to get hold of him in a hurry, we will simply send a courier over to Paris to hand-deliver the correspondence."

"That sounds like a lot of trouble," Miss Chang said.

"I'm afraid that my father is a bit old-fashioned," Prince Freddy said. "He was never very interested in technology except for battery-powered recreational devices."

"Very well," Mr. Sharma said, closing the file and standing up. "I think we have all the information we need," he said, reaching out to shake Prince Freddy's re-gloved hand. "It was a pleasure meeting you, Your Highness," Mr. Sharma said. He turned to Carl Rhodes. "It was good to see you again, Carl," he added. "We miss having you working with us here at the bank but

I am very pleased that you have found such a prestigious position with the country of Utrecht-Lorraine."

"Thank you," Carl Rhodes replied. "When do you think the bank will make a final decision?" he asked.

"I would give it a month or so," Mr. Sharma replied. "The board of directors is considering a number of projects and it takes time for them to evaluate each of these proposals." He checked his watch. "If you will excuse me, Miss Chang and I have to go to another meeting."

"Of course," Prince Freddy said, rising to his feet. "Don't be late on our account," he added.

Mr. Sharma and Miss Chang escorted Prince Freddy and Carl Rhodes to the elevator. "Thank you for coming to Shanghai, Your Highness," Miss Chang said as Prince Freddy and Carl Rhodes stepped onto the elevator. "We will be in touch."

"Thank you," Prince Freddy said. "And good luck in keeping those prospective defilers from climbing on top of you, Miss Chang," he added graciously as the doors closed.

PART FIVE

PARTYING WITH
THE COOL KIDS

CHAPTER 8

THE BRICS SUMMIT

"You're on in five."

"Four."

"Three."

"Two."

"One."

The steel guitars of a traditional Hawaiian ballad wafted across the stage as the center camera zoomed in on three people seated on barstools around a high bar tabletop emblazoned with a neon sign: *Comings and Goings*. Ken Roberts, America's favorite newscaster, was wearing a bright red and yellow Hawaiian shirt and khaki shorts and sipping a Mai Tai. To his right was the distinguished foreign correspondent, Margaret Hill, resplendent in a white cotton dress with matching sandals. Two gigantic feather wings were mounted on her back and she sipped a glass of white wine. To Ken's left was the distinguished Nobel Prize winning economist, Stanislaw Zutnik, dressed in the same tuxedo that he had worn at the BRICS gala affair and enjoying a beverage that appeared to be on fire in a gigantic mug. "Good afternoon, everyone," Ken said, as the overture faded, and the camera closed in on America's gift to television broadcasting. "Welcome to another edition of *Comings and Goings*. Today we are in the beautiful tropical paradise of Honolulu, Hawaii, where we are wrapping up our coverage of the sixteenth annual BRICS summit. With me are my distinguished colleagues, Margaret Hill, the award-winning foreign correspondent, and Stanislaw Zutnik, the world-renowned economics professor and Nobel-laureate. We have set up a makeshift studio in the Diamond Head bar of the Grand Honolulu Hotel which is located on beautiful Waikiki Beach. Today we will be wrapping up our coverage of the most recent summit by the BRICS countries which, somewhat surprisingly, has been held in Hawaii, which is, of course, part of the United States." He took a long sip on the straw of his Mai Tai. "Margaret," Ken said, turning to his right. "What is the significance of the BRICS countries deciding to hold their annual summit in Honolulu, Hawaii?"

Margaret shifted uncomfortably in her seat as one of the feathered wings swung around and hit Ken on the back of his head. "Sorry about that, Ken," Margaret said, exasperated. "I don't know why I let my designer, Eloise Wang, talk me into wearing these wings with this dress," she said, shaking her head. She turned toward the camera, shifting again as the wing swung back into place behind her, and put on her professional face: "Ken, I think this decision to hold the conference here in Honolulu was a statement by the BRICS countries that they are a legitimate player in the international banking system and are ready to challenge the global leadership of the United States and its allies, who dominate the IMF and the World Bank."

"Sort of a thumb in Washington's eye?" Ken asked, as he ordered a triple Mai Tai from a passing waiter to improve upon the efficiency of his drinking experience.

"I think so, Ken," Margaret replied, using her elbow to shove the drifting wing on her right shoulder back into place. "We have been here for the past three days listening to speech after speech by various finance ministers and heads of state from countries that either already belong to BRICS or have applied for membership to BRICS. In general, most of the speeches sound as though they were all written by the same speechwriter: They typically recite a litany of grievances against the current global economic order and stress the need to create new lending institutions that will serve the needs of the emerging economies."

Ken nodded. "Professor Zutnik, what did you think of these speeches?"

Professor Zutnik took a deep sip from the metal straw protruding from his flaming cocktail. "Well, I believe that many of these leaders view BRICS and its New Development Bank as an alternate forum in which they can play a more substantial role and obtain more favorable lending terms than might otherwise be possible with other development banks—most notably the IMF and the World Bank."

Margaret nodded at the passing waiter while pointing to her empty glass. "Professor Zutnik, I think we should mention that all of the countries that currently either belong to BRICS or that are applying for membership to BRICS also are members of both the IMF and the World Bank."

"That is true, Margaret," Professor Zutnik said, sipping his drink again as the flames popped higher and sent several embers floating into the air. "Just because you are a part of BRICS does not mean that you do not belong to the IMF and the World Bank. Indeed, I am not aware of any country that has ever left the IMF and the World Bank—because they are the dominant global multilateral lenders." Professor Zutnik giggled as a fiery bubble floated up from the bottom of his mug and popped. Both Ken and Margaret looked shocked that Professor Zutnik was capable of giggling. "Russia and China always complain about the fact that the United States can veto any loan proposal by any country submitted to the IMF or the World Bank," Professor Zutnik added, taking another sip. "But they both continue to remain in the IMF and the World Bank as do all of their fellow BRICS members." He giggled again as the flames in his mug jumped upward.

Ken looked at Professor Zutnik's flaming drink. "By the way," he asked. "What do you call that drink?"

"This is a fireball," Professor Zutnik said, taking another sip. "It is a mixture of Canadian whisky and cinnamon and flavored sugars," he added, as a waiter brought Ken his triple Mai Tai and Margaret her white wine. "Some people think the fireball is too sweet, but I happen to like its spicy burn." He giggled again. "I think I need another one," he said, turning toward another waiter who was floating by.

As the waiter placed a bowl of pretzels on the table, he accidentally knocked over Professor Zutnik's drink. A stream of flames rolled across the table as both Ken and Margaret jumped out of their chairs.

"Fire! Fire!" Professor Zutnik called out as the sleeve of his tuxedo caught fire.

"Hold on, Professor Zutnik!" Ken said, thinking quickly and using a cloth napkin to beat out the flames. "Waiter!" he called out. "We need a pitcher of water! And no ice!" A waiter quickly appeared next to the smoldering Professor Zutnik and placed the pitcher of water in front of him. Professor Zutnik quickly dunked his charred sleeve in the pitcher. "Thank you," Professor Zutnik said, suddenly visibly sober.

"Professor Zutnik, maybe we should get you to a doctor," Margaret said, concerned, as her left wing swung around and knocked over a stagehand. "I'm so sorry, Bobby," she said, bending over to help the young man to his feet. "I can't stand this outfit," she muttered, standing up. "Why can't Eloise design a simple dress that does not have angel wings or a gigantic tarantula—"

"Oh, I am fine, my dear," Professor Zutnik responded good-naturedly as he steadied himself. "I guess I am done with the fireballs for now."

"Speaking of which," Ken said, "we *do* have a show to do." The three of them returned to the table and resumed their discussion. Ken checked his notes and brushed the ashes off the tabletop. "Margaret, we were talking about the fact that no one leaves the IMF or the World Bank, even though they may be involved with other development banks such as the New Development Bank of BRICS, the African Development Bank or the Asian Development Bank."

"That is correct, Ken," Margaret replied. "Every country

wants to have as many borrowing options as possible. As countries develop and their economies mature, they become more desirable to a wider variety of lenders. Every one of these BRICS countries belongs to several different development banks. I think it is more useful to think of BRICS as another development bank that can be approached by emerging countries as opposed to a new behemoth that is going to upend the existing global financial system."

"Professor Zutnik?" Ken began before forgetting the question he was going to ask.

"I agree with Margaret," Professor Zutnik replied, eyeing the burn marks on his tuxedo and wondering if he should try to develop a taste for a less flammable drink in the future. "All countries want to have options," he said. "They do not want to be under the thumb of any given bank or development agency." Professor Zutnik noticed the stench of burned tuxedo for the first time and coughed. "India, for example, may be one of the founding members of BRICS, but I can tell you that it would sooner borrow money from the Asian Development Bank or the World Bank than to borrow those funds from the BRICS New Development Bank if it thought that it was getting a bad deal on the loan or was somehow being pushed around by China or Russia."

"I quite agree, Professor," Margaret said, sipping her wine as a dove flew into the bar and landed on her head. "Ken!" she shouted. "Get this bird off my head!" She waved her hands near the bird trying to shoo it away.

"Maybe it thinks you are its mother," Ken offered, trying to be helpful. "I mean, you are wearing those enormous wings," he pointed out.

"Ken!" Margaret snapped, wondering if Ken or the bird had the smaller brain.

"Okay, sorry," Ken said hurriedly. He reached over and gently lifted the cooing dove off Margaret's head and handed it to Bobby, who was waiting off to the side. Bobby then carried the dove out of the bar, presumably to set it free or offer it to the *sous chef* in the hotel kitchen as a low-cost pheasant under glass substitute.

"Anyway," Margaret continued as though nothing had happened. "I think we tend to focus on one development bank or another development bank and see them as competing against each other for dominance in the world economy." She ran her fingers through her hair just to make sure that the dove had not left any gifts behind. "But I am not sure that we should view the issue from the perspective of these development banks at all. Instead, I think it makes more sense to look at it as though every country is going on a shopping trip in search of bargains with the major global lenders."

"That is an interesting perspective," Professor Zutnik said, wondering if it might be a good idea to order another fireball drink. "Everyone gets caught up in the narrative about all of these possible upstart banks—including the New Development Bank—trying to replace the IMF and the World Bank when, in fact, I doubt that even the most vocal proponents of the New Development Bank such as China and Russia have such ambitions."

"Well, several of the speakers have issued some very provocative challenges during this BRICS summit," Ken pointed out.

"You would have thought from some of the speeches that the United States was treating the entire developing world as little more than a collection of knickknack vassal states—"

"They do have a flair for the dramatic," Margaret agreed. "But I think they were playing to their domestic constituencies—"

"Okay," Ken said, trying to bring some order to the discussion. "We have spent the last three days in Hawaii reporting on the BRICS summit. Perhaps one of the most touching segments was the Parade of Debtors in which representatives from thirty-five nations, who owe money to the New Development Bank, filed into the meeting hall and carried their offerings of gold, frankincense and myrrh over to the golden throne of President Xi."

A video of a line of delegates, heads bowed, filled the screen. They slowly moved up the main aisle of the room, each one setting down a box at the feet of President Xi, who acknowledged each gift with a nonchalant wave of his hand, before the delegate headed off into a side hallway. The video stopped and the camera returned to Ken. "We should point out that President Putin has been conspicuously absent from the summit due to concerns about the outstanding arrest warrant issued by the International Criminal Court." He looked at the camera. "Otherwise, he would have been in attendance as he always does very well in the tequila and vodka shots competitions." Ken shuffled his papers. "But nothing kills your buzz like the prospect of being placed under arrest and dragged off to the Hague to stand trial for crimes against humanity."

"That's true," Professor Zutnik agreed.

Ken turned back to the camera. "Although we did enjoy the pageantry of the Parade of Debtors, I think the highlight of the first day of the summit was the ceremony welcoming the new members of BRICS."

Another video clip began to play which showed the leaders of the four new member nations—Egypt, Ethiopia, Iran and the United Arab Emirates (UAE)—standing on a platform as President Xi walked over, greeted each one and placed a gold medal around his neck. The camera zoomed in to show the face of one of the medals up close. The engraved words "Official BRICS Member" were spaced around the edge of the medal and wound around a color portrait of both President Putin and President Xi at the center. The phrase "Best Friends Forever" was printed out in small type in both Cyrillic and Pinyin below their smiling faces. The camera pulled back and President Xi then handed each of the four leaders a gold card and shook their hands before walking off the stage." The video shut off and the camera returned to the *Comings and Goings* tabletop. "Professor Zutnik, what were those gold cards?" Ken asked, curious.

Professor Zutnik studied his charred sleeve for a moment. "Ken, those are the BRICS Gold Motor Club membership cards," he responded. Professor Zutnik looked at his notes. "It is a perk that is available only to the heads of state of BRICS members," he said. "Cardholders get 100 miles of free towing each year along with discounts on gasoline purchases. I believe that cardholders also receive promotional gifts from all sorts of retailers, such as clothing boutiques, candy companies and sporting goods stores."

"Do you get to keep the card after you leave office?" Margaret asked.

"That is a good question," Professor Zutnik answered. "Given the likelihood that many of these leaders may be violently killed during future military coups and popular uprisings, and thus be deprived of a peaceful retirement with their BRICS Gold Motor Club cards in hand, I would venture to say that it may not make much difference."

"Okay," Margaret said, as both of her wings swung outward in opposite directions. "The first day of the summit ended with the investiture of the four new members of BRICS and a good time was had by all."

"That is correct, Margaret," Ken answered. "So can you tell our audience what happened on the second day of the summit?" he asked.

Margaret nodded. "Although the first day was all about pomp and circumstance, the second day was replete with numerous working groups and conferences in which representatives from different BRICS countries attended meetings on a variety of topics." She glanced at the camera. "Some of the more popular gatherings were symposiums on how to give speeches chastising the United States for anything that comes to mind or lectures on ways to move large amounts of money to reliable offshore tax havens." Margaret pushed the wings back behind her. "Indeed, the seminar inviting participants to offer their most searing insults of the United State was disrupted when the Ethiopian vice president called the United States 'the Humongous Satan.' This outburst prompted the Iranian finance minister to declare that *his* country had invented the original satanic slur decades before when it branded the United States as the 'Great Satan.' The Ethiopian vice president then stuck his tongue out at the Iranian finance minister. This action prompted the Iranian finance minister to threaten to sue Ethiopia for trademark and copyright infringement. The Ethiopian vice president then warned that his country would start producing 'Death to America' t-shirts and associated protest apparel at prices far below those being offered by Iranian merchants on college campuses and at fine department stores everywhere." She rolled her eyes at the camera. "Eventually, security officers intervened, and the two antagonists were escorted out of the room." Margaret shook her head in disbelief.

"Shocking," Ken offered, wondering if he could get another triple Mai Tai.

Margaret glanced at her notes. "Professor Zutnik," she said. "Was there not a seminar in which the participants were playing a version of 'pin the tail on the donkey?'"

"Yes, Margaret," Professor Zutnik answered. "It was a seminar billed as a team building exercise for emerging nations. Hung on a wall were banners with the names of individual nations. Each banner was divided into different sections. The Russia banner, for example, had twelve boxes each containing a word such as 'benevolent', 'egalitarian' or 'freedom-loving.' The banner for India included terms such as 'philosophical', 'friendly' and 'generous.'" Both of these banners had a gold star at its very center. A blindfolded player who pinned a ribbon on the gold star would win a valuable prize, such as a motorcycle."

"What would you get just for pinning the ribbon in one of these boxes?" Ken asked, his razor-sharp mind firing on both cylinders.

"A lifetime subscription to the *People's Daily*, the official newspaper of the Central Committee of the Chinese Communist Party," Professor Zutnik replied. "I am told that it can be educational but lacks much in the way of a sports section," he added.

"Dare I ask if there was a banner for the United States?" Margaret asked, already knowing the answer.

"Of course there was," Professor Zutnik replied.

"And would it be safe to assume that terms such as 'fair-minded' or 'charitable' or even 'inspirational' were conspicuously absent from the American banner?" Margaret wondered aloud.

"That would be a safe assumption," Professor Zutnik answered, looking around for a waiter after having decided that it would make a lot of sense to order another fireball drink *sans* the flaming top.

Feeling as though she was having to extract every sentence from her learned colleague like a dentist gripping a stubborn molar with a pair of pliers, Margaret moved to the next question—which could have been anticipated by an eight-year-old child: "What sorts of words were on the banner for the United States?" she asked.

"Nothing very flattering, Professor Zutnik said, "I believe the words included 'rapacious', 'murderous' and 'predatory.'

"And was there a gold star at the center?" Margaret asked.

"No, not at all," Professor Zutnik responded. "It was the face of Satan."

"Satan?" Margaret was puzzled.

"Yes, Margaret," Professor Zutnik responded. "Satan." He leaned back in his chair. "Of course, that sent the Iranians over the edge because they felt that the depiction violated their various trademarks and copyrights relating to their 'America is the Great Satan' line of shirts, caps and protest banners. So once again the unruly Iranian players had to be escorted out of the room by the security guards."

"Were any of the other industrial democracies given a banner?" Margaret asked.

"Of course," Professor Zutnik replied. "France had a banner with terms such as 'condescending', 'rude' and 'immoral' whereas Great Britain had a banner which included words such as 'toothy', 'pretentious' and 'bigoted.'"

"So how are these derogatory banners supposed to foster a sense of shared identity or team building?" Margaret asked.

"Well, Margaret, the point is to foster a sense of identity with the BRICS countries by denigrating the United States and its allies. In other words, they are trying to build a consensus by fanning a shared hostility towards the United States and its allies."

"But that seems to be a very fragile thread with which to create an economic alliance," Margaret observed.

"True," Professor Zutnik replied, ordering another drink. "But the ringleaders of BRICS—particularly Russia and China— are going to take every opportunity they can to cast the industrial democracies as the enemy of the developing world in the hopes that they can expand their own influence throughout the global system."

"Did anyone actually pin a ribbon on the face of Satan?" Margaret asked.

"No," Professor Zutnik answered. "After the Iranians threw such a stink, nobody really wanted to take a turn and risk years of intellectual property litigation with the Iranian government by accidentally pinning a ribbon on the face of the devil." He thought for a moment. "Plus, who wants to have to worry about checking their brake lines every morning for the rest of their life?"

"That is a legitimate concern," Margaret agreed.

"No doubt," Ken added. "Besides, who *really* wants to play such a childish game in the first place?" he asked no one in particular.

Margaret nodded, deciding that it was time to move on with the broadcast. "But there was also time for levity and entertainment on the second day of the BRICS summit," she continued as another video started. "The evening culminated with a formal dinner for all of the attendees, followed by a talent show featuring performers from each of the BRICS nations. The highlight of the show was this jaw-dropping feat by the Chinese national gymnastics team." The camera followed a group of Chinese acrobats as they climbed on top of each other to form a gigantic human fist with the middle finger protruding upward.

"Margaret, are those Chinese acrobats giving the world the finger?" Ken asked, suddenly interested.

"It appears so, Ken," Margaret said. "But this would not be a big surprise as President Xi believes that China should be the leading hegemonic power in the global system. Some commentators have said that China's bullying actions towards neighboring countries, such as India, Vietnam and the Philippines, reflect a chauvinism bordering on pathological arrogance. As a result, this use of acrobats to flip off the rest of the world is very telling."

"You certainly don't see that in most gymnastic competitions," Professor Zutnik observed, having taken delivery of another fireball minus the combustible top.

A telephone rang. Margaret looked down at her feet and saw that a special guest was calling her. She retrieved her phone and answered it. "Hello?" she said, smiling. "Oh, Mrs. Roberts, it is *so* nice to hear from you!" she answered, obviously delighted to receive the call.

"Is that my mother on the phone?" Ken asked fearfully, looking as though he were about to be led off to the electric chair.

"It is, Ken!" Margaret said happily.

"Margaret, we are in the middle of a broadcast," Ken whispered between clenched teeth. "Tell Mother I will call her back," he demanded.

"Ken, she called me," Margaret said firmly. "This is my phone," she added, holding it up to demonstrate that the call did indeed come in on her phone.

"You need to hang up," Ken demanded, exercising his privilege as an alpha male.

"No, I don't," Margaret said, ignoring Ken's privilege as an alpha male. "Ken, you may not realize it, but your mother's phone call with us at the BRICS Gala Affair was the highest rated segment of the broadcast. The producers told her to call back anytime she wanted." She smiled at him. "They said she was 'broadcasting gold.'"

The color drained from Ken's face.

"Oops, sorry!" Margaret said, not sounding very contrite. "I accidentally hit the speaker button."

"Hi, Ken," Ken's mother said, her voice carrying across the set. "I haven't heard from you in over a week. Have you been sick?"

Ken steadied himself. "No, Mother, not at all. We have been very busy preparing for our broadcast from Honolulu to cover the BRICS annual summit—"

"Hawaii is such a romantic place," Mrs. Roberts pointed

out. "By the way, were you planning to take Margaret out to a nice dinner?"

"Yes, Ken," Margaret interrupted in a demure tone, obviously enjoying Ken's plight. "Were you planning to take me out to dinner?"

Ken appeared totally flustered as he fumbled for words. "Well, we have been very busy," he stammered.

"Ken, you still have to eat," Mrs. Roberts pointed out. "Otherwise, you will die of starvation, and I will never get any grandchildren." She sighed. "Surely you could spend an hour taking that beautiful woman out to a fancy restaurant."

"Oh, that is so sweet of you to say, Mrs. Roberts!" Margaret said, blushing and smiling at the same time. "I really like her," she whispered, turning to Ken. "She is so adorable!"

"But I'm allergic to feathers, Mother," Ken said lamely, as Margaret's left wing hit him on the back of the head again.

"You'll be fine, Ken," Mrs. Roberts declared. "It's not like I'm asking you to storm the beaches at Normandy," she said.

"I *am* able to take these feathers off, Ken," Margaret pointed out just in case Ken had mistakenly thought that they had been fused to her shoulders. "Eloise just has to unlock the harness," she pointed out.

Ken's mother cleared her throat. "Margaret, I know Ken can be a bit lacking in the self-starting department," Mrs. Roberts explained. "So I have booked a dinner for the two of you at the Waikiki Beachside Restaurant for this evening. They have my credit card so everything has already been taken care of—"

"That is so nice of you, Mrs. Roberts," Margaret said, clearly enjoying watching Ken moving his lips without making any sounds. "We will have a very nice time." She nudged Ken. "Right, Ken?" she said, smiling.

"Oh, yes," Ken said finally, feeling as though he has been run over by a column of German tanks. "Well, thank you, Mother," he managed. "That is a very thoughtful gesture," he added with what little sincerity he could muster.

"So very thoughtful," Margaret agreed, smiling. "It will be the highlight of our trip to Hawaii," she said.

"Ken, quit slouching!" his mother snapped as her son seemed to be sinking into his seat. "You need to sit up straight."

"Yes, Mother," Ken said, sitting up.

"By the way, Ken," his mother said. "Did your producers tell you that they want to have the two of us host a reality show together?"

Ken felt the floor shifting underneath his feet and the desk spinning around in circles. "I did not know that," he muttered finally, specks of light dancing before his eyes. "What a surprise!" he croaked, trying to manage a smile that would not have looked out of place on a mannequin.

"I was very surprised," Ken's mother continued as Margaret covered her mouth with her hand. "They said that the audience enjoyed our banter during the BRICS gala event so much that they wanted to pair us together on a television show."

"Oh, gosh," Ken said weakly, pulling the straw out of his drink and downing it in a single gulp. He then reached over and grabbed Professor Zutnik's fireball and finished it off without taking a breath. Margaret lifted her glass of white wine out of reach before Ken was able to snatch it.

"Tell us about the format for the show, Mrs. Roberts," Margaret said, clearly enjoying herself as her left wing swung forward and bumped Ken on the head again.

"Thank you, dear," Mrs. Roberts said. "From what the producers told me, they would like to do a show in which I, as Ken's mother, am able to provide him with advice on how to handle every issue or situation that arises in his life. In other words, I would share my wisdom with him to help guide him through the many problems and dilemmas that he must confront on a daily basis."

"That sounds wonderful!" Margaret said. "I am so happy for you!"

"Thank you, dear," Mrs. Roberts replied. "The producers are still discussing several possible formats but the one I like best is where I follow Ken around day and night constantly telling him what to do."

"I vote for that format," Margaret said excitedly, raising her hand in the air.

"I agree, Margaret," Mrs. Roberts said. "I don't know how else I would be able to provide continuous guidance to Ken if I am not around him 24 hours a day." She was silent for a moment. "I guess I will have to move in with him," she said finally. "But he has a big house so that should not be a problem," she added. "There are enough additional bedrooms for the film crew," she pointed out.

Margaret noticed that Ken seemed to be slipping into a catatonic state so she decided that it was time to move on with the broadcast. "Well, Mrs. Roberts, it was lovely speaking with you again," Margaret said as Ken continued to stare straight into the camera like the proverbial deer gazing into oncoming headlights. "Ken and I will both look forward to that wonderful dinner tonight. But we do have to move along so I am sorry but I will have to say goodbye for now."

"Oh, I understand, dear," Mrs. Roberts said. "The show must go on! Goodbye, Margaret," she added. "And break a leg!"

"Goodbye, Mrs. Roberts," Margaret said. She turned back toward the camera. "That was so nice hearing from your mother, Ken," Margaret said to Ken, who was still staring blankly into the camera. "Ken?" Margaret shook his arm. "Ken?" No response. "Ken?" She turned to the camera. "My colleague is a little under the weather," she said hurriedly to the viewing audience. Margaret motioned to Bobby who came over and wheeled the still-motionless Ken and his chair off of the set. Margaret watched Bobby roll her colleague out of the bar to what she presumed was either the hotel doctor or his bedroom suite. "I am sure Ken will be fine," she told the viewing audience, hoping that he would shake off his coma before dinner.

"I hope so," Professor Zutnik said, ordering another fireball with the enhanced 'flaming crown'.

"That brings us to the closing event of the BRICS summit," Margaret announced. "Today's *State of the BRICS* organization speech is being given by the President of South Africa, Cyril Ramaphosa. Each year a different head of state is tasked with the job of providing an update on the various matters affecting the BRICS organization. This year it fell to the South African president to offer his comments about BRICS and its prospects for the future. For more on this story, we now switch to our roving correspondent, Alex Marvelll."

"Hello, Margaret," Alex said, standing in an enormous room as the voice of the South African president could be heard in the background amidst the chatter of several thousand persons in the audience. Alex looked closer at the *Comings and Goings* ensemble. "Nice to see you as well, Professor Zutnik," he added. Professor Zutnik grunted amidst a long slurp on his straw. "Where's Ken?" he asked, after noticing that there were only two people on the set.

"Oh, I'm afraid he wasn't feeling very well," Margaret said.

"Well, I hope he gets better soon," Alex said good-naturedly. The camera pulled back from Alex's face to reveal him wearing a yellow t-shirt over his long sleeve dress shirt The t-shirt was emblazoned with the motto 'Death to Iran' over an outline of the country of Iran.

"Alex, what are you wearing?" Margaret asked warily.

"Oh, it's the funniest thing," Alex said. "Both Iran and Ethiopia have been sniping at each other all day," he said. "They both have stands set up outside the building and are selling t-shirts. The Ethiopians are selling 'Death to Iran' t-shirts and the Iranians are selling 'Death to Ethiopia' t-shirts." He held up a bright red t-shirt featuring yellow and black letters that said, 'Death to Ethiopia'. "Pretty cool, huh?"

"I hope this doesn't get out of hand," Margaret said cautiously.

Alex looked around at the people milling around the cavernous room. "I think everyone else is ignoring this little spat between Iran and Ethiopia," he said.

"Is anyone still selling 'Death to America' t-shirts?" Professor Zutnik wanted to know.

"The Iranians still have several racks of 'Death to America' t-shirts available but I don't think that they are very popular any-more," Alex said. "I didn't see anyone buy one today. Frankly, they looked old and faded," he added. "I don't think there is much of a market for them anymore. After all, Iran has been selling them for decades to protestors so that they could be used for staged spontaneous embassy takeovers. There are only so many 'Death to America' t-shirts that anyone is going to want for their wardrobe."

"Quite right," Professor Zutnik agreed.

"So, Alex," Margaret began. "I see the President of South Africa is still giving his speech behind you. Can you tell us some of the highlights so far?"

"Sure," Alex said. He retrieved a small notebook from his back pocket and flipped through the pages. "After offering the usual pleasantries in his opening remarks and thanking everyone for coming to the summit, President Ramaphosa then proceeded to talk in general terms about the expansion of BRICS as illus-trated by the admission of four new members—Iran, Ethiopia, Egypt and the United Arab Emirates or UAE. He also pointed out that a number of other countries have made inquiries about joining BRICS—"

"Are they going to change the name of BRICS by adding the first letter of the name of each of these four new members?" Margaret asked.

Alex shook his head. "I have not heard about any proposals to change the name of BRICS. I think it could become increas-ingly unwieldy as more nations join the ranks." He thought for a moment. I guess you could add the 'I' for Iran, the 'Es' for Egypt and Ethiopia and the 'U' for United Arab Emirates," he ventured.

"But I am not sure what sort of acronym that you would get." He thought for a moment. "You could do 'BRICISEEU' (brik-eye-see-u), for example, but I don't see how that helps the brand recognition of the organization." He suddenly looked alarmed. "Wait a second!" he said, pulling off his bespoke 'Death to Iran' Ethiopian garment and stuffing it in his pants pocket. "I see a few of the Iranians coming this way," he whispered. "No need to create an international incident" he added, as a group of individuals who appeared to be Iranians wearing 'Death to Ethiopia' t-shirts passed by in front of him.

"That was close," Alex said, relieved. "Getting back to President Ramaphosa's speech, the tone has been upbeat and optimistic. He has described BRICS and the New Development Bank as an ascending force in the global economic system, and, not surprisingly, has also taken a few shots at the United States and both the IMF and the World Bank. He seems to want to convey the idea that BRICS is the shiny new object on the world stage and that the American-dominated multilateral financial institutions, such as the IMF and the World Bank, are sclerotic and harmful to the interests of developing countries." He turned toward the stage. "President Ramaphosa is now talking about the evolution of the New Development Bank from little more than a concept in 2015 to a significant multilateral development bank in a single decade."

The camera focused on President Ramaphosa as he wiped his brow with his handkerchief. "I am pleased to tell you that we have seen the NDB grow to become one of the leading emerging markets and developing country, or EMDC, lenders that is actually owned and controlled by these very same types of countries—"

A hand shot up in the first row. "President Ramaphosa, would you consider China to be a developing country?"

President Ramaphosa was surprised at the interruption. "Sir," he said, "I am giving an address right now. This is not a question-and-answer period—"

"I understand, Mr. President," the voice responded. "But it is a simple 'yes' or 'no' question. Is it appropriate for China, which currently boasts the world's second largest economy, to call itself a developing country?"

"I believe that is how China refers to itself," President Ramaphosa said, irritated. "You would have to ask the Chinese representatives themselves." He nodded to one side and two security guards began moving toward the outstretched hand which suddenly began moving in the opposite direction and then dashed out a side door with the two guards in hot pursuit.

"My apologies for the disruption," President Ramaphosa said. "The New Development Bank will continue to expand over time. We now have nine members, including four new nations: Egypt, Iran, Ethiopia—"

"Death to Ethiopia!" yelled a voice in the audience. A hand waved a red t-shirt in the air like a towel.

President Ramaphosa raised his arms. "Please be quiet," he implored, "I am trying to talk!"

Two yellow t-shirts popped up several aisles away. "Death to Iran!" two voices shouted.

President Ramaphosa waved his hands and shouted for quiet as dozens and dozens of yellow and red t-shirts began twirling in the air amidst calls for the deaths of Iran and Ethiopia, respectively. President Ramaphosa turned the volume setting on the microphone up as high as it would go. "I see I may be running out of time," he shouted hurriedly. "Suffice it to say, that BRICS has authorized loans for nearly 100 infrastructure projects, including the construction of thousands of kilometers of roads, hundreds of bridges, tens of thousands of housing units and hundreds of kilometers of water infrastructure conduits throughout the developing world. Moreover, I am proud to say that the BRICS organization—" President Ramaphosa ducked his head as a balled-up red 'Death to Ethiopia' t-shirt sailed by his ear "—now includes more than a third of the world's land surface, more than forty percent of the world's population and more than a quarter of the world's gross domestic product." More and more red and yellow t-shirts flew back and forth among the audience along with a variety of umbrellas, briefcases, hats, plastic cups and soda cans, amidst mounting calls of death to Iran, death to Ethiopia and death to several other countries that had previously been left out of the discussion.

President Ramaphosa ducked his head as two more yellow t-shirts bounced off the front of his lectern. "In conclusion, I would like to thank you all for attending the annual BRICS summit and welcoming our new members into the BRICS organization. We look forward to a bright and prosperous future for all of our members. As the Hawaiians say, '*Aloho po*' or 'Good night.'" President Ramaphosa scrambled off the stage but was still winged by a well-placed leather shoe before disappearing down a hallway. The room was a blur of red and yellow as the t-shirts continued to fly back and forth across the screen as various audience members screamed at each other.

The camera focused back on Alex who was then smacked on the side of his head by a yellow t-shirt. "Well, things seem to be getting a little out of hand in the assembly hall," he said. "President Ramaphosa offered a very abbreviated address regarding the State of the BRICS organization, but he did the best he could, given the chaos that is now taking place behind me." Another yellow t-shirt hit Alex in the face. "Well, it's still a little messy down here, Margaret, so let's go back to you."

The screen switched back to the hotel bar where Margaret was finishing another glass of white wine and Professor Zutnik was sipping yet another flaming fireball. "Thank you, Alex," Margaret said, nervously watching a giggling Professor Zutnik as he blew into the straw and watched several flaming bubbles rise into the air before popping. "Well, we have reached the end of our coverage of the BRICS summit from Honolulu, Hawaii. We have learned a great deal about the BRICS organization and the New Development Bank and their current operations. The BRICS countries seem to believe that their organization will become an increasingly important multilateral development bank in the international arena. Whether the dominant position of the IMF and the World Bank is challenged by the BRICS countries in the future remains to be seen. Anyways, it has been my pleasure to work with Ken Roberts who is resting comfortably, Professor Zutnik who is enjoying his blazing beverage, our roving correspondent Alex Marvelll and our entire news crew. This is Margaret Hill signing off for *Comings and Goings*. Thank you for joining us this evening."

PART SIX

WILL BRICS
SUCCEED OR FAIL?

CHAPTER 9

THE PROS AND CONS OF BRICS

Some people believe that BRICS is little more than a loud-mouthed, teen-aged multilateral organization that periodically throws tantrums about the unfairness of the American-dominated global economic system. However, BRICS, along with its New Development Bank (NDB), has managed to carve out a role for itself in the international realm as an important source of development funds for emerging countries. In doing so, it has gradually muted some of its criticisms of the global order as it has become part of that very same financial system.

BRICS was reportedly born in an outburst of both unbridled enthusiasm and the overconsumption of vodka in the Rasputin tavern in Yekaterinburg, Russia (the "jewel of the Urals") in June 2009 as described in the Prologue. Although some historians claim that this festive meeting was the culmination of several prior years of negotiations among the four nations, it appears that the gathering in the tavern constituted the first formal summit between the nations. The napkin that that was initialed by President Medvedev of Russia, President Hu of China, President da Silva of Brazil and President Singh of India is a treasured document that would rival the Constitution of the United States or England's Magna Carta in historical importance except for the fact that it was used to by President Singh to blow his nose and was then discarded along with the other trash on the table when it was cleared by the busser.

Fortunately for posterity, President Medvedev, President Hu, President da Silva and President Singh met at a Famway Trade Show in New York later that year to sample the new Famway organic line of lard-based body lotions and hydrochloric acid-laced skin exfoliants and to sign a new BRIC napkin *sans* President Singh's nose mucus. This priceless document was then placed in a bulletproof glass case and is currently on display in the lobby of the Famway headquarters in Bentonville, Arkansas.

The hermetically sealed BRICS napkin is an inspiring example of the sorts of things that can be achieved when well-meaning people come together to create a new type of global institution while consuming enormous quantities of alcohol. However, opinions vary as to whether the BRICS organization can be considered an unbridled success, an unmitigated disaster or something in between the two extremes. As BRICS and the NDB are comparatively young as far as multilateral institutions are concerned, their more vocal defenders can argue with some justification that they are still experiencing growing pains and that it will take some time for them to catch up with the IMF and the World Bank, which are seen as being like the grouchy old neighbor who tells all of the children to get off of his lawn.

As with any multilateral organization, there are several pros and cons to BRICS. The positive attributes are not so great to ensure that BRICS will dislodge the IMF from its perch atop the global financial system anytime soon. However, its negative features are not so severe as to suggest that BRICS will collapse into a heap of newly-printed rubles, renminbis, rupees and reals. The truth, as with most things, is probably somewhere in the middle of the spectrum. The prognosticators who offer their opinions about the future of BRICS will probably see some of their predictions come true and others fall by the wayside. Many of them will declare the infallibility of all of the predictions that were remotely accurate and conveniently forget about all of the predictions that went awry. In any event, it is important to list several of the positive and negative features of BRICS and leave it to individual readers to consider the good and the bad, and make up their own minds about the prospects for BRICS and the NDB.

FOUR PROS OF BRICS

FIRST PRO: BIG POPULATIONS AND BIG ECONOMIES

The reason most commonly given in support of BRICS and its future prospects—by those who concern themselves with BRICS minutiae and collect trading cards featuring various BRICS bank officers—is the sheer size of its individual members. After all, China boasts the world's second largest economy and India has recently become the world's most populous country. Russia claims the world's largest landmass—even though much of its economic heft arises from the sales of commodities ranging from diamonds and gold to oil and wheat. Brazil is a rapidly developing regional superpower in South America and South Africa is, well, a country at the southern tip of the African continent where numerous hungry sharks wait for beefy tourists to swim out too far from shore.

When combined with the newest members of BRICS, which include Iran (which offers the widest variety of 'Death to Ethiopia' clothing), Ethiopia (which offers the widest selection of 'Death to Iran' clothing), Egypt (which has yet to release its own line of 'Death to [Pick A Country]' t-shirts and caps), and the United Arab Emirates (which has so much oil that it does not need to sell a line of 'Death' clothing at all), BRICS members can claim a population in excess of 3.2 billion people and more than quarter of the world's land mass and economic output.

One way to appreciate the enormity of the population of the BRICS membership is to imagine how many times 3.2 billion persons could encircle the earth if they were lined up shoulder-to-shoulder. If the circumference of the earth is 40,075 kilometers, then we could comfortably fit one person per meter or 1,000 people per kilometer. Even though some participants might find themselves shifting forward or backward a few inches here and there to get away from an adjacent participant with flatulence or diarrhea, we would still have around 1,000,000 people for every 1,000 kilometers which means that it would take approximately 40,750,000 people to span the circumference of the earth. Perfectionists who insisted on lining up all 3.2 billion people would find that these people could collectively encircle the earth at least 78 times.

Carrying out such an undertaking would pose huge logistical issues because those individuals who had to position themselves in various rivers, lakes and oceans around the world, for example, might have to tread water for weeks on end before everyone managed to get into place so that a truly accurate count could be completed. Then there would be the added complications of shark attacks, drownings, hypothermia, tidal waves, hurricanes, and jelly fish stings that would cull the number of participants, thereby necessitating that replacements be dropped in on short notice so that the integrity of this worldwide human chain could be maintained.

The BRICS countries also claim some of the largest and most dynamic economies in the world with an estimated total gross domestic product in 2023 of $25.7 trillion. China is, of course, the heavyweight of BRICS with its gross domestic product of $17.6 trillion, accounting for nearly 70 percent of the BRICS output in 2023. Although China's share of the BRICS economy may decrease somewhat with the addition of Iran, Egypt, Ethiopia and the United Arab Emirates as new members, the drop is not likely to be significant.

Of greater import would be the entry of Saudi Arabia, the world's leading oil producer, which has been offered membership in BRICS. However, the Kingdom has been somewhat cagey in its acceptance as it appears to be concerned that a full-throated endorsement of BRICS might endanger its economic and military ties to Europe and the United States. Estimates vary widely regarding how best to calculate the GDP of Saudi Arabia with the much-beloved IMF suggesting a range between $1.1 trillion to $2.1 trillion, depending on the type of metric being used. If Saudi Arabia decides to formalize its membership in BRICS, however, then it would add a GDP that is similar to that of Russia's $2.0 trillion GDP. Although not a game-changer in absolute terms with respect to the IMF and the World Bank, an active Saudi presence in BRICS would boost the organization's profile even further and perhaps convince other countries—particularly other oil-producing countries—to consider joining BRICS. It would also remind the world that the BRICS constituency (referred to as BRICS+ by those who do not want to try to create a more inclusive acronym that could ultimately consist of twenty, thirty or even more letters) consists of two of the three largest oil producing countries in the world—a geopolitical boost that will be significant for the foreseeable future due to the ongoing dependency of the world on hydrocarbons. No matter how much people may wish that the world's energy demands could be met with windmills, solar panels and fairy dust, it appears that oil will be the lubricant of the global economy for decades to come.

Anyways, the point is that the BRICS nations have to be taken seriously if only due to the sheer size of both their constituent populations and their economies. Even though China and India have spirited disagreements with each other and lob artillery shells across their shared border every so often, these intermittent skirmishes do not appear to be severe enough or frequent enough to cause the BRICS membership to splinter. On the other hand, China's ongoing rivalry with India could lead to other flashpoints in the future and embroil Russia in on-going no-win disputes in which it is required to favor one country over the other. For the time being, however, the members of BRICS have managed to maintain at least the façade of having a shared purpose and sense of unity as well as an ongoing excuse to go to swanky summits each year without having to take their spouses.

PRO TWO: NEW BRICS MEMBERS GET TO HANG OUT WITH RUSSIA AND CHINA

China and Russia did not start BRICS and the NDB as a purely altruistic endeavor because they do not have much of a record of unbridled philanthropy in the modern era. Indeed, Russia and China are far better known for their numerous exercises in reverse philanthropy in countries such as Tibet, Vietnam, Mongolia, Ukraine, Poland, Czechoslovakia, Finland, and Georgia. The unfortunate recipients of this charitable largesse were invaded by either one or the other of the afore-mentioned reverse philanthropists and, in many cases, plundered and pillaged. These exercises in reverse philanthropy were also invariably accompanied by enormous numbers of civilian deaths and injuries, which some hand-wringing critics (who were not well-versed in the benefits conferred by reverse philanthropy on recipient countries) have harshly characterized as "war crimes."

The marketing of BRICS by its founding members was tricky because neither Russia nor China are viewed as particularly warm or friendly countries by the rest of the world. After all, you can only get so much mileage from vilifying the United States over and over again—which is not unlike hitting an obliterated pinata hundreds of times long after it has given up its last piece of candy. China, in particular, despite the spectacular growth of both its economy and its arrogance over the past four decades, has found it most helpful to portray itself as a developing country that wants to lend a helping hand to other emerging countries. However, this is not the no-strings type of assistance that one might expect from a charity run by Mother Theresa because there are subtle expectations that new members will support, at least tacitly, many of the initiatives dear to China and Russia.

BRICS is first and foremost an organization that exists to promote the economic and political objectives of its founders. Although the administrative structure of BRICS is somewhat skeletal when compared to the enormous bureaucracy that has been dutifully constructed at the IMF and the World Bank over the past eighty years, it still boasts enough staffers who can reach out to other developing countries and offer touching stories about the benevolence of Russia and China and their affinity for those developing countries that they have not previously attacked or occupied. Indeed, BRICS is particularly adept at engaging in sympathetic discussions with emerging countries—many of which see their own governments overthrown on a regular basis—because its NDB is a comparatively new player in the global financial system and can be portrayed by BRICS itself as the anti-IMF and the anti-World Bank. This portrayal is rather disingenuous because the NDB—like every other multilateral development bank—is able to carry out its business only because it operates in a neo-liberal global arena that has been sustained in large part by the United States since 1945.

But Russia and China are also able to point to the growing concern many countries have expressed about the preeminence of the American dollar in world trade. A number of countries around the world have become wary of relying on American dollars because it gives the United States an inordinate amount of influence over the global banking system. Why? The pervasiveness of the American dollar enables the United States to be the banker of the world and essentially skirt many of the financial constraints that are faced by every other country. It can print almost unlimited quantities of dollars without suffering a catastrophic currency devaluation. In addition, the United States enjoys lower borrowing costs and can thus service a greater amount of debt due to the dollar's status as a reserve currency.

The dollar has been the most widely-held currency since the end of World War II and still accounts for nearly three-fifths of all foreign exchange reserves. Even though the ubiquity of the dollar has declined somewhat in recent years, it is still far more common than the Euro—which makes up about one-fifth of all foreign reserves. Although the Chinese renminbi now accounts for about three percent of all foreign exchange reserves, it is unlikely to pose a challenge to the primacy of the dollar anytime soon. Most central banks are not yet falling over themselves to increase their renminbi reserves, due in large part to concerns about China's lack of transparency in its financial dealings as well as its continuing lack of enthusiasm for the rule of law and the property rights of certain disfavored individuals and organizations.

Indeed, much of the increase in the holdings of Chinese renminbi by other countries in recent years is due to China's increasing trade with other BRICS members such as Russia and India. Russia's foreign exchange reserves, for example, are now almost exclusively denominated in Chinese renminbi. This startling development occurred due to Russia's growing reliance on China as its primary export market after sanctions were imposed by the United States and Europe in response to Russia's invasion of Ukraine. These actions effectively froze Russia out of the global banking system and cut off many of its most lucrative export markets.

China's foreign exchange reserves are far more diverse than those of Russia, but its holdings of American dollars have declined in real terms by almost half in the past decade—from about $1.3 trillion in 2013 to about $750 billion in 2024. China's flagging enthusiasm for dollars has been fueled by its desire to reduce its vulnerability to the vagaries of American politics. It also wants to encourage its fellow BRICS members to increase their use of the Chinese renminbi and, as a result, reduce their dependence on American dollars. China's reduction in its foreign reserve holdings of dollars is also due to its fear of being sanctioned if it should take actions that would arouse the ire of the United States, such as launching a full-scale invasion of Taiwan or even revealing that kung pao chicken is really made of mystery meat created in its Wuhan laboratories.

Although these sanctions initially caused the Russian economy to contract, it also prompted Russia to look southward to China and India for other ways to circumvent the sanctions and expand the markets for its products—particularly oil and gas. The Chinese, in particular, were happy to help their fellow reverse philanthropist weather the storm of being a global outcast by purchasing Russian oil and natural gas at deeply discounted prices. However, the Chinese have also been careful not to antagonize their biggest trading partners in Europe and North America. After all, the Chinese economy is far more dependent on exports than the Russian economy, which gives Moscow greater discretion to send a column of tanks crashing across a border if President Putin is having a bad day.

The use of the American dollar as a reserve currency arose not from any general affection felt by other countries towards the design of the currency or its generous use of green and black inks or even its quirky rectangular shape. The dollar became the leading reserve currency because the rest of the world fortuitously lay in ruins in 1945 and there was no other country that possessed the economic wherewithal to support an alternative to the dollar. As the dollar was the only game in town, other countries had no choice but to stock up on dollars so that they could participate in international trade. Although China and Russia are the most vocal proponents of de-dollarization today, the dollar continues to be the most common currency for carrying out international transactions because it is so widely accepted. Most of the world's currencies are in far less demand and must often be converted into American dollars before a trade can take place.

If Utrecht-Lorraine wished to purchase 1,000 croquet sets from the Limey Gaming Company in Great Britain, for example, it might offer to pay for the order using its own national currency—the vaunted *fleg*. But no matter how colorful the currency or how skillfully the portraits of Prince Freddy have been retouched, the croquet company will probably refuse to accept the *flegs* as payment. Why? Because the country of Utrecht-Lorraine is so tiny and its financial reach so limited that its currency is simply not used by very many other countries. As a result, the Limey

Gaming Company will probably insist that Utrecht-Lorraine pay for its order with either British pounds or American dollars. As a result, Prince Freddy would have to go to the vault at the palace and either dig up enough dollars to send to the company or sell off some assets such as the gold royal toe rings to get the dollars needed to pay for the croquet sets.

The problems faced by Utrecht-Lorraine if it tries to use *flegs* to purchase foreign goods is familiar to many other developing countries whose currencies are in about as much demand as the bubonic plague. Many of these countries have comparatively puny exports and are thus unable to earn a great deal of foreign exchange—which would be needed to purchase goods from other nations such as United States, Germany and Japan. As a result, these countries have no choice but to acquire currencies such as the dollar so that they can purchase highly desired products such as croquet sets.

PRO THREE: BRICS MEMBERS GET TO USE THEIR OWN CURRENCIES (SORT OF)

A valuable perk that comes with joining BRICS—aside from being able to purchase discounted handbags and coffee mugs at the BRICS gift shop in Shanghai, China—is that member countries can engage in trade with each other and use their own currencies to fund these exchanges. Or at least that is what some of the shiny brochures in the vaunted BRICS swag bags promise to prospective members who are invited to join the BRICS organization. The reality is somewhat different due to the structure of BRICS and the extent to which the currencies of the individual members are used in international trade.

The idea that BRICS members would be able to use their own currencies in trading with other BRICS members is very appealing. However, the hard truth is that it is not always possible for the smaller BRICS members to use their own currencies for their own trades. Part of the problem stems from the same lack of demand that Utrecht-Lorraine must deal with in trying to acquire world class croquet products with the thinly traded *fleg*.

However, another obstacle to the widespread use of the more tertiary currencies of BRICS members, such as Egypt, Iran or Ethiopia, is that reverse philanthropic streak that pervades the worldview of both China and Russia. They did not establish BRICS just to be nice to everyone else because they could have simply stayed in the IMF and the World Bank and periodically sent fruit baskets and fluffy baby kittens to the other members as good will gestures. Indeed, China and Russia believed that BRICS could be used to serve their own interests and enable them to increase both the sales of their products and the use of their currencies around the world.

BRICS was set up by Russia and China to reach out to other countries who believed, rightly or wrongly, that they were not being sufficiently coddled by the IMF and the World Bank. As such, BRICS was always viewed by its founding members as a vehicle for pushing back against the American monopoly on global finance and, if possible, weakening the grip of the United States on the global trading system.

The added benefit to steadily increasing the membership rolls of BRICS is that it brings more countries into the fold that can purchase China's goods and services and transact business using China's own currency (instead of the hated dollar) as the quasi-reserve currency for BRICS. This arrangement may or may not be an improvement for developing countries. Even if only a fraction of their trades with China are carried out in their own currencies—which include the celebrated Egyptian pound, the less-celebrated Ethiopian *birr* (not to be confused with the sand burr weed that has tormented barefooted pedestrians for untold centuries), and the seldom-celebrated Iranian *rial* (which is among the least desirable currencies in the world)—then they would not always have to purchase dollars to carry out their trades. China would have to recycle the currencies of these countries elsewhere, but it would be able to insist that most of its trades with other BRICS members be carried out using the *renminbi*. This arrangement would enable the new BRICS members to use their own currencies for some of their transactions while also tying them more tightly into a China-centered financial system which is not unlike being strangled by a python.

Unfortunately for many of these newer members, their currencies are not going to be used very often because they are almost worthless. The Egyptian pound, which we might associate (erroneously) with the British pound that financed the expansion of a worldwide global empire for three centuries, is worth only about 2 cents. If you have $20,000 in American dollars tucked away in your upscale mud hut along the Nile River, then you would be a millionaire in terms of Egyptian pounds. Similarly, if you are a cattle merchant in Ethiopia and have managed to earn $8,000 in American dollars from the recent sale of several head of cattle to an ambivalent vegetarian cult, then you could convert your money to Ethiopian *birrs* and enjoy your newfound status as a "birrillionaire." Unfortunately, you may not find very many people who want to sell things to you for newly-printed *birrs* as they will generally prefer those dollars that you just gave up.

The Iranian *rial* takes the concept of marginal currencies to an entirely new level. A teen-ager who managed to accumulate $100 in American dollars by doing odd jobs such as cleaning the graffiti off the billboard portraits of the supreme leader of the nation would be a multi-millionaire in Iran with about 4,200,000 *rials*. Because the Iranian government has done such an outstanding job running the economy into the ground in recent years, the Iranian *rial* is worth so little that it has become an all-purpose currency that can be used for everything from lining bird cages and wrapping gifts to blowing noses and diapering babies. The one bright spot to having such a worthless currency is that almost everyone in Iran is a "rial millionaire"—which reflects an enormous achievement in paper wealth-building that has seldom been experienced before in the modern era. The other advantage is that you can be robbed of a briefcase stuffed with *rials* while on your way home and not lose much more than the funds needed to go purchase a cup of coffee at the local *qahve khaneh*.

In short, BRICS may offer these countries opportunities to engage in trade with their fellow BRICS members but it is unlikely that they will be able to use their own currencies to fund most of these transactions. They will instead find that their trades with other BRICS members will most likely be carried out using Chinese *renminbis*. After all, China is the dominant member of BRICS and wants to encourage the use of its currency in as many intra-organizational trades as possible. But it will have to throw an occasional bone to its fellow members—particularly the ones with the more marginal economies—and allow them to use their own currencies every so often in order to keep the peace within the organization.

PRO FOUR: BRICS MEMBERSHIP MAY OFFER GREATER POLITICAL INFLUENCE

When Brazil, Russia, India and China went to the trouble to set up BRICS, they did so with the idea of combining together in order to exercise correspondingly greater influence in the global arena. After all, the world had heard Russia and China whine and complain about how the United States controlled the international financial system for years and years. Yet their combined economic heft was never enough to effectuate any significant change in the status quo. Indeed, the United States has repeatedly rejected their calls that the IMF and the World Bank be radically reformed to ensure a more "democratic" representation of the global community which, in most cases, would have meant transferring enough power to China and Russia to allow them to become first-rate wrecking ball troublemakers. Although there have been various proposals to alter the voting quotas held by the nations of the IMF in favor of developing nations, the issue has been contentious and remains unresolved. After all, nobody ever wants to give up their power and privileges voluntarily—even a teeny tiny bit. Indeed, it is possible that the countries who control the IMF and the World Bank might now point to BRICS and some of its sister multilateral development organizations and say that any disgruntled IMF or World Bank members can take their marbles elsewhere. In the diplomatic world, this is known as telling another country "to go pound sand."

If the United States and its traditional allies essentially

scuttled any further talk about "democratizing" the IMF and the World Bank, then BRICS could become even more appealing to other countries. However, it is not clear that poorer countries such as Ethiopia or Egypt are going to have much more of a voice in BRICS due to the stranglehold maintained by China and, to a lesser extent, the other founding members. Although BRICS has expanded its membership to nine and possibly ten members (if Saudi Arabia ever makes up its mind) and now boasts nearly half of the world's population, it still has 180 or so fewer members than the IMF or the World Bank.

The IMF can fly a lot more flags in front of its headquarters building than BRICS can and, in a way, can claim to be far more inclusive than BRICS. However, BRICS does provide its members with a new platform with which to challenge the prerogatives of the IMF and the World Bank—even though any such actions will have to be approved by China and Russia before they ever see the light of day. Whether the second-tier BRICS members feel that their new social club is more responsive to their interests and needs than the IMF remains to be seen. However, it is probably the case that certain issues about which select members feel very strongly about (e.g., preferring to ride horses instead of hogs in international polo matches) may be received more sympathetically by the membership body in a smaller organization like BRICS.

For newer BRICS members like Ethiopia and Iran, their affiliation with the organization may arguably amplify views that might otherwise not gain much attention or traction in the IMF or World Bank. No doubt it is also easier to deal with a handful of members—even those who tend toward more autocratic or even violent behavior—as opposed to an entire mini-United Nations at the IMF, even if the larger organization is under the benevolent thumb of the United States and the other industrial democracies. As these new BRICS members have only just received their official varsity BRICS jackets and matching caps, however, it is too early to tell if the smaller BRICS organization will be a more satisfactory outlet for them to express their views and grievances.

Finally, membership in BRICS offers its new members another source of developmental funds without requiring them to give up any rights they may currently enjoy as participants in the IMF or the World Bank. As the IMF has developed something of a reputation for engaging in excruciatingly detailed underwriting practices, BRICS is hoping to attract potential borrowers who are a reasonable credit risk—even though they may have a few blemishes on their credit report such as failing to account for missing foreign aid donations or being unable to explain why the head of state's limousine was blown up. However, the BRICS members are also aware that the NDB cannot make loans to every prospective borrower that comes along with their hand out without engaging in some sort of meaningful review process. Otherwise, the bank would soon go out of business. As a result, the NDB, like the other multilateral development banks, has to follow the same general banking principles as those embraced by the IMF and the World Bank—even though they may like to think of themselves as upstarts who will one day upset the global banking applecart.

THREE CONS OF BRICS

FIRST CON: BRICS MEMBERS HAVE CONFLICTING INTERESTS

If the leaders of countries as diverse as Brazil, Russia, India, China and South Africa were to go into a bar offering unlimited quantities of free drinks, you would not expect to see them emerge a few hours later with their arms locked, singing an uplifting hymn like *How Great Thou Art*. Indeed, we would expect that the leaders of China and India would become involved in a heated argument over the exact location of their common border and perhaps take a few swings at each other. Russia's president would try to intervene to maintain the peace and accidentally get hit in the face before threatening to destroy the world twenty times over. The president of Brazil would show off his BRICS Gold Motor Club membership card to all of the single females sitting at the bar and offer to teach them how to dance the samba while standing naked in his hotel shower stall. At the same time, the president of South Africa would get into an argument with the bartender over the lack of any South African dishes on the food menu such *as hertzoggies, bobotie*, or even *malva pudding*, likening the bar's focus on traditional pub fare such as bangers and mash, fish and chips or beef stew to an insidious form of culinary apartheid.

Even though each of the founding members of BRICS have vastly different cultural, ethnic, political, historical and economic backgrounds, they have managed to find enough common ground to create and operate the BRICS organization. Much of the catalyst for this union is their shared dislike of (if not deep hatred of) the United States and the hegemonic role it plays in the international economy. As such, the glue holding BRICS together is, to some extent, a sort of real-life manifestation of the ancient proverb offered by cross-legged wise men in numerous Academy Award-winning martial arts films, "The enemy of my enemy is my friend." Otherwise, what else would bring together fun-loving Brazil, spiritual India, angry South Africa, dour China and revanchist Russia?

But any reliance on a soundbite from a movie in which the star manages to defeat 50 armed assailants with a few deft karate moves may be unrealistic. As far as the original BRICS members are concerned, their vastly disparate backgrounds as well as the differing positions they currently occupy in the global hierarchy necessarily affect the ways in which they view the United States. In short, Russia and China, both of whom have long had designs on becoming the biggest bully on the block, see the United States as the primary obstacle to their respective dreams of global domination.

If the United States were to disappear tomorrow, however, then Russia and China—who have both declared their undying devotion to each other (at least for the moment)—would immediately turn their attention to each other. China and Russia would both begin to circle each other warily (in a metaphorical sense) while trying to figure out the best way to defeat their former best friend forever. As China and Russia have a centuries-old rivalry that has had its ups and downs and more downs and still more downs, the governments of both countries might expect that armed hostilities will eventually break out between them because they are both very disagreeable nations even on their best days. The only thing that has drawn them together is their mutual desire to supplant the existing global economic hierarchy. Their shared antipathy toward the United States has probably prevented their own disagreements with each other from boiling over into armed conflict. If there was no United States, then their recent affinity for each other would probably revert to the colder, more hostile attitude that prevailed for the past few centuries—prompted in large part by repeated Russian incursions in and, in some cases, annexations of vast swaths of Chinese territory. But Russia is Russia and it has arguably always suffered from an addiction, akin to alcohol or drug addiction, that compels it to invade other countries over and over again—an affliction that appears to have no real cure except for the capitulation by the victim country to Russia.

This hostility towards the United States reflects the zero-sum mindset of both countries. Both China and Russia view themselves as rightful heirs to the hegemonic role played by the United States for the past century. As BRICS was created with the idea of challenging the existing orthodoxy of the global banking system, both China and Russia saw it as an instrument whereby the primacy of the IMF and the World Bank could be challenged.

Brazil, India and South Africa do not necessarily have the same grandiose geopolitical ambitions as their larger and more disgruntled BRICS senior members. Indeed, they all have democratic governments and significant economic ties with the United States. However, all three countries are dominant regional powers in their respective parts of the world. Brazil is certainly the leading continental power of South America, but it lacks

Russia's pathological aggressiveness, having stopped invading its neighbors—such as Uruguay, Paraguay and Argentina—long before the end of the 19th century. As the only founding BRICS member located in the New World, Brazil is far removed from the disagreements and disputes that periodically percolate among Russia, China and India. Moreover, Brazil boasts white sandy beaches frequented by attractive bathers who—if they were to disrobe entirely to demonstrate their support for animal rights— would not necessarily cause any onlookers to turn to stone.

Now the world's most populous nation, India has been engaged in an on-going rivalry with China since the latter country was overrun by the CCP in 1949. In recent years, India has sought closer ties with the United States to deter Chinese aggression as it still resents China for having illegally seized some 38,000 square kilometers of mountainous territory along India's northern frontier during their 1962 border war. Even though China has had ample leisure time to consider India's grievance regarding China's heavy-handed behavior, China's leaders have not been able to find time in their work schedules for the past six decades to discuss the possible return of these territories. More-over, China wants to contain India's ambitions in southeast Asia and views its southern neighbor—which refused to join China's Belt and Road Initiative— as little more than a middling power with great power aspirations. It is also beset by both a declining population and an anemic economic growth rate and fears that the rapidly growing Indian economy could overtake it in the next several decades.

As the only founding member of BRICS that was a year

late in joining the party, South Africa, like Brazil, finds itself geographically isolated from Russia, China and India. However, South Africa boasts one of the most powerful military forces on the African continent and has become increasingly close with China over the past several decades. Indeed, China originally invited South Africa to join the original BRIC organization and, after the approval was given by Brazil, Russia and India, suggested that an "S" be added to the name to reflect South Africa's ascension. China considers South Africa to be the linchpin of its efforts to expand its political influence throughout the African continent. To that end, it has promoted extensive trade relations with South Africa and provided billions of dollars of loans which South Africa will probably have to pay back at some point in the future. Like India and Brazil, South Africa views itself as a regional power and had, prior to the end of apartheid rule in 1994, carried out extensive military operations in neighboring countries, particularly modern-day Namibia and Angola.

Brazil, India and South Africa do not view the United States as a mortal adversary because they do not share the global domination dreams of China and Russia. Instead they regard BRICS as an organization that will provide them with an additional source of capital for infrastructure projects while amplifying their voices on the global stage. Although sympathetic to the original calls by the founders of BRICS to reorganize the global economy, Brazil, India and South Africa want to maintain their current affiliations with the IMF and the World Bank while taking advantage of their positions in BRICS to secure loans and other types of development assistance.

SECOND CON: BRICS IS SIMILAR TO MOST OTHER BANKS

Although the leaders of the original BRICS members have their differences and may get into petty spats that occasionally erupt into military operations against each other, they all view BRICS as an organization that can be used to redress perceived inequities in the international system. Similarly, the NDB is portrayed as a lender that will be more sympathetic to the borrowing needs of developing countries. Whether the NDB is able to transcend the traditional banking model is debatable because it is funded by the capital contributions of the BRICS members and must engage in profitable lending activities in order to stay afloat.

Brazil, Russia, India, China and South Africa, each originally contributed $10 billion to the NDB when it was set up in 2014. They also agreed to make an additional contribution of $10 billion ($2 billion per member) in seven equal installments to the NDB and to be on the hook for another $50 billion of callable capital. In other words, if there were financial shortfalls in the operations of the BRICS organization that could not be met by existing cash reserves and a diligent search under the cushions of the lobby couches for spare change, then each of the five BRICS members would step up and write a check for their share of the debt. If the BRICS holiday party in Shanghai, China, went over budget by $10 million, for example, then each of the five original members would be subject to a capital call of $2 million and the person responsible for planning the actual party would be transferred to a remote outpost in Siberia and never seen again.

Fortunately, there have been no capital calls to date and the BRICS members have been fairly disciplined in their management of organizational expenses—particularly executive expense accounts. However, there was some concerns about President Putin's expense account which included a recent entry for "$600,000 for 2,000 artillery shells." Fortunately, the matter was quickly resolved when Putin revealed that the artillery shells were being purchased for a "bitchin'" fireworks display to celebrate his eldest son's birthday party, which was going to be held in eastern Ukraine. Putin then sent the payment to the BRICS controller so that the party could go on as scheduled.

As an added precaution, the BRICS members also approved the Contingency Reserve Agreement (CRA), which was set up to provide a source of liquidity for countries experiencing financial distress. Unlike the NDB—which was funded in equal shares by all five members—the CRA was funded primarily by China, which contributed 41% of the initial capital contribution. Russia, Brazil and India each contributed 18% of the initial capital contribution and South Africa—which had left its wallet back in Cape Town—supplied the remaining 5%.

The idea for the Contingency Reserve Agreement was not new to BRICS as the IMF has been doling out funds for decades to help debtor nations overcome short-term financial crises brought on by such things as unexpectedly high ammunition costs incurred while bankrolling roving terrorist groups. These funds are not viewed as actual loans but instead short-term cash infusions to help countries stabilize their economies. If Kazakhstan is suffering from a currency crisis due to its being unable to sell its government bonds, for example, then it could go to the NDB and get a bag of cash to help it through the rough times. The extra cash could also help to cover the $800,000 check that it needs to issue to pay for the five mobile missile launchers that it is sending to commemorate the birthday of Putin's eldest son in Ukraine.

Given the fact that the five BRICS members have made enormous investments in the NDB, it seems plausible that they would expect to make a profit on their contributions. Otherwise, BRICS would be nothing more than a glitzy foreign aid program—which would not be very much fun because there would be absolutely no prospect of being paid back. If you are the owner of any bank, including the NDB, then you will want to make sure that the recipient acknowledges that the money needs to be paid back. Otherwise, you can let them know your collection specialists from New Jersey will be coming over to pay them a visit.

The appeals of the BRICS members to developing countries around the world suggest that they are more sympathetic to the concerns of these prospective borrowers than the cold-hearted scrooges who oversee the IMF and the World Bank. But a bank is a bank and any loan issued by the NDB to any borrower—regardless of whether it is Ethiopia or Iran or even Utrecht-Lorraine—is going to include interest and other charges such as postage and handling. After all, the BRICS members want to make money on their loans because they gave up the opportunity to spend the billions of dollars that they contributed to the NDB in the first place on themselves. But the prospect of controlling an important multilateral development bank does offer a certain psychic pleasure to its owners that is difficult to overestimate.

The real question is whether the NDB can be any different than any other multilateral development bank, or even the IMF itself, in the eyes of the world's borrowers. If the NDB is to be a profitable bank, then it is difficult to see how it will be able to consistently offer more advantageous terms (e.g., lower interest rates, fewer closing costs) than its competitors. But the BRICS members may still be able to attract borrowers by marketing the NDB as a bank owned by developing countries that is making loans to other developing countries.

The NDB can also promise a somewhat less arduous underwriting process than is typically required by the IMF. Part of this difference arises from the fact that the NDB has a smaller staff for processing loans and does comparatively less research on prospective borrowers when compared to the IMF and the World Bank. As the IMF and the World Bank have spent eight decades accumulating staff and office supplies, many employees there will have a hand in the underwriting process for each loan. Because BRICS and the NDB are relative newcomers to the global banking business, they have not been around long enough to build up a truly bloated bureaucracy. Although the NDB does examine the economic conditions of each of the applicants, it also gives significant weight to the scope of the infrastructure projects themselves and the extent to which companies from one or more of the BRICS nations can be employed in the construction of these projects.

A loan applicant such as the African country of Angola, for example, will have to provide information about the country's economy to the NDB staff so that they can get some sense of the likelihood that the loan can be repaid. However, the NDB will also consider the nature of the infrastructure project itself and the benefits that the project can be expected to provide to the borrower. If Angola wants to use the funds to build roads, bridges, water distribution systems or even renewable energy facilities, then it may not be very difficult to get the loan approved.

What if Angola wants to go in a different direction, however, and build a vanity project—like a full-scale replica of the Versailles palace in the capital city of Luanda to serve as the official presidential residence? Based on the prior projects funded by the NDB, the bank's underwriters might be a little less enthusiastic about funding the construction of a palace having 2,300 rooms and covering 721,000 square feet. The bank's ardor might be further dampened after it learns that the palace project would also include a faithful reproduction of the 2,000 acres of gardens at Versailles featuring hundreds of statues and fountains, dozens of lakes and waterways, and several hundred thousand trees and plants. It would also include a full-time staff of actors and actresses who would wander about the grounds babbling in French while playing historical characters such as King Louis XIV of France and Marie Antoinette of "Let them eat cake" fame.

Even though Angola might argue that the extensive gardens would be far more attractive than the capital city of Luanda (much of which would, sadly, have to be bulldozed to make room for the new presidential palace and gardens), the NDB might conclude that this project would not fit within the parameters of its usual infrastructure projects. If nothing else, the estimated $20 billion dollar price tag for the project would probably sink it as far as the bank was concerned. Indeed, the costs of funding the construction of a new Versailles in Luanda would probably sink the NDB as well.

At the end of the day, the NDB might not be able to offer a more charitable banking experience because it, like every other bank, has to cover its expenses, pay the salaries of its employees and, most importantly, avoid making bad loans. Despite the fiery rhetoric that accompanied the creation of both BRICS and the NDB, the bank itself has to deal with the same constraints and conditions that face every other development bank. As a result, the NDB cannot veer too far from the traditional banking model or give a middle finger salute to the norms of the global banking system.

THIRD CON: BRICS IS A MISHMASH OF COUNTRIES CONTROLLED BY CHINA

BRICS has been portrayed by its founding members as a unified bloc of developing countries who have come together to offer an alternative source of funds for financing infrastructure projects in the developing world. However, the founding members of BRICS are all very different countries with disparate cultures, histories, ethnicities, economies and political systems. Furthermore, they occupy vastly different rungs in the international hierarchy—with some bordering on superpower status, others claiming regional power rankings and still others being little more than subsistence-level nations barely able to feed their own populations. As such, the BRICS members lack the cohesiveness of more economically homogeneous organizations such as the G-7, a group which includes the United States, Canada, Japan, France, Germany, Italy, and the United Kingdom. Moreover, BRICS is an amorphous organization that is charged with advancing the interests of its members even though it lacks any authority to bind member states in the way that the members of NATO, for example, are legally obligated to come to the defense of an attacked member.

In some ways, BRICS is more like a club than a formal organization in which members with very different backgrounds and perspectives join together every year at their annual summit to discuss issues of concern to them and toss out a few insults at the G-7 countries as well as the IMF and the World Bank.

The themes of self-sufficiency and development pervade everything about BRICS. However, there is the uncomfortable truth that BRICS is not an organization in which all of the members (original and otherwise) have an equal say in the way it is operated. After all, China and Russia were the original forces behind the creation of BRICS and the NDB; they were not really interested in creating a benevolent organization that would spread joy, happiness and pork fried rice throughout the world for free. China's extraordinarily large contribution to the CRA also foreshadowed something more than a desire to help others with no thought of any personal reward.

Although the United States has been criticized for years by Russia and China for refusing to give up its veto powers in the IMF and the World Bank, there is little doubt that no development project at the NDB can go forward without the consent of China and Russia. In recent years, Russia's involvement in the Ukraine War and its turn to China as a customer for its oil and natural gas exports have highlighted the extent to which Russia's dependency on China has increased. At the same time, China has taken the helm at BRICS to expand its own political influence among emerging nations while encouraging the wider use of its currency in trades with other members.

China's Belt and Road Initiative, which was originally launched by President Xi in 2013, is the world's largest infrastructure finance program. To date, it has funded more than $1 trillion in the construction of roads, railways, power plants, bridges, ports, and other energy and transportation projects throughout Africa, Asia and South America. Somewhat surprisingly, for the first few years of the program, Russia was the biggest recipient of these funds. An added benefit for China is that many Chinese firms have oversaw the construction of these infrastructure projects—which has been a sore spot with many participating countries that had hoped that their funds would be used to employ more of their own restless citizens for these projects.

Despite some marginal economic benefits that have been realized from these infrastructure projects, the Belt and Road Initiative has been criticized for trapping many borrowers into loans that they cannot pay back, due to the sheer amounts of the loans and their associated costs, as well as the disappointing returns on these investments. A number of the projects such as coal plants and mining operations have also resulted in increased environmental degradation throughout much of the developing world.

Unlike China's Belt and Road Initiative, the NDB offers a source of funding from a separate multilateral development bank—but the NDB (like BRICS itself) is arguably controlled by China. The NDB offer a less visibly nationalistic institution through which China can continue to pursue its objectives to increase its influence throughout the rest of the developing world without appearing to be so blatantly geared toward China's own self-interest. As a result, the Belt and Road Initiative and the NDB have been used in tandem to enable Chinese state companies to engage in large-scale construction projects around the world and create new markets for Chinese products.

Both the Belt and Road Initiative and the NDB appear to be serving as twin vessels for China to expand its geopolitical reach even as China continues to portray itself as merely another developing country standing in solidarity with the rest of the world's emerging nations. Both appear to be instruments of Chinese statecraft intended to expand China's power at the expense of both its adversaries, especially the United States, as well as its current buddies, including Russia. What remains to be seen is whether this massive investment by China over the past decade will ultimately pay off and help it to become the undisputed global superpower or whether the vagaries of politics and economics will end up severely impacting the success of these projects and leave China with a string of worldwide infrastructure ventures that ultimately provide it with little in the way of international prestige or tangible strategic benefits.

A CONVERSATION WITH PRESIDENT XI AND PRESIDENT PUTIN

A brass quintet from Franz Joseph Hayden's *Trumpet Concerto* blasted in the air as a single camera zoomed in to focus on a gray-haired man wearing glasses set in a *faux* tortoise shell frame. He was seated in the middle of a makeshift set with a backdrop that looked like it had been decorated by chimpanzees flinging chunks of animal waste onto a canvas. The man was wearing a blue suit and yellow tie and holding a clipboard. He was flanked on one side by two men, one of whom was seated, the other standing behind the chair. On the other side, there was an empty chair with a framed picture of a bare-chested man sitting on a horse.

Standing behind the unoccupied chair was another man holding a cell phone. All three of the gentlemen were dressed in dark business suits. The music faded out as the man with the clipboard addressed his audience, which was not very difficult as there was only a three-person film crew in front of him.

"Good evening, everyone," he began. "Welcome to Hollywood, California, and yet another edition of *World Affairs*," he announced. "My name is Rodney Cheswick and I am your host for this evening. We are honored to welcome to our show two of the most important leaders in the world today." He gestured to his left. "President Xi Jinping of the People's Republic of China." Xi nodded his headed slightly. "And President Vladimir Putin of the Russian Federation—or rather a picture of President Putin—who is appearing via telephone today due to the still unresolved outstanding warrant that was issued for his arrest by the International Criminal Court in 2023 for crimes against humanity." Putin's photograph stared impassively at the camera. "Very well, gentlemen." Cheswick looked at the men standing behind Xi. "I see that each of you brought your translators to the program," he observed. President Xi grunted.

"President Xi said that he is pleased to be here with you, Mr. Cheswick," the man standing behind President Xi said.

"Thank you, President Xi," Cheswick replied pleasantly, checking his notes. "We appreciate that you and your translator, and President Putin's translator and his portrait-quality photograph have traveled all the way around the world to appear on our show—" Putin offered a comment over the phone.

"Mr. Cheswick," Putin's translator said. "President Putin

would like to have our parking ticket validated." He handed a voucher to Cheswick.

"Oh, yes, of course," Cheswick said, retrieving several adhesive stamps from his jacket pocket and affixing them to the voucher before handing it back to the translator. "We certainly don't want to have President Putin's car towed," he added.

"Mr. Cheswick, *you* would not be very happy if President Putin's car was towed," Putin's translator said ominously, pocketing the ticket.

"Well, let's get right to it," Cheswick said, looking furtively at both the translator and the photograph of President Putin. He turned back toward the camera. "*World Affairs* provides a forum in which our guests discuss various topics that are of interest to our viewing audience—which may include matters ranging from foreign affairs and national security to popular culture and politics. Today the subject is BRICS—the organization founded by Brazil, Russia, India, China and South Africa—and its lending arm, the New Development Bank—"

President Xi's translator waved his hand. "President Xi would like to know if you are friends with any movie stars," he asked.

Cheswick nodded. "Well, this is Hollywood, the film capital of the world, and I do cross paths with many celebrities—"

"He would like to meet several of your most famous actresses," Xi's translator said. He bent over so that Xi could whisper in his ear. "Do you happen to know Miss Shari Eubank?" the translator asked after standing up. "She was the radiant star in Russ Meyer's classic movie *Supervixens.*"

"Shari Eubank? Shari Eubank?" Cheswick shook his head.

"No, I don't believe so," he said apologetically. "Does she have a background in the theater?" he asked.

The translator conferred with his boss. "President Xi does not think that Miss Eubank was involved in any Broadway productions," he replied. Xi reached into his pocket and handed his translator a card, who in turn passed it over to Cheswick. It featured a picture of an attractive brown-haired woman with an extremely extroverted upper body whose cantilevered form was an engineering marvel of cutting-edge underwire technology. He flipped the card over and read the following: "Shari Eubank Fan Club: Beijing Chapter. Charter Member: Xi Jinping". Cheswick handed the card back to the translator who returned it to President Xi. "President Xi considers himself to be something of an aficionado of Miss Eubank's artistic works, but he is unaware of any stage performance she might have given—clothed or otherwise." The translator shrugged his shoulders and then bent over again. "President Xi wanted to know if you might have heard why Miss Eubank never received an Academy Award for any of her movie roles."

"I am afraid not," Cheswick said. "But there are many fine actresses who have given extraordinary performances and never received an Academy Award—"

"True," Xi's translator agreed. "Life can be very unfair."

"However, I will do my best to see if we can track Miss Eubank down and arrange for her to meet with President Xi," Cheswick promised.

"Thank you, Mr. Cheswick," Xi's translator replied, grateful for Cheswick's "can-do" attitude.

"Perhaps we should move on," Cheswick said, watching the

program director wave his hand in a circular motion and mouthing the word "focus" or "faster" or "fired" some other "f" word that he could not quite discern.

"What about Uschi Digard or Colleen Brennan?" the translator asked, parroting Xi's grunts. "They are both accomplished actresses who appeared in *Supervixens* along with Shari Eubank," he added, hoping that the additional information would help clear the fog.

"I am afraid I have never heard of a movie called *Supervixens*," Cheswick said. "I believe female foxes are called vixens," he said to himself, recalling an obscure fact from his ninth-grade biology class. "Can you tell me a little bit about the plot?" he asked, always eager to add to his knowledge about American cinema.

"Of course," the translator replied. He spoke with President Xi for a moment. "President Xi said that *Supervixens* is one of Mr. Meyer's more controversial works due to its extreme violence, but it does offer a poignant story of a man fleeing across the country after being charged for a murder he did not commit and being pursued over and over again by buxom nymphomaniacs." President Xi whispered to his translator again. "It is sort of an updated version of John Steinbeck's *The Grapes of Wrath*," the translator explained. "But with a less grubby cast," he added.

"I am sorry I am not familiar with that movie," Cheswick said, worried that his encyclopedic knowledge of popular films might have a few gaps. He was going to ask where female foxes figured into the storyline, but he thought better of it.

President Xi cleared his throat. The translator stood up again. "President Xi wants to know if you might be able to introduce him to any of the actresses who appeared in the Russ Meyer's film *Beneath the Valley of the Ultra-Vixens?*"

There was an embarrassed silence and Cheswick tried unsuccessfully to remember any mention of "ultra" female foxes in his ninth-grade biology class. "Like who?" Cheswick finally asked.

"Miss Kitten Navidad?" the translator said. "She was a very voluptuous, red-headed actress." Xi offered another comment. "President Xi said that she was one of the most cerebral method actresses in the adult movie industry," the translator added. "Unlike Miss Eubanks who—like Grace Kelly—appeared in only a few movies before leaving the business, Miss Navidad was a busy bee whose career spanned several decades and included over a hundred classic movies including such blockbusters as *Girls on Girls*, *Eroticise*, and *Buford's Beach Bunnies*. Indeed, President Xi has directed his Minister of Culture to begin an ambitious film restoration project called *The Russ Meyers Universe* which aims to restore every Russ Meyers film ever made—using a combination of both manual and digital techniques—and make them all available to the public at a multiplex theater currently under construction near Tiananmen Square in Beijing. President Xi feels it is important that we preserve the most precious aspects of modern culture—regardless of nationality. His only regret is that Mr. Meyers did not live to see his movies receive the proper recognition that they deserved."

Putin offered a quick comment. "President Putin believes that Miss Navidad passed away several years ago," Putin's translator said a minute later.

President Xi's translator conveyed the sad news to the Chinese leader. President Xi looked visibly upset and wiped his eyes with a handkerchief. His translator tried to comfort him before returning to the host. "President Xi is very sorry to hear about the passing of Miss Kitten Navidad but he would also like to meet Miss Ann Marie if she is available. She appeared in both *Super-vixens* and *Beneath the Valley of the Ultra-Vixens* so she clearly was an extraordinary actress. President Xi has always appreciated the enthusiasm she brought to her scenes, particularly when she was in bed bouncing up and down on top of her male co-stars."

"Surely you are not referring to Ann-Margaret?" Cheswick said.

"Who is Ann-Margaret?" Xi's translator asked, puzzled.

"Never mind," Cheswick replied. "I will see what I can do to find Miss Ann Marie," he promised.

Xi's translator bent over again and then resurfaced. "President Xi understands that Russ Meyer's movies may not be as widely known as the works of other popular directors such as Steven Spielberg and Francis Ford Coppola. Perhaps you have heard of Don Edmond's masterpiece *Ilsa, She Wolf of the SS*?" President Xi muttered a few words. Xi's translator continued: "It stars Miss Dyanne Thorne as Ilsa, a sadistic and sexually insatiable Nazi prison camp commander." The translator stopped while President Xi added a few additional comments. "President Xi enjoyed it not only for Miss Thorne's high-spirited nudity but also for its true-life depiction of the wartime conditions in Hitler's Europe. He believes that the sequels—*Ilsa: Harem Keeper of the Oil Sheiks* and *Ilsa: the Wicked Warden*—were able to maintain that same level of cinematic quality despite what several critics referred to as an over-reliance on group shower scenes—"

President Putin offered a comment, and his translator shook

his head. Xi's translator conferred with Putin's translator for a moment. He then conveyed the message to President Xi, who began to weep.

"Is Miss Thorne also dead?" Cheswick wanted to know, fearing the worst. President Xi nodded between sobs. "I am so sorry, Mr. President," Cheswick said, genuinely touched by Xi's deep sense of loss. "Is there any other actress that we might try to contact on behalf of President Xi?" Cheswick asked, hoping to snap President Xi out of his funk.

Xi's translator conferred with his boss for a moment. "How about Miss Candy Samples?" he asked. "Her movies include *Prison Girls* and *Bouncin' in the USA*—"

"*Ded*," said the Russian leader over the phone as Putin's translator shook his head. Putin did not sound very concerned by this tragic loss of acting talent.

"Miss Haji?" Xi's translator continued. "She starred in *Faster, Pussycat! Kill! Kill!* and *Double D Avengers*," he added, trying to be helpful.

"*Ded*," Putin said, very matter-of-factly.

"Miss Raven De La Croix?" Xi's translator queried. "President Xi found her performance in *Up* to be mesmerizing," he added.

"*Ne mertv*," was the response. "Not dead," said Putin's translator. "At least not yet." Xi's translator updated President Xi on Miss De La Croix's apparent state of non-deadness.

"Miss Tura Satarna?" Xi's translator asked. "She appeared in classics such as *The Doll Squad* and *Sugar Boxx*," he added.

"*Ded*," was the response.

"Miss June Mack? Miss Susan Bernard?"

"*Ded* and *ded*."

President Xi shook his head sadly as he sank back into his seat, apparently despondent that the "golden age" of American cinema had, indeed, passed into the backwaters of history. He wiped his eyes several times and steadied himself.

Cheswick returned to his notebook. "Gentlemen, we seem to have gotten a little off topic," he said. "Perhaps we can return to the main subject matter of the show and discuss the BRICS organization and the New Development Bank."

"*Da,*" said Putin over a blast of static.

Cheswick turned to Putin's photograph. "President Putin, one of the most significant political developments in recent years was the creation of the intergovernmental organization known as BRICS by Brazil, Russia, India, China and South Africa in 2009. What were the primary reasons behind this decision to join together in this new enterprise?"

Putin's translator spoke into the phone and then waited for the response. "President Putin said that BRICS was set up to foster economic cooperation amongst its members and thereby enable them to have a greater impact on global events," the translator responded. "It was also formed to enable countries such as China and Russia to challenge the dominance of Western banking institutions such as the World Bank and the IMF," Putin's translator added. "Wait a minute," he said, as Putin rambled on. "BRICS was envisioned to be a forum in which members could coordinate their economic policies with their diplomatic overtures to protect their own interests as well as those of developing countries throughout the world," Putin's translator added.

"I see," Cheswick said. "Was that the reason for the establishment of the New Development Bank in 2015 by BRICS?"

he asked. "To serve as a counterweight to the IMF and the World Bank?"

President Xi waited patiently as his translator spoke and then responded. "The New Development Bank was formed by the original BRICS members to facilitate the mobilization of funds in order to finance infrastructure and sustainable development projects throughout the developing world," Xi's translator said. "Although there are several regional development banks, the founding members of BRICS did not feel that these other development banks looked at the world economy as a whole. As a result, the New Development Bank was not limited to making loans in a single part of the world such as Asia or Europe but— like the IMF and the World Bank—was set up to make loans throughout the entire world.

President Xi held up a pen. "Mr. Cheswick," Xi's translator began. "President Xi would like to take a moment to tell your viewers that they can receive an official BRICS writing pen just like the one being held by President XI *for free* if they know a president or a prime minister of a developing country who needs to borrow a few hundred million dollars to build a dam or a power plant. All they must do is to refer that head of state to the New Development Bank." President Xi pulled out a piece of paper and held it up over his head and scrawled a few words on the side facing him. "President Xi would like to point out that the BRICS pen has a unique pumping system that pushes ink out through the nib even when you are writing upside down." Xi added a few comments which the translator passed on. "President Xi would like to add that you can write with this pen while swimming underwater or sitting in a hyperbaric chamber or running through a burning building or jumping out of an airplane with a parachute—"

"I am not sure I could write anything if I were plummeting to earth," Cheswick said, laughing nervously.

"By the way," Putin's translator interrupted. "President Putin agrees with President Xi that the BRICS pen is a precision-crafted writing instrument that offers unparalleled writing comfort. In fact, President Putin has used BRICS pens numerous times to sign important documents to declare war on whomever he wants or to exile noisy dissidents to the gulag for the rest of their lives—"

"It is a shame that you have to refer a head of state to the New Development Bank to get one of these fine pens," Cheswick said, suddenly wanting a BRICS pen.

"Well, you can get a *free* BRICS pen for referring a prospective borrower to the New Development Bank," Xi's translator said. "However, if you do not know any presidents or kings or autocrats personally, then it might be quicker to pay $100 or the equivalent in *renminbi* or *rubles* or *euros* and purchase a BRICS pen for your own personal use. You can go in person to the BRICS merchandise store located at the New Development Bank headquarters in Shanghai, China, or you can go online and visit the official BRICS website where you can purchase this pen and all sorts of other branded merchandise such as hats, sweatshirts, socks and basketballs."

"Well, that sounds like a wonderful idea," Cheswick said, making a note to remind himself to order a pen after the show. "Otherwise, I wouldn't be able to get a BRICS pen because I really don't know any heads of state who are planning to apply for a development loan."

President Xi handed the pen to Cheswick. "Please accept this pen as a token of President Xi's friendship," Xi's translator said.

"Doesn't he need his pen?" Cheswick asked.

"Oh, he has thousands of them at home," Xi's translator responded. "He will not be running out of writing implements anytime soon."

"Well, please tell President Xi that I thank him for his kind generosity," Cheswick said, wondering when he might be able to crawl into a hyperbaric chamber to test out the pen.

"You're welcome," Xi's translator said. President Xi smiled slightly.

Cheswick held the pen in his hand and marveled at the precision balance of the barrel. He pointed it up toward the ceiling as though he were trying to write upside down. Suddenly the barrel separated, and the ink cascaded out and splashed into his lap, forming a big blue stain across his crotch.

"Oh, dear," President Xi's translator said. "I thought the gasket problem had been fixed." He turned to Cheswick. "President Xi is deeply sorry for the malfunction. He will be very happy to pay for the dry cleaning—" The translator dug into his pocket and retrieved a slip of paper. "Here is a voucher entitling you to have your clothing dry cleaned for free at the BRICS laundromat in Shanghai. Just present the voucher when you leave your clothing with the attendant and there will be no charge."

"Thank you for your concern," Cheswick said, looking down and noticing that his lap looked like it was covered by a blue apron. "It's barely noticeable," he said, putting his best foot forward. He took the voucher from the translator and stuck it in his jacket pocket. "I will be sure to stop by the BRICS laundromat the next time I am in Shanghai," he declared.

"Very good," Xi's translator said, satisfied that a diplomatic incident had been averted.

President Putin coughed loudly and spoke for a moment. Putin's translator turned to Cheswick. "President Putin would also like to return to the question regarding the founding of the New Development Bank. President Putin, like his good friend, President Xi, both believe that the interests of Russia and China and the other BRICS members have been underrepresented in the IMF and the World Bank." He waited for Putin to finish a very noisy outburst. "President Putin believes that a country such as Russia—which has one of the largest nuclear arsenals in the world and is capable of wiping out human civilization dozens of times over—should have more than 2.7 percent of the total quota and voting shares in the IMF."

Cheswick nodded. "Understood," he remarked. "So Russia feels that it has not been respected by the international community—particularly the United States—"

The translator nodded and waited for Putin to take a breath. "President Putin says that Russia is the largest country in the world and boasts a thousand-year history which has seen outstanding contributions in science, mathematics, music and literature. Yet Russia has less than three percent of the vote at the IMF. President Putin says that you only need to look at the globe to get a true sense of the vastness of the Russian Federation." The translator waited for Putin to finish his thoughts. "Russia has never been treated with respect at the IMF or the World Bank. As a result, it had no choice but to start a new bank that would reflect more accurately the capabilities of itself and the other founding members."

President Xi's translator jumped in: "President Xi concurs with President Putin and would like to point out that the People's Republic of China, which boasts the world's second-largest economy and a population of 1.3 billion persons, only has 6.4 percent of the total quota and voting shares at the IMF. Believe it or not, this amount is slightly less than the total quota and voting share held by Japan—which has an economy that is only about one-fourth the size of that of China and a population that is less than one-tenth that of China."

"I can see why you might be a tad bit irritated," Cheswick said sympathetically. "Did either of your governments ever petition the IMF to adjust your quota and voting shares so that they would be more aligned with the current state of affairs in the world?"

"Oh, we tried that a few times," Putin's translator said. "The IMF agreed to some minor modifications but 'You Know Who' still has the veto on everything—"

"You mean the United States?" Cheswick asked innocently.

"Of course I mean the United States," Putin's translator answered. "Who else would be powerful enough to rig the IMF?" He took a deep breath. "Anyways," Putin's translator continued. "Both President Xi and I realized that we were never going to get an even playing field at the IMF because the United States was never going to give up its privileged status. Not only does the United States have the veto, but it has a quota and voting shares that are nearly three times that of China and more than five times that of Russia. In short, the political power of the United States at the IMF is far in excess of its actual economic power in the real world—"

"That is very interesting," Cheswick said, feigning enthusiasm as the conversation continued.

Putin's translator paused for a moment. "Anyways, President Xi and I and the other original BRICS members agreed that we needed to seize the moment and create our own version of the IMF and the World Bank from the ground-up—which we now know as the New Development Bank."

"Well, everything that I have read in the New Development Bank's brochures says that it is a lending institution that wants to underwrite infrastructure projects throughout the developing world—"

"That is correct, " both translators said at the same time. They looked at each other and giggled.

"So BRICS began with five original members and has now added at least four more members in Egypt, Ethiopia, Iran and the United Arab Emirates." Cheswick shifted in his chair. "BRICS now has arguably two global powers, three or four regional powers and several emerging economies mashed together under the BRICS banner—"

Putin's translator nodded his head furiously as his boss yelled over the phone. "President Putin wants to point out that Saudi Arabia has agreed to become a member of BRICS—"

"Has it?" Cheswick asked. "My understanding is that the Saudis were offered membership in BRICS and that they accepted the offer but then backed off and said that they would have to think about it. What is going on here?"

Putin's translator's shoulders sagged. "It has been so exhausting dealing with the Saudis," he said. "President Putin and President Xi have spent so much time trying to persuade the Saudis to join the BRICS organization. But they seem to be playing with our affections. The Saudis say they want to join BRICS but then they tell us they are worried that it will upset the United States and the other Western powers—"

"Are there any other countries planning to join BRICS?" Cheswick asked.

"Oh, we have big plans for the future," President Xi's translator said. "We recently agreed to admit up to 13 new members to BRICS."

"Really?" said Cheswick, impressed. "Which countries?" he asked.

President Xi's translator consulted with his boss. "Algeria, Belarus, Bolivia, Cuba, Indonesia, Kazakhstan, Malaysia, Nigeria, Thailand, Turkey, Uganda, Uzbekistan and Vietnam. Venezuela also tried to get in but Brazil threw a fit and vetoed its application." He waited for Xi to finish. "This rapid expansion in BRICS is proof of the value that this organization can provide to other developing countries whose voices might otherwise be ignored by the IMF and the World Bank."

"That is a very impressive increase in the BRICS membership—" Cheswick observed. "However, it does raise the question as to whether this expansion in the BRICS membership will dilute the influence of the founding members—particularly China and Russia. Gentlemen?"

President Xi waited for his translator to finish. He then shook his head and laughed. The translator laughed with his boss and waited for his response: "President Xi says that you,

Mr. Cheswick, are very funny. The founding members have contributed tens of billions of dollars to BRICS and the New Development Bank and their voices shall continue to be heard in recognition of their enormous financial stake." Xi pulled on the sleeve of his translator. "President Xi said that the concerns of all of the BRICS members will continue to be heard but, ultimately, the decisions regarding its administration and orientation will be made by the founding members—"

"Is BRICS not an organization in which every member has an equal voice?" Cheswick inquired.

"Only if they each contribute a few billion dollars to the till," President Xi's translator responded. "See?" he added. "Democracy in action."

Putin offered a few sentences over the phone. "President Putin said that the founding members must necessarily have some type of control over BRICS and the New Development Bank because it would be chaotic to subject all decisions to the entire membership—particularly in view of the fact that BRICS may be expanding to nearly two dozen members," Putin's translator explained.

"Are you looking for new members who can plunk down several billions of dollars and achieve the status of a founding member?" Cheswick asked, blotting his pants with some crumpled paper. "Would you want one or more of the Western powers to join BRICS?"

Putin launched into a lengthy discussion which was followed by his translator's regurgitation: "President Putin said that BRICS has been sufficiently funded by its founding members and has no need for new infusions of capital. He does not see any reason to invite one or more of the Western powers to join BRICS at this time because it might create divided loyalties and obscure the original reasons for setting up BRICS and the New Development Bank in the first place—"

"Which is?" Cheswick asked.

"To create a financial network that does not rely on American dollars to fund its transactions—" Putin's translator continued.

"Do you want to wean yourself and your fellow members off of American dollars entirely?" Cheswick said.

"Yes," Putin's translator responded. "The long-term objective is for all intra-trade transactions within BRICS to be carried out using the currencies of one or more of the BRICS members themselves. In this way, we can insulate ourselves from using the dollar and, by implication, being subject to whatever sanctions the American government tries to impose on any of the member nations of BRICS."

"Do you want BRICS and the New Development Bank to supplant the IMF and the World Bank?" Cheswick asked, wondering if it would be better for him to dye his pants blue to match the ink stain.

Putin spoke for a few minutes. "President Putin believes that there is more than enough room for the IMF and the World Bank to co-exist with BRICS and the New Development Bank. All of the countries who belong to BRICS are also members of the IMF and the World Bank so we have interests in both organizations. Moreover, some of the BRICS members belong to other regional development banks such as the African Development Bank and the Asian Development Bank so there are a lot of cross-cutting loyalties. However, the difference from my point of view is that

BRICS was founded by five countries whose interests are not appropriately represented in the IMF and the World Bank." Putin had another thought. "Membership in any development bank is voluntary and each country can decide if that particular organization serves its interests."

"Do you foresee the need to leave the IMF or the World Bank?"

"*Nyet,*" said Putin directly. His translator continued: "We will continue to strengthen BRICS and the New Development Bank but we also want to be able to avail ourselves of the resources—particularly the research facilities—provided by the IMF to all of its members. There is no point in getting into a cold war with the IMF because it is still the dominant lender in the global economy." He was thoughtful. "The New Development Bank is barely a decade old so we do have much to learn from the IMF and the World Bank. However, we are making enormous progress and will continue to expand our membership in the future."

President Xi cleared his throat. "BRICS and the New Development Bank are more closely geared toward development and infrastructure loans which are targeted at developing countries," Xi's translator said. "The IMF engages in other types of activities such as currency stabilization programs which are really outside the scope of the BRICS mandate. We want the New Development Bank to fund specific projects so that there is a beginning and an end. We do not want to provide open-ended lines of credit to borrowers." Putin's translator waited for a moment. "President Putin has seen the problems caused by unending credit lines in dealing with his own family members as well as various high-ranking officials in the Politburo, so he does not want to have entire nations on the dole—"

"That's understandable," Cheswick concurred.

"Plus, who wants to babysit these countries?" Putin's translator said. "Do you know how many employees we would have to hire to monitor these countries on an on-going basis? We try to run a lean and mean operation which means minimizing our staff so that it frees up more money for loans."

Cheswick was thoughtful for a moment. "The United States government has reportedly taken a very dim view of the rhetoric by the BRICS countries about reducing the primacy of the dollar in international trade. In fact, the American president has recently called for enormous tariffs to be imposed on products imported from any BRICS member due to the stated aim of your organization to de-dollarize the global economy."

"It was a joke," said Putin's translator after a long silence. "Everyone was having a little bit of fun. President Putin thinks it may have been the Brazilian president who talked about de-dollarizing the global economy because he did have a few drinks at the summit." He waited for President Putin to finish a rambling statement. "But President Putin would like to point out that these very same dollars have been used as a weapon to shut down the Russian economy and its banking system merely because our military forces intervened to rescue Ukraine from the clutches of the Czech Republic."

"I don't believe the Czech Republic tried to take over Ukraine," Cheswick said. "In fact, the only footage I have seen of any military forces invading Ukraine has been that of the Russian army sending its tanks across the border in the spring of 2022—"

"The Czechs are very wily," Putin's translator continued. "They want you to focus on something like a Russian tank column rolling into Ukraine while they are secretly planning to occupy Kyiv using soldiers disguised as members of the Ukrainian national hockey team—" He waited for Putin to finish an additional statement that seemed to go on for several minutes without Putin taking a breath. "President Putin believes that magicians employ these very same diversionary tactics when they perform sleight of hand tricks," he added, judiciously editing out Putin's calls for nuclear strikes on Los Angeles.

"That sounds a little farfetched to me," Cheswick said dubiously. "However, I am curious what President Xi thinks about the threat by the United States to impose enormous increases on tariffs on goods imported into the United States—which would certainly include those products manufactured in China—"

President Xi's translator waited for his boss to finish his response. "President Xi would like to point out that China is a fragile, developing country that is still recovering from centuries of exploitation by foreign powers. As such, it must have access to foreign markets so that it may industrialize and one day become a leading global economic power—"

"China already has the world's second largest economy," Cheswick pointed out. "In fact, I believe that China is the leading manufacturer of such products as steel, electronics, cars and heavy machinery—"

"Well, we have had a very good year," Xi's translator explained. "Before this year, however, things were not going so well. In any event, China opposes any attempt by the United

States to increase tariffs on its products because it could lead to a global trade war."

Cheswick consulted his notes. "But China exports about $425 billion of goods to the United States and the United States exports only about $150 billion of goods to China. By my reckoning, China has a trade surplus with the United States of about $275 billion—"

"I don't think it is that enormous," Xi's translator said nervously. "Maybe your report contained an error such as an extra '0' or two. I mean, if you move the decimal point to the left two places, China's trade surplus with the United States is only $2.75 billion." He waited for President Xi to finish talking. "President Xi believes that $2.75 billion is little more than a rounding error—"

"I don't think we are talking about a couple of billion dollars," Cheswick said as President Putin asked his translator something about the frequency with which broadcasters fall out of the windows of tall buildings in the United States.

"If we assume that the numbers are correct and China has a trade surplus of $275 billion with the United States, then is it not the case that the United States has enormous leverage with China?" Cheswick looked at President Xi who was now glancing at his watch and wondering about the frequency with which broadcasters get run over by taxicabs in the United States. "If the United States were to double all tariffs on any products imported from China, then that would likely cause an enormous drop in exports to the United States and possibly lead to widespread factory closings and mass unemployment in China—"

"It would also lead to higher prices in the United States,"

Xi's translator said. "A tariff raises the price of a good. American consumers will pay a higher price for the same good—"

"But that good may not be made by China," Cheswick said. "It might be made in the United States," he added. Xi's translator stared blankly ahead. President Xi fired off a quick comment. "President Xi would like to switch the topic to something less contentious such as the recent loan of two giant pandas to the Los Angeles Zoo."

"I do love the giant pandas," Cheswick said happily. "They are such happy-go-lucky animals that are generally docile except for when they rip the heads off of humans who look at them the wrong way—"

"No, giant pandas are extremely friendly," Xi's translator protested. "President Xi is not aware of any incidents in which they have decapitated a human being." Xi's translator shook his head. "President Xi is not interested in talking about giant pandas anymore," he stated wearily.

"Okay," Cheswick said agreeably. "We can talk about something a little less controversial." He flipped through his notebook. "President Xi, let me ask you about China's so-called 'debt trap diplomacy,'" Cheswick began.

President Xi's face suddenly turned bright red. He pulled his translator down by the collar and fired off several comments. "President Xi takes exception to your characterization of loans by China as 'debt traps,'" Xi's translator said angrily. "You have insulted President Xi and must return the pen," he added, grabbing the pieces of the pen from Cheswick and getting blue ink over his hands.

"It was a simple question," Cheswick pointed. "Do you agree

that the loans made by China have amounted to traps that burden developing countries with debts they cannot pay?"

President Xi shook his head angrily. "No, President Xi vehemently disagrees that any of the loans issued by China are unfair in any way," Xi's translator said. "President Xi would like to point out that loans approved by China do not require debtor nations to restructure their economies—which is often a condition of loans issued by the IMF and the World Bank. China leaves it to the governments of the borrowing countries to determine how best to manage their own economic affairs and pay back the loans—"

"Some might say that these countries were not very good at self-management in the first place or they would not otherwise need the money—" Cheswick interjected.

"Mr. Cheswick, your sources have not provided you with very accurate information," Putin's translator said, jumping into the verbal morass after being prompted by a vocal outburst from his boss. "China's loans are easier to secure than those issued by the IMF and the World Bank. I would compare it to the difference between a mosquito bite and a colonoscopy. The IMF can be excruciatingly detailed in its underwriting of loans for prospective borrowers. Many countries who have obtained loans either from China itself or the New Development Bank would not have been able to obtain approval for their projects if they were submitted to the IMF."

"I see," Cheswick said, not regretting the loss of his pen fragments. "But is it not the case that many loans by China have been approved subject to the condition that the projects have to use Chinese-made materials such as steel and be built by Chinese workers? In other words, is it not the case that the debtor countries in these types of loans have little say in the selection of the construction companies that will build the projects—which is not typically an issue with IMF and World Bank loans."

"So?" both translators asked at the same time.

"So the debtor country does not get to supply much of the construction material for the project and also sees its own construction firms shut out of the project. As a result, there is not much benefit to the local economy because both the materials and the constructions workers are being brought into the country to build the project."

President Xi looked very unhappy and President Putin's picture remained impassive. "President Xi is not enjoying this interview very much," Xi's translator said finally. "President Xi must excuse himself as he has to attend a reception at the Chinese consulate in Los Angeles." President Xi stood up and motioned for the translator to follow him. Cheswick stood up and offered his hand but it was ignored. "Just make sure that you contact those actresses for President Xi," the translator said as he followed President Xi offstage.

President Putin's translator looked around nervously for a moment until Putin shouted an order at him. "*Da, ser,*" he said, picking up Putin's portrait and hurrying off the stage.

The camera closed in on Cheswick. "Well, I would like to thank my guests, President Xi Jinping of the People's Republic of China and President Vladimir Putin of the Russian Federation for taking the time to talk with us today on *World Affairs*. We will do the best we can to contact the actresses mentioned by President Xi so that he may meet with them before he returns to China. And I will probably be throwing out my trousers as

I doubt that any dry cleaner will be able to get this ink strain out." He looked sadly at the blue splash across his lap. "We look forward to seeing all of you on our next episode of *World Affairs*."

Hayden's *Trumpet Concerto* resumed and continued to blare away as the credits rolled and the screen slowly faded to black.

www.ingramcontent.com/pod-product-compliance
Lightning Source LLC
Chambersburg PA
CBHW022102210326
41518CB00039B/364